Glenn Dickey's 49ers

Glenn Dicke

THE RISE, FALL, AND REBIRTH OF T

PRIMA PUBLISHING
3000 LAVA RIDGE COURT · ROSEVILLE, CA 95661
(800) 632-8676 · WWW.PRIMALIFESTYLES.COM

y's 49ers

HE NFL'S GREATEST DYNASTY

Glenn Dickey

PRIMA PUBLISHING and colophon are registered trademarks of Prima Communications, Inc.

Library of Congress Cataloging-in-Publication Data

Dickey, Glenn.
Glenn Dickey's 49ers : the rise, fall, and rebirth of the nfl's greatest dynasty / Glenn Dickey
    p.   cm.
  Includes index.
  ISBN 0-7615-2232-8
  1. San Francisco 49ers (Football team)—History.   I. Title: Glenn Dickey's 49ers. II. Title.

GV956.S3 D518 2000
796.357'64'0979461—dc21

                                      00-027434
                                         CIP

00 01 02 HH 10 9 8 7 6 5 4 3 2 1

Printed in the United States of America

HOW TO ORDER

Single copies may be ordered from Prima Publishing, 3000 Lava Ridge Court, Roseville, CA 95661; telephone (800) 632-8676, ext. 4444. Quantity discounts are also available. On your letterhead, include information concerning the intended use of the books and the number of books you wish to purchase.

Visit us online at www.primalifestyles.com

TO NANCY AND SCOTT, MY INSPIRATION

CONTENTS

INTRODUCTION

THE 1990s started with the San Francisco 49ers on top of the football world. They had just demolished the Denver Broncos, 55–10, in the Super Bowl, their fourth Super Bowl triumph in nine seasons.

Entering the millennium, though, they were in disarray, their flamboyant owner banished from football, their legendary coach/general manager trying in vain to regain his once magic touch with players, their chief executive gone to Cleveland, their great quarterback considering retirement because of repeated concussions.

And the team had disintegrated, falling to the bottom of the NFL with little hope that it would rise again any time soon.

What happened? The salary cap was the natural villain. Designed to even the economic competition, the cap had helped bring the free-spending 49ers down, as it had the Dallas Cowboys earlier. In fact, the cap evasions the 49ers had pioneered finally backfired on them.

But more than anything else, this is a very human story of how men blinded by ego put their own interests ahead of the team's interests, bringing about an almost inevitable disaster. The same men who had been most instrumental in the rise of the team also played significant roles in the team's precipitous decline, and attempts to place blame on others were rampant.

As a columnist for the *San Francisco Chronicle* during this period, I watched the whole story unfold, and probably 80 percent of this book is based on personal observations and the many one-on-

one conversations I had with the principals in this drama. Much of the information I gleaned in those conversations was intended for background use at the time, and only now can it be revealed. And even now, some of the information and opinions are so sensitive that the participants do not want to be quoted directly. I have respected their wishes, but anonymous material comes only from those I have known and trusted for many years.

There were many great times during this period and I have detailed them, because it is impossible to fully understand how the team finally disintegrated without knowing how the problems that eventually resulted in the team's demise started to show themselves even during the greatest triumphs.

Victory covers a multitude of problems, and so most of the 49ers' internal squabbles were overshadowed by their long run of success, starting with their first Super Bowl win in 1981 and continuing a stretch that ran through 1998—17 seasons with at least 10 wins, including an NFL record 16 straight, and 16 playoff appearances in those 18 years.

Even during those years of great success, though, there was tension. Star quarterback Joe Montana and coach Bill Walsh each thought he should be the one getting the major share of the credit for the team's early success; and they clashed, publicly and privately. A later battle for playing time between Montana and Steve Young split fans, players, and 49er executives.

But most of the tension was created by owner Eddie De-Bartolo. Some thought DeBartolo's obsession with winning was the sand that created the oyster. Perhaps so, but he also drove Walsh out of coaching early, a circumstance that set into play events and decisions that eventually caused the 49ers' slide. Eddie's split with one-time friend Carmen Policy, who had held the organization together after Walsh's departure, also drove Policy out of the organization. And finally, his own excesses brought DeBartolo crashing to earth, involved in a Louisiana gambling probe and forced to divest himself of the team that had been his identity.

All of these events were foreshadowed by the very first press conference held by DeBartolo after the team was purchased in 1977. Through the team's media guide, DeBartolo spread the story in the high-flying 1980s and '90s that he had taken over a team in disarray and brought it to the top. In fact, he had taken over a team that was on the way back up, but the actions of the man he first hired to run the franchise drove it to the bottom. The decline and fall of the 49ers 22 years later mirrored that same path by DeBartolo, starting with the very first day.

CHAPTER ONE

Enter Eddie

STANDING IN front of a hostile audience of fans and media at the March 1977 press conference announcing the sale of the San Francisco 49ers to the DeBartolo Corporation, Eddie DeBartolo was bristling with anger. He was insulted when writers questioned his moves; at age 30, he'd never had that experience before. His father was a rich man; and as the firstborn and a male, Eddie had always had anything he wanted. His father had bought the 49ers for him as a toy, and Eddie was going to run it his way. He all but told his audience to stuff it, saying he would run the 49ers as a business.

That wasn't what 49er fans wanted to hear. They were already in a state of shock over the news that the team was going to be sold to a company that was, though highly successful as a major builder of shopping centers, largely unknown in the Bay Area.

Although as cosmopolitan as any city in the United States, San Francisco also has its provincial aspect: San Franciscans regularly congratulate themselves on having the good sense to live in the city, and virtually the first question reporters ask prominent visitors is what they think of the city.

Eddie was too young and too spoiled to have any sense of the city. In Youngstown, Ohio, where the DeBartolo Corporation was an overwhelming presence, DeBartolo family members were all treated with near reverence. Eddie hadn't bothered to do any research on San Francisco, so he didn't realize his reception there would be any different. He didn't utter the usual paeans to the city and, in fact, said right up front that he would continue to live in Youngstown. That was heresy, and it was the beginning of a relationship with San Franciscans that was always a wary one for both sides. Many fans would come to love Eddie, believing that his money had created a winner, even though the first Super Bowl team had one of the lowest payrolls in the league. Many others, however, have always been uncomfortable with Eddie's rough edges—the hard drinking, the gambling, and the legal problems, including a sexual assault case and an assault on a Packers fan after a playoff loss in Green Bay.

For his part, Eddie would never be comfortable in San Francisco, and he would rarely appear at parties in the city, even those honoring the 49ers. When the 49ers were campaigning to get a new stadium in 1997, Carmen Policy, by then the club's president, had to virtually drag Eddie to North Beach, a place where one would expect him to feel comfortable, considering its large population of Italians and their descendants. Once there, Eddie had a good time, because Policy steered him into bars where patrons would buy him drinks, always Eddie's idea of a good time.

When his father died in 1994, and with his mother already dead, Eddie no longer had to live in Youngstown. But when he moved, it was to Atherton, 30 miles south of San Francisco on the Peninsula, and his only ventures into San Francisco were to the 49er games at Candlestick Park, on the southern boundary of the city.

All of that lay in the future in 1977, but both 49er fans and the media representatives at Eddie's first press conference could sense trouble ahead, with outsiders taking control of a team very special to San Franciscans and, indeed, to most of northern California.

The 49ers were the first major league professional team in northern California, 12 years ahead of the Giants; and unlike the Giants, they were a San Francisco team from the beginning. The Giants would move out from New York, the Warriors would move out from Philadelphia, but the 49ers had never played anywhere else. And, from the start, they had a strong local focus.

> Many fans would come to love Eddie, believing that his money had created a winner.

Their first coach was Lawrence (Buck) Shaw, who had been a great college coach at Santa Clara, 45 miles south of San Francisco. The first 49ers team, in 1946, consisted largely of players from either the local colleges (the offensive stars, quarterback Frank Albert and fullback Norm Standlee, were both former Stanford players) or from the teams that had represented military bases in the area during World War II.

Shaw, who had a creative offensive mind but little regard for defense, brought in offensive stars and ignored the defense. With quarterbacks like Albert, Y. A. Tittle, and John Brodie; receivers like Alyn Beals, Gordy Soltau, Billy Wilson, and R. C. Owens; and runners like Hugh McElhenny, Joe Perry, John Henry Johnson, and John Stryzkalski, the 49ers had no problems scoring. Their 1954 backfield of Tittle, McElhenny, Perry, and Johnson (all of whom are in the Pro Football Hall of Fame) was known as the "Million Dollar Backfield." That would probably translate to $40 million today. Because the defense was so weak, the 49ers often found themselves in games where even five touchdowns weren't enough to win, but nobody could say the games weren't exciting.

Their first conference, the All America Football Conference, was only marginally major league; but the NFL absorbed the 49ers when that conference folded, and the 49ers were unquestionably major league from that point.

By 1977, they had yet to win a league championship, but they were San Francisco's own. From the start, they had been owned by the Morabito family, Tony and younger brother Vic, and then by their widows after both men died of heart attacks in their 50s. Their current president was Lou Spadia, a lifelong San Franciscan who had been with the team since its inception.

And now they were going to be owned by outsiders, who seemed to have little in common with the Morabitos but an Italian heritage. To make it worse, these outsiders were going to bring in a general manager, Joe Thomas, who had a reputation of being a good football man but whose ego was out of control.

Thomas was originally from a small town in Ohio, not far from Youngstown, and he was a family friend; but what apparently got him the job was a recommendation from Al Davis, the only man who could compete with Thomas for the reputation as the most hated man in football.

As usual with Davis, his reasons for being involved in the 49ers' sale were complex.

NFL salaries had taken a big jump because of competition with the AFL in the previous decade. As a result, the Morabito widows, Jo (Tony) and Jane (Vic) knew they could no longer compete financially and had decided in 1976 to put the club up for sale. "They were right in that decision," said Spadia. "That was their only source of income."

The 49ers had always been run like a family business; and Spadia, who had been allowed to buy 5 percent of the team earlier by Tony Morabito, had never had a contract, because there had been no need for one. Now, though, club attorney Marshall Leahy, aware that a new owner probably would not run the same kind of operation, advised the widows to give Spadia a five-year contract that would take effect the day of the sale. That provision would pay off in a big way for Spadia later.

Wayne Valley, who had sold his ownership interest in the Oakland Raiders to Davis after a bitter power struggle, put in a bid to buy the club, and the sale was so near completion that Spadia had let Valley look at the team's financial records. But minority owner Franklin Mieuli, who also owned a basketball team, the Golden State Warriors, exercised a clause that allowed him to put in a preemptive bid for the team. Mieuli could not come up with the financing to buy the team, but when he stepped forward, Valley dropped out.

There was speculation, neither confirmed nor denied by Davis, that he had encouraged Mieuli's bid to thwart Valley. Davis and Valley had fought for years over the Raiders, and Davis could often be a petty, vindictive man toward his enemies, of whom he had many. When the club once again went on the market, Davis volunteered his services to help find a buyer. He brought the DeBartolos to the 49ers' owners and earned a $100,000 finder's fee, though there were some who wondered how difficult it could have been to find the DeBartolos, who were building shopping centers around the country and were already involved in horse racing and hockey.

Ed DeBartolo, Sr., bought the 49ers for his son, who knew nothing about football and had never even been in charge of a separate entity within the DeBartolo Corporation. Clearly, Eddie needed help, and Joe Thomas seemed to be the man who could provide that help.

Thomas probably couldn't have found a general manager's job with any other NFL team. Only new owners, like the DeBartolos, who had not previously been involved in the league and weren't aware of the problems he had caused wherever he had been, would have hired him.

Thomas earned his reputation as a good judge of talent from his work as personnel director at Minnesota and Miami, largely because he had convinced some football writers that he was responsible for the success of those organizations. Roger Stanton, who published the influential *Football News*, was probably the biggest Thomas booster. Within the NFL, football people thought the success of the Minnesota and Miami organizations was primarily due to Jim Finks and Don Shula, respectively; but Thomas's reputation got him the opportunity he was seeking, and he was named general manager of the Baltimore Colts in 1972 after Robert Irsay purchased the team.

Thomas was up to his armpits in confrontation and controversy almost from the moment he was hired.

He fired coach Howard Schnellenberger just three games into the 1974 season, and Irsay told Thomas to take his place on the sidelines. Reluctantly, Thomas did, and the Colts went 2–9 the rest of the season under Thomas.

Thomas went back to the front office the next season, when Ted Marchibroda became the coach, but his confrontations with Marchibroda were so heated that Marchibroda quit early in the season. When the players all backed the coach, Thomas was forced to plead with Marchibroda to return.

> Thomas was up to his armpits in confrontation and controversy almost from the moment he was hired.

Irsay also allowed Thomas to represent the team at NFL owners' meetings. "He was both arrogant and dumb," said one owner who observed him at those meetings. "Everything had to be explained to him three or four times because he couldn't understand anything we voted on."

Meanwhile, Thomas had alienated the Baltimore fans by disposing of many veteran players, including legendary quarterback Johnny Unitas. Thomas was right about Unitas, who had been reduced to a below-average quarterback by age and injuries, but the graceless way he dumped the most famous player in franchise history enraged the fans.

This was the man the DeBartolos were bringing to San Francisco. It didn't take a crystal ball to see the trouble ahead.

CHAPTER TWO

The Education of Eddie

THE FIRST of DeBartolo's casualties would be coach/general manager Monte Clark, who had brought the 49ers back to respectability in the 1976 season, when they finished 8–6 and played better than that, losing two games in overtime and two more by less than a touchdown. If the 49ers had had a more reliable kicker than Steve Mick-Mayer, who earned the nickname "Miss-a-Mile" when he missed 10 of his last 18 field goal attempts and 4 of 30 point-after-touchdown attempts, they would have made the play-offs easily.

Clark, 39 when he was hired, was the youngest head coach in the NFL, and he was one of three potential coaches Lou Spadia had interviewed after firing Dick Nolan at the end of the 1975 season. Mike White, then the head coach at the University of California, Berkeley, was the second. The third was Bill Walsh, then the offensive coordinator for the Cincinnati Bengals. But when Spadia talked about Walsh to Paul Brown, the Bengals' coach, he was warned, "Don't touch him with a 10-foot pole."

Spadia chose Clark, who had been given total authority, including the final decision on both drafts and trades. "That was the only way we could get him," said Spadia. "We had never given a coach that kind of authority before, but I thought it was important because, with the club for sale, Monte's job would be defined no matter who bought the team."

Don Shula, under whom Clark had coached at Miami, had that kind of authority with the Dolphins, and he advised Clark to get it, too. "He kept telling me to make sure I had the authority to do what I wanted," said Clark. "I had turned down Kansas City because they wouldn't give me that authority."

As general manager, Thomas would have authority over player trades and draft selections. Clark knew he couldn't continue with Thomas calling the shots, especially since he had firsthand experience with Thomas at Miami, when Thomas was player personnel director there.

Clark remembered one telling incident about Thomas at Miami. The coaches were discussing an upcoming draft and they thought they'd play a joke on Thomas, putting a totally bogus name up on the draft board. When Thomas saw the name, instead of asking who the player was, he pretended to know, giving the fictional player different attributes.

"If there was one man in the world I wouldn't have turned my future over to, it was Joe Thomas," said Clark. "With Joe, you never know what's going to happen next. You might love a guy, and he's gone the next day, or he brings in a guy you don't want.

"I was on the staff at Miami with Howard Schnellenberger, and I saw what happened to Howard at Baltimore with Joe Thomas. I just wanted no part of the man.

"I tried to tell the DeBartolos what San Francisco was like. I told them, you're going to have to operate with class and dignity, and Joe Thomas is not going to fly here. I predicted exactly what would happen, and I didn't want to be a part of that."

The DeBartolos tried to work out a new contract with Clark that would have left him as the coach, perhaps with a salary increase but without any authority on player moves. Talking with friends after those negotiations, Clark said, "The only way I would stay is if I was over Thomas, and my first move would be to fire the SOB."

That wasn't at all what the DeBartolos had in mind. They wanted Thomas to be in charge of all player moves. If he had accepted that arrangement, Clark said later, "I'd have felt like I had 'SOLD' written across my forehead."

An Unmitigated Disaster

AND SO Eddie fired Clark at the press conference called to introduce the new ownership.

The sale of the 49ers elicited so much interest that the press conference had to be shifted from the Fountain Room of the Fairmont Hotel to the larger Venetian Room, where top-name entertainers performed nightly. Elegant three-color invitations were sent out, complete with an RSVP note. The DeBartolos had intended it to be a warm and friendly occasion, a chance to impress San Franciscans with their class and competence. It didn't turn out that way.

With his father watching from the back of the room, Eddie made some innocuous opening remarks about wanting to put a winner on the field, and that sentiment was applauded; but he stepped into a hornet's nest when he announced that Clark had been fired.

"Mr. Clark's contract was in direct conflict with that of our general manager," Eddie said. "I tried, over six sessions, to work it out. I ate my guts out trying to make it work. But Monte would not redefine his duties as they exist in the present contract. It was his position that to do so would render his methods and approach as a coach ineffective, and therefore, he requested that his existing contract be honored.

"His contract has three years to run. We will honor it to the fullest extent. That is the way the DeBartolo Corporation does business."

The questions started to come, fast and furious. Why was he firing the coach who seemed to have the 49ers on the track to success?

Eddie was defiant. He made no attempt to win over his audience, telling them only that his way was the only way.

"Joe Thomas was a friend of ours long before we intended to get into football," he said, "and some time ago, we let him know that if we became involved, he would run the football part. I wanted Monte Clark as coach—but only as coach. Even if Thomas were not involved, I would have wanted to renegotiate Monte's contract. No coach in the National Football League received such authority in trades, drafts, and waivers."

> Eddie was defiant. He made no attempt to win over his audience, telling them only that his way was the only way.

Of course, Shula had such authority, but before anybody could raise that point, Eddie continued by asking, rhetorically, "Does everybody here realize this is a business, not a playtoy? With an investment of $17 million and more, we are not here to placate personalities. We have to run the team our way. . . ."

By this time, the room was buzzing, but there was more to come, more lecturing to the audience that the DeBartolo Corporation knew what needed to be done, even though nobody in the company had ever been involved with a football team before. Eddie's status as an absentee landlord, calling the shots from Youngstown, was another blow.

The questions continued to come. Didn't he know Thomas's reputation in the football world? Eddie dismissed the stories as inaccurate reporting by the media, not a sensitive or astute remark in that particular setting. "You'd have to be on the scene to know the whole picture," he said, though he had been nowhere near the scene himself. "We're convinced Mr. Thomas will get along just fine with all of us here."

Quite likely, Eddie never made a worse prediction in his life. Thomas didn't get along with anybody, not the fans, not the media, not the players, past or present. He was an unmitigated disaster.

Joe Thomas, Dictator

MY FIRST indication of what was in store came in a meeting with Thomas at his office in the 49ers' practice facility, then in Redwood City. I had requested an interview because I wanted to ask him about the controversies in his past, as well as his plans for the 49ers. To that point, my knowledge of Thomas was limited to what I had read and heard, and my impressions were ambivalent: His methods seemed rough, but I thought he had done a good job in Baltimore in getting rid of unproductive veterans and bringing in good young players.

I left his office in a daze, four hours later, after being subjected to an almost nonstop monologue; in all that time, I doubt that I said 30 words, and I certainly wasn't able to truly interview him. He went over every aspect of his life, even his personal life (that part of the monologue was short, because he had none). He even told me that he and his wife owned only a few pieces of furniture. He went over virtually every player move he had ever made, with special attention to his decision to get rid of Unitas in Baltimore. Though I was dealing at the time with ego-driven personalities like Al Davis and Charlie Finley, Thomas was unique in my experience.

There's an old saying, "Be careful what you wish for." If Thomas had remained as a player personnel director, with somebody above him in control, he probably would have done fine. But he wanted complete control. In Baltimore, he had been challenged by his coaches, and his owner slapped him down when he fired his first coach. In San Francisco, he would hire only coaches who were subservient, and his owner was more than 2,000 miles away. He had total control and, with that control, he turned a team that was on the verge of making the playoffs into one that was the worst in the league, no better than an expansion team.

His player judgment seemed to desert him. He released Jim Plunkett, who had come to the 49ers in a costly trade worked out before Clark joined the team; the Raiders picked up Plunkett off the waiver wire, and he later led them to two Super Bowl triumphs. Thomas gave up five draft picks over a three-year period, including his No. 1 in 1979, for O. J. Simpson, whose knee injuries had robbed him of his great ability. That No. 1 pick was the very first pick in the '79 draft, but Buffalo had it, not the 49ers. His first draft was a total washout—not one player who ever made a significant contribution. His second draft produced four players (from 15 choices) who later played on Super Bowl winners—offensive linemen Fred Quillan and Walt Downing, linebacker Dan Bunz and defensive lineman Archie Reese—but no stars. The first pick, tight end Ken MacAfee, was a total bust. Thomas didn't have a chance for a third draft.

The coaches were all nondescript men who should never have risen above the level of assistants—Ken Meyer in 1977, Pete McCulley and Fred O'Connor in '78, McCulley for the first nine games, O'Connor the last seven. Because players knew Thomas had all the authority—he even dictated who should start from week to week—they had no respect for their coaches.

Thomas desperately made player changes, on the roster and in the starting lineup, but nothing worked. The 49ers got worse and worse, falling from 8–6 in Clark's last year to 5–9 in Thomas's first season. In 1978, the NFL season was expanded to 16 games, which gave the 49ers a chance to set a franchise record for most losses, with a 2–14 mark. The frantic Thomas lectured players in the locker room after virtually every loss.

For more than 20 years, Spadia had worked hard to forge a bond between the community and the 49ers. One example: When then mayor Joe Alioto came to the 49ers with an idea for a "Youth Fund" that would be used to help fund athletic programs for youngsters, Spadia agreed to use some of the ticket revenue for the program. It was under Spadia, too, that the 49ers began a promotion campaign that honored season ticket buyers as "49er Faithful." In two years, though, Thomas almost totally undid all the good Spadia had done over a much longer time.

> [Thomas] turned a team that was on the verge of making the playoffs into one that was the worst in the league, no better than an expansion team.

Spadia was retained by the De-Bartolos as community relations director, but Thomas did not designate an office nor even a desk for the former club president at the 49ers' facility. "Why don't you work out of your home, Lou?" he suggested. It was a very bad period for Spadia, who had just lost his wife to cancer. Nonetheless, he continued to meet with civic leaders to try to put together common programs with the team, but Thomas never honored Spadia's commitment to any civic cause. Finally, after one year, he fired Spadia. "He fired Jim Plunkett and me the same week," said Spadia, wryly. "One of those was a mistake."

Thomas stormed out of meetings with the city's Park and Recreation Commission, which has responsibility for approving ticket prices for 49er games, and he insulted season ticket holders. He fired several employees, including long-time public relations director George McFadden. He changed all the locks and put up bars on the windows at 49er headquarters, and he threw away pictures and souvenirs of anything that had existed before he came on the scene, including the "10-year club" plaque on the dressing room wall, which honored players who had spent at least 10 years with the 49ers. He was totally out of control.

Some of his actions were incredibly petty. His new home on the Peninsula was smaller than the one he'd had in Baltimore, so he sold a couple of beat-up couches to the team and put them in the dressing room. In the past, assistant coaches had earned small fees for appearing on the postgame radio shows, but Thomas told Bill Shaw, then general manager of KSFO, that the money should go to him and the coaches would appear on the show for nothing.

Most fans weren't aware of everything Thomas was doing behind the scenes, but they certainly knew who was responsible for the team's decline. At every home game, fans put up signs reading, "Blame Joe Thomas" and "Thomas Must Go." Thomas instructed stadium security men to destroy the signs. A group of fans formed an organization called "Doubting Thomases" that was aimed at getting rid of Thomas. The barrage of criticism from media and fans, along with the realization that the team was getting worse and worse, made Thomas paranoid. When San Francisco mayor George Moscone was assassinated on November 27, 1978, Thomas became convinced that somebody would try to shoot him as well, at the game scheduled that night at Candlestick Park, and he wanted the game canceled. The game was played and nobody shot at Thomas. And, of course, the 49ers lost, 24–7 to the Pittsburgh Steelers.

Eddie's first response to this uproar was the same as at his original press conference: defiance. He announced that he was extending Thomas's contract for four years!

> The barrage of criticism from media and fans, along with the realization that the team was getting worse and worse, made Thomas paranoid.

"Because of all the turmoil, all the press criticism, I thought it was important to make a statement," he explained later. "If I had it to do all over again, no, I wouldn't have done it."

But Eddie didn't sign the new contract, and Thomas knew he was in trouble. After a 49er loss to the St. Louis Cardinals, he charged into the dressing room and told players, "If I'm going down the tubes, I'm going to take you with me."

After that Monday night game when Thomas feared being shot, Eddie fired Thomas, later recalling the incident as the first time he had fired anybody; apparently, he had forgotten about Clark.

Enter Bill Walsh

EVEN BEFORE he fired Thomas, Eddie had talked to Bill Walsh, then coaching at Stanford, about coming to the 49ers as head coach; Ron Barr, who did the Stanford play-by-play, set up a meeting between the two. Walsh, who had earlier declined a feeler from Thomas, told DeBartolo he hadn't changed his mind. He knew he couldn't coach under Thomas.

Walsh, though, had had his eye on an NFL head-coaching job for years. Not knowing that Paul Brown didn't think he was head-coaching material, he had expected to get the job in Cincinnati when Brown retired, but that went to Bill (Tiger) Johnson, a former 49er player and assistant coach before he went to Cincinnati. Brown apparently also discouraged the Seattle Seahawks and New York Jets, as well as the 49ers, from pursuing Walsh.

Over Brown's objections, Walsh then went to the San Diego Chargers for a year as offensive coordinator. With the blessing of Chargers coach Tommy Prothro, he left in 1977 to become head coach at Stanford for two years. He took Stanford to bowl games in each of those years, convincing the doubters that he could be a head coach; and after his first season, he had serious discussions with the Chicago Bears and Los Angeles Rams about head-coaching jobs.

The Bears offered him a contract for more than $100,000 a year, a good salary in those days and double what he was getting with Stanford. He turned down the job because he didn't want to go to Chicago. Walsh was a native Californian, from the Los Angeles area, who had gone to school at San Jose State, and his time in the Midwest at Cincinnati had convinced him he'd rather live in California. "I don't even know why I talked to them, when I knew I wouldn't take the job," he told me later. "Sometimes, you do things for your ego."

He was much closer to taking the Rams job, replacing Chuck Knox, and there were even premature reports in Bay Area newspapers that he would. Walsh had his doubts, though, because he respected Knox; if Rams owner Carroll Rosenbloom wasn't happy with Knox, Walsh reasoned, would he be any happier with him? There were also newspapermen in the Los Angeles area who were campaigning for George Allen, who had been a successful coach with the Rams earlier. Stanford pressured Walsh to make a decision, and he decided to stay. The Rams hired Allen—but then fired him during the exhibition season, confirming Walsh's doubts about the stability of the situation.

Though Walsh had backed out on those two opportunities, it was obvious he was ready to go to the NFL if he got the right offer. As soon as Eddie fired Thomas, he called Walsh to set up a meeting at the Fairmont Hotel, with Carmen Policy also there.

Before Policy left Youngstown for the meeting, he had been called into the office of Ed DeBartolo, Sr. "I want you to watch Eddie to make sure he doesn't offer this coach too much money," the senior DeBartolo told Policy. "Don't let him go over $120,000."

But Eddie had made up his mind before the meeting was held. After Walsh had talked with DeBartolo and Policy about his plans for the team, Eddie asked him how much salary he wanted. Walsh said $160,000, more than triple his Stanford salary, never dreaming he'd get that much. "You've got it," said Eddie.

Policy gulped, wondering what he would tell the senior DeBartolo. "But Senior never asked me directly," said Policy. "I'm sure he knew, but when we started winning, it didn't bother him."

The original plan was that Walsh would then find a general manager, but as he talked to football people around the league, he learned that the 49ers' reputation was so bad that it seemed unlikely that he could find a reputable man to take the job.

Walsh's memory is that Eddie then said to him, "Why don't you do both jobs?" Perhaps it happened that way, but Walsh had always felt strongly that the coach should be the one who has the ultimate authority in player moves. It's likely that Walsh first suggested the idea that he do both jobs, and he did them both brilliantly for the next 10 years. But whichever way it happened, the Eddie DeBartolo who had not been willing, even in theory, to give a coach that kind of authority two years earlier, had changed his mind.

Eddie was learning.

CHAPTER THREE

The Walsh Years Begin

LONG BEFORE he became a head coach, Bill Walsh had earned a reputation within the football world for having a brilliant offensive mind. Paul Brown had turned the Bengals' offense over to Walsh in Cincinnati, a fact significant in itself because Brown had had some great offenses with Otto Graham, Marion Motley, Dante Lavelli, and Mac Speedie in Cleveland. The system Walsh developed was able to utilize the talents of widely disparate quarterbacks. He had Virgil Carter, a gifted athlete with a weak arm, rolling out and throwing short passes. He had strong-armed quarterbacks like Greg Cook and Ken Anderson throwing long passes to speedy receivers like Isaac Curtis. All three quarterbacks led the conference in quarterback ratings.

To help his quarterbacks, Walsh started a system of "scripting" plays before each game, first 15, then 20, then 25. The script wasn't followed exactly. "If the fourth play is supposed to be a long pass but somehow, our first three plays get us inside the opponent's 10, we're obviously not going to throw deep," noted Walsh. The quarterback always had the authority to audible out of a call if he saw a change in the defense. But Walsh's intent was to list specific plays in which the team had confidence, plays that they were more likely to run well; in a typical game, they'd usually run about 80 percent of the scripted plays among the first 25.

By the time Walsh came to the 49ers, NFL coaches were becoming more sophisticated in charting the tendencies of other teams—what they were likely to run on third-and-short or what they liked to run inside the 20, for instance—by using computers. Walsh's "script" nullified the advantages of that system because his teams were running predetermined plays instead of plays designed for specific situations or against specific defenses. To make it even more baffling, Walsh set up his game plans on four-game rotations. Since opposing teams would get films/videos only from the 49ers' last three games, his game plan would feature plays he hadn't used in those games.

Mistaken Judgments

YET, FOR all his imagination, Walsh did not become an NFL head coach until he was 47, which was also the age when Vince Lombardi got his first shot, with the Green Bay Packers. Both men made the most of their belated opportunities.

Why did it take so long for Walsh? In part, the fault lay with Brown, who told the 49ers and any other interested team that Walsh was not head-coaching material. Brown's opinion was respected because he was a great coach and innovator. Many of the practices that are common in pro football today began with Brown. Among them: coaches calling the plays from the sidelines; extensive classroom meetings to look at films and videos as preparation for the game; teams staying together in hotels the night before home games, not just on the road. Walsh himself has always credited Brown with having the most influence on his career.

Brown reportedly advised other teams that Walsh wasn't strong enough to deal with the players. He couldn't have been more wrong. As 49ers' head coach, Walsh proved himself to be tough to the point of ruthlessness. He released starting offensive tackle Ron Singleton for instance, after Singleton argued with him at practice during training camp; he told aides Billy Wilson and R. C. Owens to clean out Singleton's locker and get him on a plane. He routinely forced veterans into retirement earlier than they had planned because he thought it was better for the team. Players feared him.

Only occasionally did Walsh's iron hand fail him. The first time was with linebacker Thomas (Hollywood) Henderson, who had tremendous physical ability but had tested the patience of Cowboys' coach Tom Landry because of his erratic behavior. Walsh traded for him, knowing that Henderson was much better physically than his other linebackers and thinking he could make him a consistent player.

> As 49ers' head coach, Walsh proved himself to be tough to the point of ruthlessness.

Walsh didn't realize that Henderson's erratic behavior stemmed from an addiction to cocaine. Walsh came from a generation in which the use of recreational drugs was unknown; alcohol was the drug of choice. Drinking was usually done in a social context, at bars, parties, meals, so abuse was usually obvious to others. Athletes who were abusing cocaine, as Henderson was doing, usually did it in the privacy of their home or hotel room. Those who knew the signs recognized Henderson's problem, but Walsh was totally blind to it.

Even though Walsh rarely socialized with players, he invited Henderson to his home for dinner one night. Henderson kept excusing himself to go to the bathroom, leading Walsh to conclude that he had a serious bladder problem. Henderson, of course, was snorting cocaine in the bathroom.

Within a short time, it became difficult just to get Henderson on the practice field. He had to be released.

The other player who caused Walsh fits was offensive tackle

Bubba Paris, drafted in 1982 to correct an obvious weakness on the team. Bubba's addiction was food, in great quantity. Walsh thought Paris would be a great player if he could keep his weight below 300 pounds. For Bubba, that was an impossible goal.

Teammates passed around Bubba stories, such as the time his pregnant wife sent Bubba out for doughnuts. By the time he returned, only one of the original dozen remained. Conditioning coach Jerry Attaway was supposed to be monitoring Bubba's weight in the off-season, but when asked how he was doing, Attaway noted wryly that the only way to succeed would be to lock Paris in the county jail.

Hoping to control Bubba's weight with an off-season conditioning program, Attaway enlisted the help of Ben Parks, a junior college track coach who had worked with other 49ers on off-season programs. Parks picked up Bubba at his home the first two mornings. The third morning, the drapes were drawn and nobody answered the doorbell or the telephone. Bubba had opted out of the program.

In camp during one period, Bubba's weight stayed around 296–297 for several days, though he appeared heavier. The mystery was solved when the coach who was weighing Bubba realized that Bubba was leaning on the Coke machine next to the scale.

Another time in camp, Attaway was baffled because, though he was monitoring Paris's food at each meal, Bubba's weight kept climbing. Then Walsh got a call from the maid cleaning up Bubba's room. "What should I do with the chicken bones?" she asked. Bubba had been ordering out from the Colonel, and the bones were piled up in his closet.

"The Professor"

BEFORE WALSH proved himself at Stanford, NFL coaches and general managers were receptive to Brown's message that Walsh was too soft to be a good head coach, because the 1970s were a macho time. The Pittsburgh Steelers were the best team of the era, and there was nothing fancy about the way they played. Their defensive line was known as the "Steel Curtain," because it was impossible to get through. Middle linebacker Jack Lambert would clothesline receivers who came across the middle. Cornerback Mel Blount was a vicious tackler who caused receivers to drop catchable passes because they anticipated a Blount hit.

> Even when he [Walsh] started winning Super Bowls with the 49ers, the most frequently used descriptive word was "finesse," and that was not a compliment.

Though Walsh's offense was successful, it was often derided because it depended on deception. Even when he started winning Super Bowls with the 49ers, the most frequently used descriptive word was "finesse," and that was not a compliment.

NFL teams wanted a coach who looked and acted like Mike Ditka, not one who looked like a professor. And so Walsh had to wait much longer than he should have for his chance.

Later, Walsh said he thought he was the victim of the "old boys' network," to which he did not belong. "The NFL is opening up a lot now," he said after his first Super Bowl triumph, "but for a time, it was a very tight little circle. Jobs got passed around to the same people—and I wasn't one of those people.

"I was determined that I was going to work as hard as I could at my job and not get in the business of campaigning for a head job and then being disappointed when I didn't get it. I feel I've improved as a coach just about every year."

Sometimes, what seem to be bad breaks at the time turn out to be beneficial in the long run, and that certainly was true for Walsh. If he had been hired for the Bengals' job, he would have had to escape the shadow of Brown, who still had control of player per-

THE WALSH YEARS BEGIN • 23

sonnel decisions. If he'd come to the 49ers in 1976, he'd have run head-on into Joe Thomas the next year, as Monte Clark did, and he would certainly have made the same decision Clark did. If he'd gone to the Rams, he probably would not have fared any better than George Allen.

Coming to the 49ers when he did, Walsh had the chance to show everything he could do, without any interference. Because the team had been so bad, nobody with a reputation wanted the job, so he had complete authority. Even Eddie DeBartolo didn't interfere during the first three years, though Eddie would give Walsh plenty of grief in years to come.

Many years later, when Walsh was working NFL games on television after his Hall of Fame coaching career had ended, Brown approached him and said, "Bill, I was wrong." But, there was no apology for the anguish he had caused.

Walsh's organizational ability was as important as his coaching to the 49ers, who had been left in shambles by Thomas. Walsh would build an organization that was a model for other teams and even for other businesses, defining jobs with precision and then hiring people who could fit those specifications.

> Walsh would build an organization that was a model for other teams, defining jobs with precision and then hiring people who could fit those specifications.

When DeBartolo hired Walsh, he expected the coach to find a compatible general manager. The leading candidate appeared to be Don Klosterman, who had front office experience in the NFL and whose background was in California; he had been a record-setting quarterback at Loyola (Los Angeles) years before.

Walsh later said that the organization was in such disarray that he couldn't find anybody he wanted who was willing to work for the 49ers. It was also difficult to find a competent man who was willing to take on the role Walsh envisioned. The general manager had always been a rung above the coach on the organizational ladder; the GM could fire the coach, but not vice versa. That was never the way Walsh envisioned the separation of powers. He always felt that the coach should have the final word on players, which is the ultimate power within a sports organization.

He presented an idea to DeBartolo: that Walsh be general manager as well as coach, bringing in another executive to work on details while he made the major decisions. DeBartolo really had no choice but to agree. Because of the Thomas fiasco, Eddie's public image was scraping bottom. His only redeeming virtue at the moment was that he had hired a local hero. If it got out that he was butting heads with Walsh already, his image would plummet to below ground level.

> While others had underestimated him, Walsh had overestimated his ability to make an immediate difference.

So, Walsh started to bring in men he had known for a long time and whom he trusted. His first chief administrative aide was John Ralston, who had been head coach for Stanford in the 1960s and early 1970s, when Walsh was on the staff for a time, and who had taken Stanford to two successive Rose Bowls. Ralston left after a year to pursue business offers, and John McVay, who had been head of player personnel, moved up to become Walsh's assistant.

Walsh and McVay complemented each other perfectly. McVay, a former coach who had been fired by the New York Giants, no longer wanted to coach. He was a very knowledgeable football man who had a great eye for details—the perfect No. 2 man, who always knew the often-complicated league rules regarding waivers, trades, and injury lists. Perhaps most important of all, he shunned the spotlight. He wanted Walsh to get credit, not him, and that arrangement was perfectly satisfactory to Walsh. Typically, Walsh would have the idea and McVay would carry it out. It was, for instance, McVay's phone calls that made it possible for the 49ers to trade for Fred Dean in 1981 and for Walsh to do the draft-day juggling in 1986 that produced the best draft of Walsh's career.

Walsh knew it was important to reestablish the 49ers' link with the community, and he got players out frequently for public appearances. He, too, went out in public as much as possible. Because he had gone to San Jose State and coached at both Cal and Stanford, he understood the area and its residents.

More than almost any other football coach, Walsh had a social conscience. During his 49er career, he made a conscious effort to bring minorities into the organization, including a program that brought in black coaches. That, too, was important, especially in a city become increasingly known for its politically correct attitude.

It would take time for others to realize the extent of Walsh's influence on the 49ers and the community. The early focus was on his coaching, and the results were disappointing, to Walsh at least as much as to the fans. While others had underestimated him, Walsh had overestimated his ability to make an immediate difference, partly because he hadn't realized quite how bad a team he was inheriting and partly because, in just two years away from the NFL, he had forgotten how much better the pro game was than the college game he had been coaching. When the 49ers had another 2–14 season in Walsh's first year, it was a tremendous shock to him.

"I really thought we could come in and make a big difference that first year," he said later. "We had done it at Stanford.

"But in college, you can literally outsmart people. We had nothing on defense at Stanford that first year, but we would load up against the run until we stopped that and force teams to throw the ball, and they were generally inept at that.

"And then, when we played LSU in a bowl game, well, we

were flabbergasted at the way they would telegraph their plays. They ran them the same way all the time, so we knew exactly what they would do.

"But, you don't get that kind of break in the pro game. Teams don't give anything away, and when teams are physically superior to you, they just keep pounding away until you break."

But though the 49ers record in Walsh's first year was the same as the year before, a dismal 2–14, progress was being made. Realizing he couldn't make the big strides he had thought possible earlier, Walsh settled for small improvements. "Some people say a loss is a loss," Walsh said in training camp, "but I don't buy that. If I have to lose, I'd rather lose by one point than 30. You have to look for improvement."

Meanwhile, he was installing not just an offensive system but a complete management system with the 49ers, building the framework for future success. Though Walsh made all the important decisions for the 49ers, he did it only after getting input from everybody. He held separate meetings with coaches and scouts, so that neither group would be influenced by the other, and he insisted that all of them speak up; if a coach or scout was silent, Walsh would solicit his opinion." He hired Dr. Harry Edwards to work up psychological tests for potential draft picks and to counsel players, particularly the black players. Preparing for the draft, and knowing he couldn't possibly view all the film/video on prospects, he instructed scouts to put together a strip of a player's 10 best and 10 worst plays, so he could get an idea of the player's range of ability. He told coaches and scouts to evaluate players not just in terms of their ability but also in terms of how they could help the 49ers; it did no good to draft a good player who didn't fit the 49er system.

His practices, following the Brown example, were totally organized, with specific times allotted to each drill. Other coaches believed in working on specific plays until they were learned and then going on to others. Walsh put everything in at once. He didn't worry that players would stumble in the exhibition season because they weren't totally familiar with the plays: He was preparing for the regular season, when they would know the plays.

His practices were also shorter than those of other teams because he had players spending more time in meetings, going over plays from his voluminous playbook and looking at film. Walsh believed firmly that mental preparation was vital because a confused player wouldn't do the job physically. Walsh reduced the 49ers' physical workouts as the season went on because he wanted to keep his team as fresh as possible. In the championship years, the 49ers would always be at their best late in the season, when other teams were wearing down.

Because his squad was so weak that first year, Walsh scoured the waiver wires each week in training camp, looking for released players who might help. He would bring in players and work them out during the lunch break. If he thought a player would be a significant upgrade, he signed him; otherwise, he sent the player on his way, before anybody else knew he was there. Most of the players who were worked out didn't make it, but Walsh did pick up two players who became starters for Super Bowl teams, free safety Dwight Hicks and defensive end Dwaine (Pee Wee) Board. Steelers' coach Chuck Knox had released Board because he was loyal to his veteran defensive linemen, though they were fading. Walsh would never make that mistake.

Walsh's System: Against the Grain

FOR YEARS, football people marveled at the fact that offensive line coach Bobb McKittrick produced outstanding offensive lines with players who were not high draft picks. McKittrick was an outstanding coach, of course, but Walsh's system emphasized quickness in the offensive linemen. He often used the analogy of a boxer consistently beating his opponent to the punch and wearing

him down—and it was relatively easy to find smaller, quicker linemen because everybody else was going after the behemoths.
Similarly, Walsh's requirements for a quarterback emphasized athletic ability and football intelligence, not the arm strength that was
coveted by other teams, and he wound up with two of the best
quarterbacks in NFL history.

Walsh's offensive system required an unusual amount of study
for a quarterback because there were so many more options; but
once the quarterback learned it, he was certain to succeed because
he had so many potential receivers on every play. "Any decent
quarterback should be able to complete at least 60 percent of his
passes in this offense," Steve Young would say years later.

One distinctive aspect of Walsh's offense was the fact the 49ers
seldom had a play where a receiver went one way and the quarterback threw another, as often happens with other teams. On each
play, receivers had specific routes, broken only if the quarterback
got in trouble and had to scramble. Since the quarterback always
knew where a receiver would be, there was no reason to make an errant
throw.

> Even though the 49ers were still losing in 1979, they were much more exciting because their offense was productive.

There was enough flexibility built
in the system to go to the long
pass with the right receiver—Isaac
Curtis in Cincinnati, Jerry Rice in
San Francisco—but the short- and
medium-range passes were the key to
the system, because a high percentage
of swing passes to running backs
were often little more than long handoffs. His offense was also a
defensive weapon because, by controlling the ball for long periods,
the offense gave the 49er defense a chance to rest and to be more
effective.

Even though the 49ers were still losing in 1979, they were
much more exciting because their offense was productive; quar-

terback Steve DeBerg set a club record with 347 completions (in 578 attempts).

DeBerg, who was still playing in the league 19 years later, had a strong and accurate arm, and he was a good student of the game who picked up Walsh's offense quickly. But Walsh was always lukewarm in his praise of DeBerg—he seldom commented on DeBerg without referring to his "gross errors"—and it was obvious that DeBerg would not be his long-term quarterback.

DeBerg had one failing: He was terribly slow. The 49ers had to pass frequently because they were usually trailing, and he faced a ferocious pass rush. Unable to get away from the rush, DeBerg would often have to throw blindly. He threw only 21 interceptions in 1979, 3.8 percent of his attempts (anything below 5 is considered good for a quarterback, though in Walsh's system, the interception percentages are generally lower). But they all seemed to be critical. Of course, because the 49ers needed all the points they could get, every interception would be critical.

Walsh also had a little breathing room because he had a very good relationship with the media when he first came in. He was a breath of fresh air. He didn't talk in the usual coaching clichés, but expressed himself in clear, precise language. Later in his coaching career, he would become much more calculated and cautious in what he said, but that first year, he said what he thought. Not many coaches have ever done so.

Reporters also enjoyed the Walsh style of offensive football. The team might still be losing, but there were big plays to write about, athletes to interview. There was also some hope that the team would get better. In the Thomas years, the trend had been down, and the games had been abysmally dull. Indeed, one of the two games the 49ers had won in Thomas's second and last year, 6–3 over Tampa Bay, was cited by most who had seen it as the absolute worst game they had ever seen.

The next season, 1980, the 49ers opened with three straight wins, more than they'd had in each of the previous two seasons.

But in the third win, Board was injured and lost for the season. "I'd rather have lost the game than to have lost Dwaine Board," Walsh said.

His pessimism was justified. Without Board pressuring the quarterback, the 49ers weak secondary was exposed and they lost eight straight, including a gruesome 59–15 loss to the Dallas Cowboys in which star running back Paul Hofer was injured and lost for the season. Walsh called it the worst period of his life. "We weren't too thrilled about it, either," noted offensive guard Randy Cross, who would later play for three Super Bowl champions in his great career.

The season ended on a positive note, though, as the 49ers bounced back to win three of their last five. The most noteworthy was a 38–35 overtime win over New Orleans, in which they overcame a 35–7 halftime lead by the Saints, the greatest comeback in a regular-season game in NFL history.

And, more important, Walsh had found his quarterback.

CHAPTER FOUR

Walsh's Quarterback

EVERYBODY WANTS to be known as the one who discovered Joe Montana. John Ralston, an executive with the 49ers the year Montana was drafted, and Tony Razzano, college scouting director for the team, have each claimed that Bill Walsh had to be talked into drafting Montana. Their story is that Walsh wanted to draft Steve Dils, who had been his quarterback at Stanford and the NCAA passing champion in 1978. In Ralston's version, he was the one who convinced Walsh. In Razzano's version, he is naturally the hero.

Ralston and Razzano certainly recommended Montana, as did John McVay, personnel director at the time, but Walsh didn't have to be talked into the decision and he had never intended to draft Dils. He told me that before the 1979 draft.

Walsh and I had a special relationship while he coached the 49ers, which eventually led to our collaborating on a book about his career, *Building a Champion*, after he retired. I was excited by his intelligence and creativity, two attributes that were in short supply in the football world. He appreciated my interest in his philosophy and also the fact that I was writing a column for the

San Francisco Chronicle, which had a higher circulation in northern California than any other four papers combined. You can decide which factor was more important to him.

Our relationship was strengthened in his first year with the 49ers when I wrote of the progress he was making, despite the record, and predicted that he would make the 49ers a contender. Other writers thought I was crazy, but I saw a coach who was both organized and creative, and one to whom players responded. He didn't have the talent to win with that team, but when he got good players, he'd win.

Walsh shared his hopes and ideas with me, which greatly furthered my football education. Many times, he preferred to talk off the record, because he didn't want his thoughts to be made public, especially when he was critical of a player. I was willing to use his thoughts under my byline, because I trusted his judgment. I got burned only once. Early in Dwight Clark's career, Walsh feared that Dwight wouldn't last because he was taking so much punishment, and he told me he was going to try to get another receiver so he could bring Clark off the bench. I wrote that it would be better for the 49ers and Clark if he were the third receiver. After Clark made the most famous catch in 49ers history in the 1982 NFC Championship game against Dallas, I was scolded for years by readers who "remembered" my writing that Clark should be third-string, though NFL rosters are not deep enough for a third string.

In one of these off-the-record talks before the 1979 draft, Walsh had praised Dils's intelligence and courage but doubted that he had the physical ability to be a standout in the NFL. He didn't want to downgrade his former quarterback publicly, but he also wanted me to understand why the 49ers wouldn't draft Dils, whom he projected as no more than a backup quarterback in the NFL.

Walsh said nothing about Montana at that time, but shortly afterward, I talked to former 49er quarterback John Brodie, who had sat next to Montana at a sports banquet and had been impressed by Montana's quiet confidence. Brodie had recommended Montana to Walsh—and learned that Walsh had already worked out Montana and was prepared to draft him.

Beyond that, there are two things everybody knows about Bill Walsh: (1) He's a great judge of quarterbacks, and (2) he has absolute faith in his own evaluations, even if they run contrary to others'. Ralston and Razzano, alone or in combination, would not have been able to talk him into picking Montana if Joe had not been the one he sought.

The 1979 Draft

WHEN WALSH first started looking at the draft, though, the quarterback he really liked was Phil Simms. But because the 49ers had no first-round pick (gone in the O. J. Simpson trade), he knew he didn't have a shot at Simms, who would go to the New York Giants on the first round. So, he had to look elsewhere for a quarterback.

He went on a nationwide search, trying out every quarterback who was considered a top prospect. One result of the search was that he found a wide receiver. At Clemson to work out Steve Fuller, he asked Dwight Clark to catch Fuller's passes. Walsh was not impressed with Fuller, but he had always liked big receivers and he had always liked big receivers and he had always liked big receivers and he was pleasantly surprised by Clark, who had not even been listed among the top 50 receivers in scouting reports. He would draft Clark on the 10th round, and Clark would set pass-receiving records for the 49ers.

> There are two things everybody knows about Bill Walsh:
> (1) He's a great judge of quarterbacks, and
> (2) he has absolute faith in his own evaluations.

Montana was the last on his list, but Walsh had been intrigued by what he knew of Joe's collegiate career. At times, Montana had been benched by Notre Dame coach Dan Devine for his inconsistent play, but he had also shown moments of brilliance, most notably in the Cotton Bowl in his senior year, when he brought his team back from a 34–12 fourth-quarter deficit to a 35–34 win over Houston.

Walsh went to the Los Angeles area with a dual purpose: to work out UCLA running back James Owens and Montana. He projected Owens, who had sprinter's speed, as a wide receiver, and later selected him on the second round, the 49ers' first pick of the 1979 draft. Owens was a mistake, but drafting Montana and Clark made that draft a great one for the Niners.

> Walsh's system emphasized accuracy, not arm strength, and he was confident that he could make Montana a consistent performer.

Watching Montana work out that day, Walsh was excited as he projected what Joe could mean to the 49ers. Though Walsh had been successful working with slow-footed quarterbacks—he resurrected Dan Fouts's career in San Diego and started Fouts on the way to what became a Hall of Fame career—he preferred quarterbacks who were quick-footed enough to elude the pass rush and make plays when the normal play had broken down.

"You could see his ability right away," Walsh told me years later. "It's so important that a quarterback be able to get back quickly and set up, and then be able to improvise if the play breaks down. I sensed just watching Joe in that workout that he'd be able to do that in time, though he surprised me by how quickly he learned everything."

Walsh always had his own criteria for judging players, especially quarterbacks. Montana was downgraded by most NFL scouts and coaches because of his inconsistent college career and because they thought he lacked the arm strength to be a successful NFL quarterback. But Walsh's system emphasized accuracy, not arm strength, and he was confident that he could make Montana a consistent performer. "When you looked at his comebacks, you saw what he was capable of, and I just felt that, with constant work in practice, we could get him to a point where he could do that consistently. And, of course, that's what happened."

Because Montana was not highly regarded by others, Walsh felt he could wait to draft him. When Brodie heard on the radio that the 49ers had gone first for Owens, he called 49er headquarters to ask Walsh why he hadn't taken Montana. Walsh reassured him with information he had obtained from his contacts in the league: that no other team thought of Montana as higher than a fifth- or sixth-round pick. Some years later, Gil Brandt of the Dallas Cowboys said the Cowboys were ready to take Montana on the third round. The Cowboys never had the chance. The 49ers had the first pick on the third round and took Montana.

> When Montana became successful, the question was often asked: Did Montana make the Walsh system look good, or did the Walsh system make Montana?

Developing Montana

WHEN MONTANA became successful, the question was often asked: Did Montana make the Walsh system look good, or did the Walsh system make Montana? The two men had different answers to that question, but the truth probably is a combination.

Montana was certainly fortunate to come to the 49ers at that particular moment, to a coach who appreciated his ability and had the system to use it. His career would have been quite different if he had gone to another team, especially if it had been as a sixth-round pick. If he had gone to a team whose coach thought his quarterback should have a cannon for an arm, he probably would have been cut in training camp.

Quarterback evaluations are really that quixotic in the NFL. Jim Plunkett was cut by the 49ers and went on to win two Super Bowls for the Raiders. Johnny Unitas was playing semipro ball and was signed by the Baltimore Colts only because of an injury to starter George Shaw. As recently as the 1999 season, Kurt Warner was put on the expansion draft list by the St. Louis Rams; fortunately for the Rams, the Cleveland Browns didn't take him, and so he was there when Trent Green was injured and knocked out for the season.

So Montana got a chance with Walsh that he might not have had otherwise, and he made the most of it. Walsh has probably coached more successful quarterbacks than any other coach in NFL history, but there is no question that Montana had the best career of them all. He could bring out nuances in the Walsh system that no other quarterback could. His ability to hit receivers in stride made it possible for receivers to run for significant yardage after the catch, a key element in the Walsh offense that television announcers turned into a graphic. His nimble feet enabled him to elude the rush and get the extra time he needed to complete a pass; indeed, in his early years, he was more dangerous when he was flushed from the pocket. He had an unparalleled ability to see the field and make the right decision.

It didn't come all at once. Walsh limited Montana's options at first. Usually, that meant using just one side of the field, so Montana might have the option of looking deep down the sideline first, to the tight end hooking over the middle second and to a running back swinging out of the backfield if the first two receivers weren't open. It wasn't until the 1984 season that Walsh gave Montana everything.

Walsh also picked his spots very carefully with Montana, using him only in specific situations in his rookie season, a tactic that gave Montana the chance to look good and build up his confidence as well as the team's confidence in him. He would usually put in Montana only when the 49ers were inside their opponent's 20, for instance, and he would call a play, usually a rollout, on which Montana had just one receiver. The receiver would usually be open, but if he wasn't, Montana could run. In either case, the chance that Montana might throw an interception, which would have been devastating both to him and the team, was reduced to almost zero. And, in fact, he threw 23 passes that rookie season, but no interceptions.

Walsh used subterfuge to disguise his plans early in Montana's second season. Before the third game of the season, Steve DeBerg developed laryngitis, and the 49ers equipped him with a voice-amplifier so he could call signals in the game. When the 49ers reached the Jets 10 early in the game, DeBerg pointed to the voice box, indicating he was having problems, and came out of the game. Montana came in and ran a bootleg for a touchdown. There was nothing wrong with DeBerg's voice box; the whole procedure had been planned before the game by Walsh, who reasoned that the Jets would be caught off base by it. "It shouldn't have taken a rocket scientist to realize Joe was going to run a bootleg," said guard Randy Cross, "but the Jets couldn't figure it out."

"Napalm and Nitroglycerin"

WALSH'S MANEUVERING made it obvious to everybody, including the quarterbacks, that DeBerg was being eased out of the picture, but DeBerg remained the starter until just after the halfway point of the 1980 season. Though Walsh never admitted it, he probably didn't want Montana to experience the devastating losses that were piling up.

DeBerg was a strong leader, and he wasn't happy on the bench. "Steve DeBerg might have been the most competitive person I've ever known," said Randy Cross, "and he brought that out in Joe. Putting those two guys together was like mixing napalm with nitroglycerine.

"I remember one time we were staying at this roach-infested hotel in New Orleans and they had one of those video games where you pushed the players around with your hand. They played for three hours, just beating on the thing, and they had big bruises on their palms by the end. They were like that with everything. It was obvious one of them would have to go."

And it was also obvious which one would go. Fearing that some players might believe DeBerg should be the starter, which would have split the team, Walsh traded DeBerg after the 1980 season and then traded for Guy Benjamin, who had been his quarterback at Stanford in 1977, to be Montana's backup.

> "Steve DeBerg might have been the most competitive person I've ever known, and he brought that out in Joe. Putting those two guys together was like mixing napalm with nitroglycerin."
>
> —Randy Cross

Walsh's system was important to Montana for another reason that would become obvious in the 1981 season: Because Walsh called all the plays, the quarterback didn't have to be a vocal leader. In the past, leadership ability had been required of quarterbacks; and there were some quarterbacks with marginal passing ability—Bobby Layne, Joe Kapp—who were successful because they were such strong leaders. Montana was quiet, nothing like the Layne–Kapp model or even DeBerg, but he led by example. Starting with the 1981 season, players came to have extraordinary confidence in him.

The 1981 Draft

BUT MONTANA couldn't do it alone. Walsh had to make a decision before the 1981 draft: Was he going to settle for the same kind of team the 49ers had had so often in their first 15 years, with a great offense and no defense, or would he try to improve the defense, so he could have the foundation for a contending team?

He opted for defense, with results beyond what even he could have predicted, in his first really successful draft.

Identifying the main problem hadn't been difficult: the defensive backfield. The majority of players Walsh had picked off the waiver list for tryouts had been defensive backs, but free safety Dwight Hicks was the only one who had stuck—and he was the only legitimate NFL player who had started in the defensive backfield in Walsh's two seasons. Walsh had been so desperate that he had even tried James Owens there in spot situations, but Owens had failed. Because projections for the 1982 draft were that it would be short of defensive-back prospects, 1981 would have to be the year the 49ers addressed the problem. So Walsh drafted four defensive backs—Ronnie Lott, Eric Wright, Carlton Williamson, and Lynn Thomas—among his first five picks. It was unusual for a team to concentrate on one position that way, but Walsh thought he had no choice.

After their 6–10 season in 1980, the 49ers were drafting eighth, high enough to get a good player but probably not high enough, Walsh thought, to get one of the two outstanding defensive backs who were on his wish list, safeties Kenny Easley of UCLA and Ronnie Lott of USC. So Walsh talked with Easley's agent, Leigh Steinberg, and told him how much he wanted to draft Easley. Steinberg wrote a letter to the teams ahead of the 49ers and said Easley wouldn't play for them if he were drafted. The Seattle Seahawks called Steinberg's bluff and drafted Easley; and for a time, it seemed Lott would be gone, too.

Each draft day, though, has its surprises. That year, it was the St. Louis Cardinals, a team that often made quixotic picks, who passed up Pittsburgh linebacker Hugh Green and drafted Alabama linebacker E. J. Junior. Tampa Bay, which would probably have taken Lott, then grabbed Green, and the 49ers quickly picked Lott.

The selections could not have worked better for the 49ers. Easley was a fine player, but his career was cut short by a kidney problem. Lott became as important to the 49ers on the defensive side of the ball as Montana was on the offensive side. They also became very close friends, traveling together with their families in the off-season.

Wright was almost as important a selection, and a 49er find. George Seifert, then the defensive back coach for the 49ers, had been impressed with Wright when he was a coach at the Senior Bowl. Wright was not highly regarded by others, but he became a great corner opposite Lott—probably an even better cover man, though not the hitter Lott was, until his career was prematurely ended by a groin injury.

Williamson gave the 49ers a third rookie starter, at strong safety, and Thomas contributed as the fifth defensive back in the "nickel" coverage.

Walsh made one other significant defensive change that off-season, signing veteran linebacker Jack (Hacksaw) Reynolds, who had been released by the Los Angeles Rams.

Reynolds was a genuine character. He earned his nickname when he destroyed an old car with a hacksaw in a rage after losing a college game that had kept his Tennessee team from going to a bowl game. His way of preparing for games was to dress several hours before his teammates and sit in the empty locker room waiting for them. When the 49ers played at home, he'd drive up the freeway while dressed in his uniform, eliciting stares from passing drivers.

Walsh liked to bring in veteran leaders to guide his younger players, and Reynolds was a perfect fit for this team, with the competitive fire that his nickname suggested. His physical skills had eroded, but he was a smart player who used his knowledge to position himself to make big plays.

And so the 49ers were ready for a season in which they would shock everybody, including themselves.

CHAPTER FIVE

The Magical Season

THE 1981 season was a magical one for the 49ers, especially after the rocky road the franchise had traveled the previous four seasons. Joe Montana came of age, the rookie defensive backs were spectacular, and Bill Walsh showed for the first time what a special coach he was.

Walsh enjoyed himself in a way he never would again. He even got a little playful at the end. He didn't travel with the team to the Super Bowl because he had gone ahead to make an appearance at a dinner in Washington, D.C., and when players arrived at their Detroit hotel, a white-haired bellman came hustling out to the team bus to get their bags. It took the players a few minutes to realize the "bellman" was Walsh, who had borrowed the uniform.

Walsh has always had an excellent sense of humor, but his wit is subtle, not given to the slapstick and practical jokes that constitute locker room humor, so his little charade amused and relaxed his players, which was his intent.

After the 1981 season, Walsh would fall victim to the image problem, as successful coaches often do in the NFL, whose propaganda machine is at turbo level at all times. Tom Landry was

"Stoneface." Mike Ditka was the man in a constant rage, at players, at fans, at the media. Walsh became "The Genius."

There would be no more self-deprecating gags for the rest of his career, as Walsh struggled mightily to live up to the description. It didn't bother him that he was depicted as intellectually superior to his fellow coaches, because he had always believed he was, but it was a challenge to always look professorial, whether at dinners or on the sidelines.

Walsh was different. Unlike most coaches, he had serious interests beyond the playing field, particularly in the political realm; and he had friends like former Secretary of State George Schultz, who later would roam the sidelines when Walsh returned for a second tour as Stanford coach, and naval hero James Stockdale, who was Ross Perot's running mate in the 1992 presidential campaign and who had been a North Vietnamese prisoner of war during the Vietnam War.

> Tom Landry was "Stoneface." Mike Ditka was the man in a constant rage, at players, at fans, at the media. Walsh became "The Genius."

But there was nothing he enjoyed more than putting together a game plan, especially if it included something nobody else had. According to his assistants, a certain look would appear on Walsh's face during coaches' meetings, and it would be only minutes before he would excuse himself to go write down a new play that had just popped into his head. His wife, Geri, knew those moments too; he once absentmindedly wrote down a play on her shoulder while they were at dinner. One time I was at a dinner with Walsh and Cal coach Bruce Snyder. When Snyder asked about a play, Walsh diagrammed it on the tablecloth.

The number of coaches in football history with Walsh's offensive imagination could be counted on the fingers of one hand.

Old-timers talk of Clark Shaughnessy, who invented the T formation with the Chicago Bears and Stanford and was a brilliant defensive strategist too. Sid Gillman is the father of the modern passing game, with the Los Angeles Rams and San Diego Chargers, and he loved to exchange ideas with Walsh. Mike Shanahan has expanded on Walsh's offense with the Denver Broncos

Walsh the Coach

WALSH'S BEST coaching year was 1981. His other Super Bowl champions owed as much to his general manager's skills as his coaching, because he built superb teams, among the best of all time. In 1981, he had two great players, Montana and Ronnie Lott, and several good ones, but he also had some conspicuous weaknesses to overcome. He had a 247-pound guard, Dan Audick, playing left tackle, so he had Montana rolling out to the right side, because he knew Audick couldn't block his man for long. He had mediocre running backs (the 49ers' leading rusher that year, Ricky Patton, had only 547 yards for the season, and he was released before the next year), so he used swing passes to the backs as "long handoffs" that kept the offense moving in the same way as runs.

Watching Walsh guide the 49ers to a Super Bowl championship was a chance to get a football education free, as he consistently outcoached the man on the other sidelines. It wasn't just his playcalling, which was probably better that season than at any other time during his 49er career, but also the way he dictated what other teams did. Other coaches talked of "taking what the defense gives us"; but Walsh forced defenses to try to cope with him, because he took advantage of the macho thinking of most coaches. In the early 1980s, coaches still liked to talk of football being about "blocking and tackling," the clear implication being that strategy was for girls' softball. The result was a largely predictable game, which played into Walsh's hands; he consistently did the unexpected, even if that were only passing on first down instead of running, as every other team did. He threw short while others were throwing long, but he also coached receivers to run after the catch, so the short passes that were much easier to complete often turned into long gains.

In 1981, Walsh simply befuddled other coaches. Probably the most telling games were the ones the 49ers played against the Dallas Cowboys. Tom Landry was reputedly an innovator, but Walsh exposed him as an inflexible coach who won because he had superior players, not a better system. In 1981 Landry's players were still superior to the ones Walsh had, but the 49ers beat the Cowboys twice that season, once by a lopsided margin; and Landry was reduced to talking about Walsh doing it "with mirrors."

Other coaches referred to the 49ers by the F word—finesse—implying that the 49ers weren't real football players but were relying on trickery and deception. While deception was a big part of Walsh's offense, it wasn't at the expense of physical effort. It would be hard, for instance, to tell any receiver hit by Ronnie Lott that Lott was a "finesse" player. Lott told interviewers that a good part of what Walsh said to the team concerned physical play, and Walsh had hung a motto in the dressing room: I WILL NOT BE OUT-HIT AT ANY TIME THIS SEASON. "That was kind of a college thing," noted Dwight Clark, the 49ers' top receiver, "but it worked. Even the receivers, Freddie [Solomon] and I, we were going to go out and really hit people."

In his interviews, Walsh stressed the need for physical play, but the message didn't get through. As long as Walsh coached the 49ers, his teams were always referred to as "finesse" teams. At first, both Walsh and the players resented the implication that they weren't very physical, but they all soon realized that it was an advantage, because teams were unprepared for the physical side of the 49ers' game. In practice, they'd laugh at opponents who thought the 49ers weren't a strong physical team, and in games, they'd make those opponents pay for their miscalculation.

> Walsh is a control freak, and he attempted to control the media as well as his players and assistant coaches.

That came later. As the 1981 season opened, the 49ers seemed no better than they'd been, going 1–2. Walsh's mood turned paranoid; he worried that the media was preparing to call for his firing after two unsuccessful seasons. Ten years later, when we worked together on a book, he mentioned a writer who had prepared a four-part series on what was supposed to be Walsh's end as a 49ers' coach. Supposedly, the first part ran and the others didn't, but Walsh wouldn't say even then who the writer was; and if the first article appeared, it had no impact.

In fact, most of the writers covering the team greatly admired and liked Walsh, because he was so different from his supposed peers, more articulate and original. Because there were relatively few writers or TV and radio people around the team, it was a comfortable relationship; in training camp, Walsh would often have a glass of wine with writers after the afternoon practice.

Even so, signs of the problems he would later have with the media—when there were so many more covering the team and reporters came to resent his manipulations—were already beginning to show. Walsh is a control freak, and he attempted to control the media as well as his players and assistant coaches.

Even at that early stage, writers couldn't always be controlled, which frustrated Walsh. "I kept hearing how dull we were," he told me later that season, "and I knew some people were licking their chops, ready for us to fall. If we had, if the players had become disheartened by criticism, I don't know where we would have gone from there. I thought to myself, 'Give us a chance. Give this city a chance. San Francisco needs a team it can be proud of. Don't tear us down.'"

The beginning of the season was soon forgotten, though, as the 49ers won their next seven straight and became the darlings of San Francisco. The second win, which brought them over .500 for the season, was significant because it came on the road, in Washington, D.C., reversing a pattern that had seen the 49ers almost always losing on the road (26 of their last 28) and starting a pattern that would make them even more successful on the road than at home during their championship years in the 1980s. It was also a lopsided win, 30–17, after the 49ers had led 30–3 at one point—the kind of victory that hadn't been seen since 1976.

Fred Dean

THAT WIN, though, wasn't as important as the acquisition of Fred Dean, who gave the 49ers an awesome pass rusher.

Dean was originally a second-round draft pick of the San Diego Chargers, who took advantage of Dean and his inexperienced agent and signed him to an eight-year contract, with only minimal raises from year to year. He quickly became a Pro Bowl player and tried to renegotiate his contract, but the Chargers would not agree. So, he refused to report. The Chargers had no choice but to trade him, and the 49ers got him.

Dean was an incredible physical package, with great quickness and an unbelievably strong upper body for a man who weighed only 228 pounds, not much for a defensive lineman. It was natural strength, derived from manual labor in his youth, not work in the weight room. "Whenever I feel like exercising," he said, "I lie down until the feeling goes away." While other players lifted weights, he sat on the stool in front of his locker, puffing on a menthol cigarette. That bizarre training regime worked for Dean, who could dart around offensive linemen before they could solidly block him or who could throw a lineman to the side to clear his path. "I feel I can get to the quarterback any time I want," he said.

The first game Dean played for the 49ers was against the Cowboys—a game that was probably the most significant in 49er history to that date because the team absolutely crushed the Cowboys, 45–14.

Walsh wasn't surprised by the win, though the final margin was unexpected. "The one thing we (the coaches) have to worry about is that we don't start worrying about having to out-think the Cowboys," he told me in his office after his weekly press conference/lunch. "We're good enough now to stay with them physically."

They were more than good enough in this game. They scored the first time they got the ball, driving 61 yards after the opening kickoff, with Joe Montana passing to Fred Solomon for the score. They scored the second time, with Paul Hofer going the final four yards. They recovered a Dallas fumble at the Cowboys' 4 and scored a third touchdown. Then Ray Wersching kicked a field goal, to make it 24–0.

At that point, the Cowboys didn't even have a first down!

It was the 49ers' biggest margin of victory since they had beaten the Chicago Bears, 34–0, in 1974, and the Cowboys' biggest loss since 1970. The statistics reflected the 49ers' dominance: They had 23 first downs and 440 yards, the Cowboys had 10 and 192.

Dean also made his presence felt, sacking Dallas quarterback Danny White three times in the first half and four in the game. He was also forcing a change in the defensive philosophy of Chuck Studley. Before Dean's arrival, the 49ers had generally played a 3–4 (three defensive linemen, four linebackers), a defense in which the linemen generally just hold up the offensive linemen to keep them from blocking the linebackers, while the linebackers rush the passer from the outside and make tackles on running plays on the inside. Studley first used Dean just on obvious passing downs, usually the third, but Dean was so effective that he was quickly playing more and more, so the 49ers' basic defense became a 4–3.

Probably the best example of Dean's value came against the Los Angeles Rams in the eighth game of the season, at Candlestick. Walsh had always said that one key to success in the NFL was the ability to sack the quarterback in the fourth quarter, and there was no better example than this game.

The 49ers, one game ahead of the Rams in the standings, had a 20–17 lead going into the fourth quarter, when their offense went south, giving the Rams the ball five times in good field position, three times inside the 50. The Rams didn't get a point out of those five opportunities, and four times Dean was the principal reason.

It went like this:

- On third-and-five from the San Francisco 37, Dean and Jim Stuckey combined to sack Pat Haden and force a punt.

- On third-and-five from the San Francisco 46, Dean's pressure forced Haden into the arms of Lawrence Pillars, forcing a punt.

- On third-and-10 from the San Francisco 34, with just under three minutes remaining, Dean sacked Haden again, forcing still another punt.

- On the Rams' last drive, Dean sacked Haden twice. Haden kept the drive alive with his passing until the

Rams had third-and-10 on the San Francisco 31, with 46 seconds left. No doubt concerned about another sack, Haden called a draw and Dean stopped Mike Guman after a four-yard gain. Frank Corral missed a field-goal attempt, and the 49ers had won the game.

Walsh's Message

HIS ABILITY to motivate players was one of the primary factors in Walsh's success, especially since he often did it in unusual ways.

One example came after the Dallas game. ABC-TV executives, aware that the Cowboys and Rams were matched up in a special Sunday night game later that week, chose not to show highlights of the 49ers' smashing win over the Cowboys at halftime of the Monday night game.

That gave Walsh a chance to send a message to his team, and the message went through the media. At his Tuesday press conference, Walsh blasted ABC and the rest of the NFL.

His ability to motivate players was one of the primary factors in Walsh's success, especially since he often did it in unusual ways.

"We're not accepted nationally, obviously," he said. "The football elitists, jockstrap elitists don't consider us in the comfort zone. There are power sources, influence sources in the National Football League, 45-year-old men who are football groupies who prefer that we not exist so they can hold on to their football contracts and associations or power groups.

"It's obviously a business and they (ABC) need the Los Angeles–Dallas game to be a big game, to fight the excellent movies on Sunday night TV. It's obvious, it's blatant. In my opinion, it's a disservice to the public."

The message to his players was clear: It's still us against them.

Walsh sent the same message directly three games later, against the Steelers in Pittsburgh.

This game was very important to owner Eddie DeBartolo, who still lived in nearby Youngstown, Ohio, and, he said, had grown up as a Steelers fan. Eddie had been teased unmercifully by friends because his team had been soundly beaten by the teams closest to his home: The Steelers had won in Pittsburgh in 1977, 27–0, and in San Francisco in 1978, 24–7; and the Browns had won in Cleveland in 1978 by the same 24–7 score. Eddie desperately wanted a 49er win to get his friends off his back.

More important for Walsh and his players, the 49ers needed to prove they could be as tough as the Steelers, who were as physically strong as any team in the NFL, though not quite as good as the team that had won its fourth Super Bowl in a six-year span just two seasons before. The 49ers also needed to prove they could play well in a hostile environment; the Steelers were especially good against NFC teams, with a 15–2 mark at home since the AFC–NFC merger.

Before the game, Walsh told his players of British troops in Burma retreating before the Japanese in World War II. The Japanese were killing the rear troops and the total British group was down to about a thousand when they came up against a mountain and had to stop and fight. Walsh compared his team to the British troops. "We're 45 against 50,000 [fans]," he said, "and we have to fight back."

Melodramatic, of course, but his players certainly took it to heart. Led by strong safety Carlton Williamson, who knocked out two Steeler receivers after they had caught passes, they played the Steelers so viciously that fights broke out throughout the game.

"We had to be physical to survive," said Walsh. "The fights were not ragged, cheap shots. They were hard-hitting plays where we would not back off, and neither would they. The fights showed up early. I interpret that as positive. It means we played head-to-head from the start and didn't resort to fighting when we were behind."

The 49ers also won the game, 17–14.

Playoffs at Last

WITH A 13–3 record, the 49ers won their division easily and played the New York Giants in the first playoff game at Candlestick.

The Giants presented two problems: linebacker Lawrence Taylor, who was a fearsome pass rusher from the outside, and running back Rob Carpenter, who enabled the Giants to control games and run down the clock when they had the lead.

Most teams tried to neutralize Taylor by running the ball, but that often just made him more effective because, if they couldn't get enough yardage running, they'd be forced into obvious passing downs and Taylor would fly to the quarterback.

So, Walsh drew up his game "script" with 16 pass plays in the first 22. And, because he knew the Giants would be looking for short passes, he had long passes scripted.

And he also made certain that Taylor was always blocked. Sometimes he had Dwight Clark (a wide receiver but big enough and tough enough to block Taylor) or tight end Charle Young opposite Taylor. "Taylor's biggest success has come against teams that haven't lined up somebody in his face," noted CBS announcer and former coach Hank Stram. When no blocker was directly in front of Taylor, Walsh had guard John Ayers drop back to block Taylor when he came for the passer, reasoning that no back could hope to block Taylor one-on-one.

Carpenter? Walsh figured that if the 49ers got off to a lead, the Giants would have to throw more than they wanted to, and Carpenter would not be a big factor.

The game worked exactly as Walsh had planned. Taylor was

completely frustrated and often dropped back in pass coverage, instead of rushing the passer, which was his game. The 49ers often fooled the Giants, with fake reverses (and, later, the real thing), with play-action fakes, with two wide receivers lined up in the backfield. The Giants' defenders were so confused that Clark caught one pass when he was 20 yards in the open.

The 49ers got off to an early lead and never trailed. Carpenter was never a factor and the 49ers won, 38–24.

The rest of the football world saw the 49ers just one game away from the real Super Bowl. But their fans knew better: The real Super Bowl would be played the next week in San Francisco, the 49ers against the hated Dallas Cowboys.

CHAPTER SIX

The *Real* Super Bowl

THE DALLAS Cowboys were poster boys for arrogance; years before, they had adopted the marketing slogan "America's Team."

In San Francisco, they were hated. The Cowboys had beaten the 49ers two years running, 1970 and 1971, in the NFC championship game. The next year, in a playoff game leading up to the championship game, the Cowboys had delivered an even more devastating blow, with Roger Staubach leading a comeback in which the Cowboys scored two touchdowns in the final five minutes to overcome the 49ers. It sounded like hyperbole outside the Bay Area, but to 49er fans, the NFC championship truly was the *real* Super Bowl.

None of the 1981 players had been on the earlier 49er teams, so they didn't share the anti-Cowboy sentiment at first, but they soon got the message. "That was all we heard that week," said Dwight Clark, who would become part of the biggest play in 49er history.

Clark was perhaps the most interesting story on the 49ers, because he had been such a surprise, coming to the 49ers as a 10th-round draft pick after an undistinguished college career at Clemson, during which he caught just 33 passes in three years. His chief claim to fame was that he was dating a former Miss America, Shawn Weatherly.

Dwight had had no expectations of a pro career; when he was drafted, he thought he'd come to training camp and, when he was cut, play the best golf courses in California and then go home to South Carolina. A good student, he had majored in economics and expected to have a career in business.

He'd come to the right team, with the right coach. Clark had been downrated because he didn't have a sprinter's speed, but Walsh was more interested in his "football speed." Clark never got caught from behind in the open field—and he had touchdown receptions as long as 78 yards.

At 6'4", 210, Clark also had the size Walsh liked in his receivers. Because the rules had changed to reduce contact from defenders on receivers, some teams were going to smaller, faster receivers— the Miami Dolphins would become famous for their "smurfs" in the 1984 season—but Walsh liked big receivers who could use their bodies to screen off defensive backs and make the catches necessary to keep his ball-control offense going. "He's a receiver who can catch the ball in any situation and in any kind of weather," Walsh noted at the time Clark was drafted.

More than other coaches, Walsh also wanted his receivers to block, and Clark had the body for that as well. Defensive backs learned to hate him, because he would drive them into the ground.

Clark surprised himself by making the team in his first season, and he broke into the starting lineup for the last three games, catching 18 passes during the season.

The next year, he started 12 of the 16 games and caught 82 passes, eight for touchdowns; but it was in 1981 that Clark really came into his own, leading the NFC with 85 catches. He and his buddy Joe Montana were almost entirely the 49er offense.

Clark's size enabled Walsh to use him in more ways than he could use the other wide receiver, Fred Solomon. Sometimes Clark would line up as a second tight end, and he caught the type of third-down passes over the middle that would usually be a tight end's responsibility. Other times, he would be flanked out to one side or the other, and Walsh sometimes lined him up in the backfield. Wherever he lined up, Clark was always double-teamed, and he took a terrific beating when he caught the ball. "When you're young," said Clark, "you can take more punishment. Maybe if I'd been older . . ." But Dwight also gave as good as he got, and he would play nine seasons with the 49ers, retiring with what was then a club record for catches.

> Dwight [Clark] also gave as good as he got, and he would play nine seasons with the 49ers, retiring with what was then a club record for catches.

If they didn't already realize it from the fans' attitude, Clark and his teammates caught the importance of a win over Dallas from their coach, who railed at "the Goddamn Cowboys" in an early-week talk to his team. Walsh didn't have to fake emotion this time. He truly hated the Cowboys and their attitude, which had been demonstrated again the previous week after a 38–0 rout of the Tampa Bay Buccaneers. "I guess you could say we were awesome," said Dallas linebacker D. D. Lewis.

Awesome? Perhaps. But the Cowboys were only .500 in their biggest games: 5–4 in conference championship games, 2–3 in the Super Bowl.

Landry Exposed

THE 49ERS had the coaching edge in this game. Landry ran both the offense and the defense for the Cowboys; and, though it didn't become obvious until years later, when the talent level dipped, he really wasn't very good at either. The biggest offensive plays in the 1970s had usually been audibles called by Roger Staubach—but Staubach was no longer there. Defensively, the Cowboys had a system called the "Flex," which demanded total discipline because players had responsibility for a specific area, and they reacted to their "reads" of whether the play would be a run or a pass. The theory was that opponents couldn't exploit a hole because a Cowboy defender would always be there, but Walsh knew he could exploit the inflexibility of the system, either by deception or formation. He fooled the Dallas defense by pulling a guard, which made defenders think run, and then having Montana pass. He used different formations to get the receiver who would be Montana's primary target into one-on-one coverage. "We could get a receiver open any time we wanted," he later said.

Walsh and his assistant coaches were very confident. Offensive line coach Bobb McKittrick thought the 49ers would score at least four touchdowns. Offensive coordinator Sam Wyche said after the game, "The offense felt good about how we matched up with their defense."

That wasn't just postgame bravado; they were expressing these beliefs to the players all week. "You could hear their confidence in the way they were talking," said Clark, "and the closer the game got, instead of getting more uptight, Bill and Sam and all the rest of the coaches seemed to get more confident and more loose about the game, like they knew we were better, and they knew we should win."

The game was a terrific one, as the 49ers and Cowboys went after each other in three hours of almost nonstop action, with six lead changes, spectacular plays, controversial calls, and a gut-wrenching drive at the end that not only won the game but also defined the careers of Montana and Clark.

The 49ers scored first on a Montana to Solomon pass, but the Cowboys came back with a Rafael Septien field goal and a touchdown pass, after a recovered fumble, from Danny White to Tony Hill. The teams had scored a combined 17 points and it was still the first quarter.

In the second quarter, the 49ers regained the lead with a touch-down pass from Montana to Clark, but the Cowboys came back with a go-ahead touchdown, helped greatly by a couple of bad calls. Walsh always felt that NFL officials were intimidated by Dallas general manager Tex Schramm, who was on the competi-tion committee and was so close to NFL commissioner Pete Rozelle that he was nicknamed the "assistant commissioner"—and these calls made it seem that Walsh was right.

The first call came on a pass from White to Hill that was ruled complete on the San Francisco 47, though Hill seemed out of bounds. "He was clearly out of bounds," said Walsh later. "It wasn't even close. He was standing next to me when he caught it."

The next call was even worse. Ronnie Lott intercepted a long pass from White to Drew Pearson but was called for interference, giving the Cowboys the ball on the San Francisco 12. Television replays showed that Pearson had been behind Lott and was climb-ing over him to get to the ball; if interference was called, it should have been offensive.

Trying to explain the call later, side judge Dean Look claimed that Lott had bumped Pearson upfield while moving in front of him. But the flag wasn't thrown at that point. It was only later, when Lott intercepted the pass, that the flag was thrown, and the ball was placed at the spot of the interception, not upfield where Look said Lott had bumped Pearson. Clearly, Look was trying to deflect criticism for a call that was indefensible.

With that help, the Cowboys took a 17–14 halftime lead on a Tony Dorsett sweep.

It went back and forth that way until the 49ers were pinned back on their own 11 by a punt with just under five minutes remaining, trailing 27–21. Though they had a statistical edge on the Cowboys, their dream season seemed about to end. Clark went on the field thinking, "We have to go 89 yards against the Dallas Cowboys? How the hell are we going to do that?"

But Clark also remembers how brilliant Walsh was in that period. "I don't ever remember being around an offensive coordinator who was so on top of the game. He was so far ahead of everybody. Like that last drive against Dallas. We'd been throwing the ball all day and suddenly, we were running it."

Walsh realized that the Cowboys were in the "prevent defense," with six defensive backs and only three defensive linemen. That not only gave Montana extra time to throw but opened up some running lanes. (After the game, Dallas defensive coordinator Ernie Stautner was criticized for this decision. Landry never spoke up but, in fact, it was his call.)

Then came "The Catch."

The 49ers were not supposed to have a running attack, but Walsh had an ace-in-the-hole, Lenvil Elliott, who had started his career in 1973 at Cincinnati when Walsh was there. Once a very explosive runner, Elliott was 30 and coming off knee surgery, and he hadn't played all season. But Walsh had activated him for the playoffs because Elliott was reliable and a good pass receiver, and he had fresh legs.

Two Elliott runs, for 11 and seven yards, got the 49ers' drive going; and a little later in the drive, Walsh called a reverse to Solomon that went for 14 yards. That forced the Cowboys into a more normal defense.

With 1:15 left, the 49ers were on the Dallas 13 with a first down. On the first play, Solomon was free in the end zone but Montana's pass sailed wide. Walsh screamed in frustration on the sideline—"I never thought we'd get that opportunity again"—but regained his composure in time to call another Elliott sweep, which gained seven yards.

Then came "The Catch." Clark described it this way years later: "Joe's first option was to hit Freddie Solomon on a quick out; I was supposed to get in the way [screen] of Freddie's defender." If that wasn't there, Joe would drift out and I'd run a delayed hook pattern. When I looked back, if Joe was looking at me, I would slide along the back of the end zone. When we practiced it, Joe was told to throw the ball so that it either went out of bounds or the receiver could jump up and catch it."

On the sidelines, Walsh was saying, though he couldn't be heard by his players, "If it's not there, throw it out of bounds. We've got another play."

As Ed (Too Tall) Jones chased him, Montana threw the ball high into the right corner of the end zone. Cornerback Everson Walls thought the ball was going out of bounds, but Dwight leaped high and caught it. After the game, Jones insisted that Montana was trying to throw the ball away, which still bothers Clark. "We'd practiced that play since training camp. Our first touchdown came on that play, except that Freddie was the receiver that time."

What is usually forgotten is that the Cowboys still had time to win the game with a field goal after Clark's catch. But the 49ers had two great defensive plays left. Eric Wright made a one-handed tackle on Pearson, who might otherwise have gone all the way for a touchdown; and, with the ball on the San Francisco 44 and 38 seconds remaining, Lawrence Pillars forced a White fumble, which was recovered by Jim Stuckey. The 49ers were going to the Super Bowl.

There was an amusing aftermath to the Montana-Clark play. In the off-season, Montana and Clark were at dinner with Clark's girlfriend Ashley, who later became his wife. A constant stream of well-wishers came by to tell Montana and Clark what a great play that was. Ashley, who was not a football fan and had not seen either that game or the Super Bowl, finally asked, "What the hell was it that you guys did that was so great?"

The Super Bowl: "Us Against Them"

WALSH HAD a unique problem in preparing for the Super Bowl: He feared a letdown, especially since the opponent was the Cincinnati Bengals, whom the 49ers had handled easily in the regular season in a 21–3 win. Without the natural stimulus of the Cowboys as opponents, he had to find another adversary to continue his "us against them" theme. This time, it was the NFL. Because the game would be played in Pontiac, Michigan, in the middle of winter, both teams had to practice inside the Silverdome. The 49ers lost a coin flip to decide practice times, so they got the morning practice, with a press conference preceding the practice at 8 A.M. The league had rejected Walsh's suggestion that the 49ers use the University of Michigan's indoor facilities in Ann Arbor. NFL executive director Don Weiss told Walsh the league had considered all factors in making its decision. That gave Walsh the hook he needed.

> Without the natural stimulus of the Cowboys as opponents, [Walsh] had to find another adversary to continue his "us against them" theme.

"Well, they didn't take into account the fact that one team is traveling across three time zones to the game and the other will be staying in the same time zone," he said. "We'll be talking to the press at 5 o'clock by our body clocks."

This was strictly a psychological exercise. Walsh knew that practicing in the morning would make it easier for his players to adjust their internal time clocks to the Eastern time zone.

In fact, he was more relaxed than he'd been at any time during the season. "I can see the end in sight now," he said. "When you get to the end of the season, you don't have to be as guarded in your statements."

The 49ers at the time were operating in a cramped facility in

Redwood City, using a trailer for press conferences; years later, they would move to palatial headquarters in Santa Clara. The facility was totally overrun by media that week, a few days before the 49ers would leave for Pontiac, and Walsh's press conference had run an hour and a half long. Yet, as we talked in his office, just before he did an interview with KCBS play-by-play announcer Don Klein, he seemed in no hurry.

"It means that I'll have to stay later tonight to work on my game plan," he said, "but you just have to accept that as part of the job."

Walsh always had a big advantage when his team played an opponent for the second time because he would have an answer for anything that had worked for the other team in the first game, while the opposing coach usually didn't have a clue as to what Walsh was doing.

"We study their game films at least three times more than we do anyone else," said Jerry Glanville, then defensive coordinator for Atlanta, which played the 49ers twice each season. "We thought they were running the best offense even before they were winning."

Walsh was also certain to come up with a new twist in every game. For this one, it was an unbalanced line, which completely confused the Cincinnati defense in the first half. The 49er defense had some twists, too. Fred Dean was used as a roving linebacker, lining up in a different spot each time, which made it difficult to find him, let alone block him. And the 49ers would wait until the Bengals came to the line of scrimmage before they lined up defensively, with middle linebacker Jack (Hacksaw) Reynolds calling the alignment.

Few Super Bowls are truly memorable, and this one was no exception. For the players, just getting to the game was more of an adventure than the game itself.

A motorcade for then Vice President George Bush, combined with the inevitable snow from a Midwestern winter, had totally snarled traffic coming into the game. The bus carrying Walsh and half the team got caught in the mess, and a trip that was supposed to take 25 minutes from the hotel took an hour and a half. The players who had come to the stadium in taxis were waiting in the dressing room and wondering when the rest of the team would show up.

Walsh was worried, too, but he was determined not to let his players know. He joked with them, pretending he was listening to the game on the radio and told them, "The trainer's calling the plays."

"I've never in my life been in that situation," he said, "where you're in traffic bumper-to-bumper, police can't clear out the cars, you can't see the stadium, and you're supposed to be on the field in 30 minutes. It takes the players 25 minutes to dress. I thought of telling everybody to get off and hold on to each other's arms, and maybe we could ski cross-country."

It wasn't quite that desperate a situation; the bus got to the stadium at 2:40 and, though players had to rush to get dressed, they were on the field by the obligatory 3:05.

Before that, Walsh kept a lighthearted façade. "When he came into the dressing room, he was laughing and joking, saying things like, "Did we think we were going to have to go without him?" said Clark. "He asked us who was trying to take over." Walsh also told the 49ers to put on their special song, "This Is It," by Kenny Loggins, which Montana had suggested.

His approach worked. The 49ers came at the Bengals aggressively and took a 20–0 lead back to the dressing room at halftime.

It couldn't stay that way, and the Bengals made a nice comeback in the second half, closing the gap to 20–14. They might even have gone ahead but for a great goal-line stand in the third quarter, when the Bengals had second-and-goal at the San Francisco one. After the Bengals had been stopped cold on two successive runs, they had one more shot. There was no question that 250-pound fullback Pete Johnson would get the ball. Johnson usually ran to the left side, behind massive tackle Anthony Munoz, but Cincinnati offensive coordinator Lindy Infante thought the 49ers would be expecting that, so he called the play to go to the right side.

The Super Bowl became more than a goal: It was the standard.

But Reynolds had the play figured. "The backfield was set up that way," he said after the game. When Johnson headed into the hole, preceded by running back Charles Alexander as a blocker, linebacker Dan Bunz hit Alexander so hard he knocked him back into Johnson. The entire 49er defensive line, along with Bunz (who had lost the chin strap to his helmet with his hit) and Reynolds, collapsed in a heap atop Johnson, just short of the goal line. On the top of the pile, Archie Reese kicked his legs in joy. The 49ers had held.

In the fourth quarter, the 49er offense started moving again, getting close enough for Ray Wersching to kick two field goals and put the game out of reach. The Bengals did score another touchdown, but it was with just 16 seconds left; and an attempted onsides kick failed. The game ended with the 49ers up, 26–21. They had won their first Super Bowl.

For Walsh, it was total vindication for the years he'd spent trying to get a head-coaching job and for his first two years with the 49ers. "If I'd had to wait 20 years for this, it would be worth it," he said. "This is the highlight of my life. This is a group of men who do not have great talent, but they have great inspiration. No one could take us this year."

For Eddie DeBartolo, it was also vindication. He had taken a great deal of abuse in the five years he had owned the 49ers. He had admitted a terrible mistake when he fired Joe Thomas, but had redeemed himself by hiring Walsh. Those of us observing Eddie thought the experience had humbled and matured him.

We were dead wrong.

When the 49ers were losing, Eddie had been supportive of Walsh, largely because he had no choice. He still knew nothing about football and had no contacts; he couldn't fire Walsh because he wouldn't have known whom to hire to replace him.

Once the 49ers reached the pinnacle, Eddie forgot about the hard times. The Super Bowl became more than a goal: It was the standard. Anything less would not be tolerated. For the rest of his coaching career with the 49ers, Walsh had to live with the fact that Eddie would go into a rage at every loss, and Walsh would go to bed wondering if he'd have a job when he woke up.

CHAPTER SEVEN

A Nightmare in 1982

ED DEBARTOLO, Sr., commonly called Senior by friends and associates, had always had somebody watching his rambunctious son. When Eddie was in college, at Notre Dame, his father had a contact on the football coaching staff who would report on him; because the DeBartolos were big contributors to Notre Dame and especially the athletic program, there was always somebody who would oblige, though Eddie did not play football. At home, he could watch Eddie himself, with the help of Carmen Policy. When Policy moved into a full-time position in the 49ers' office, he stayed close to Eddie when Eddie came out from Youngstown; but before that, Senior relied on club employees. He always had one man he could call and ask, "How's Eddie?"

There were frequent conversations between father and son when Eddie was in Youngstown. Eddie's behavior troubled Senior because they were such opposites. The father was frugal and conservative, quiet and restrained in public, an old-world gentleman who treated everybody courteously. His son was a wild man, a hard-drinking womanizer who gambled excessively and put on embarrassing displays in public. But whatever scolding Senior gave his son in private, he never put any shackles on his public behavior.

Eddie's most public behavior was his gambling. The casinos loved him because he could be expected to lose hundreds of thousands when he gambled, and they often created "honors" for him to get him into the casino.

One such occasion came in spring 1982, after the 49ers' win in the Super Bowl. Bally's in Las Vegas invited Eddie to be honored with a special presentation, and Eddie flew in his private plane from the owners' meetings with his usual entourage of 30-plus—this time including Bill Walsh, general manager John McVay, club vice president Ken Flower, and their wives, as well as O. J. Simpson. When they checked in, they were each given an envelope containing $500 of gambling money from Eddie, who was always very generous to those who partied with him.

Before the ceremony, Eddie and O. J. went to the baccarat table, and Eddie persuaded Walsh to come along. Walsh was uncomfortable sitting at the table, because the presence of the three quickly drew a crowd, but Eddie kept shoving money at him to bet. An observer estimated that Walsh might have had as much as $20,000 sitting in front of him at one point. It was chicken feed for Eddie, who was gambling much more.

At the ceremony, Eddie was presented with a mockup of the Superdome, though it was not clear what that had to do with the 49ers. The room was noisy because the hotel management had instructed employees to fill up the back tables, to make the crowd seem larger. Eddie, who had already been drinking for several hours, was thrilled by the attention.

After the ceremony, Eddie went back to the tables, as the Bally people had anticipated. Soon he was losing heavily. One of his entourage whispered to him, "Eddie, they're playing you for a sucker." DeBartolo realized the truth of the statement and rose in a rage from the table, announcing that he was leaving the hotel and flying back to San Francisco on his private plane. Walsh, McVay, and Flower had already gone to bed, but Eddie didn't forget them. When Walsh woke up the next morning, there was a message for him at the front desk. DeBartolo had chartered a Learjet that would fly Walsh, McVay, Flower, and their wives back to San Francisco.

That was the Good Eddie and the Bad Eddie in one encompassing package.

There was another incident in a later year, when he was supposed to be honored by the Hilton in Las Vegas. When he and his entourage arrived, one of them looked at the hotel register and said, "We're not being comped." In fact, they *were* getting free bookings—hotel/casinos were delighted to pay for DeBartolo's stay because they more than recouped the cost of his room from his gambling losses—but the booking was entered in a different fashion, for bookkeeping purposes. Before the clerk could explain the discrepancy, Eddie instructed one of his group to call a cab, and they went to the Thunderbird.

Hilton executive Henri Lewin called DeBartolo to explain, and by the time of the event, Eddie was up on the podium with his arm around Barron Hilton.

But the Hilton casino didn't get his business.

Eddie didn't spend much time in the 49er offices—business bored him—but when he did, he would sweep in with his entourage, expecting everybody to stop what they were doing and fawn over him. In return, employees knew they could expect fat Christmas bonuses, as much as $32,000 for top executives after the 1984 Super Bowl season.

But those who had to work with him on civic projects more than earned their money. Eddie was never comfortable at public events—except those honoring him in Las Vegas—and he would usually duck out on them, even when his presence had been advertised. After the 1986 season, for instance, the City of Hope held a "roast" of Joe Montana that was a huge event, with more than 1,000 people attending at the Moscone Center in San Francisco. There were so many roasters, including me, that the event lasted beyond midnight. DeBartolo was scheduled to be one of the roasters, but a couple of weeks in advance, he told those scheduling the event that he would not appear. He ridiculed the sponsoring organization, saying he had an unhappy experience with it in Youngstown and making anti-Semitic remarks about the organization's executives.

He was notorious within the 49er organization for making promises of financial support in alcohol-induced moments of goodwill at banquets, only to call a 49er employee in the morning and say, "Get me out of this."

Some incidents were amusing, such as the time he had a form letter sent out to the Reverend John LoSchiavo, at the time president of the University of San Francisco, a Catholic university, inviting him to watch the next 49er home game from the DeBartolo box. LoSchiavo called the 49ers and said dryly, "I think there's been a mistake with this invitation. It's for me and my wife. Is it all right if I bring another priest instead?"

> [Eddie] was notorious for making promises of financial support in alcohol-induced moments of goodwill.

Other incidents were not at all amusing. When the city of San Francisco planned a civic function honoring the 49ers on the occasion of their 40th anniversary in 1986, DeBartolo refused to be a part of it because the Morabito widows would also be there. "What did they ever do for the 49ers?" he snarled to a club employee. He and Walsh, who didn't want to cross DeBartolo by attending, submitted videos saying they regretted not being able to make the event.

When NFL Films planned a video celebrating the 49ers' history, DeBartolo didn't want any mention of the Morabitos in that either. NFL Films finally came up with a compromise he accepted: The early history was done in black and white, with color used for the DeBartolo years.

Sometimes it seemed as if Eddie's actions were all based on whims, and friends would become enemies for no logical reason.

It happened with Carmen Policy in the mid-1990s. In the mid-1980s, it happened to Ken Flower, who had been doing everything from arranging broadcasting contracts (the 49ers had the highest local contracts in the league) to selling luxury suites, and who was close enough to Eddie to be invited on trips like the ones to Las Vegas. In the fall of '86, Policy called from Youngstown to tell Flower that he was out. Walsh, a close friend of Flower's, told him that he thought the problem could be worked out, but it wasn't: John McVay told Flower that he would be through as of January 1, 1987. No reason was ever given. Flower later sued for wrongful termination, and DeBartolo settled for a year's salary plus legal expenses.

> His respect for Walsh increased after the Super Bowl win, and for the next few months, Walsh could do no wrong in Eddie's eyes.

Even before the Super Bowl win in '81, Walsh had a different relationship with DeBartolo. Though Eddie would sometimes mutter "He's not as smart as he thinks he is" behind Walsh's back, he was deferential to him in face-to-face meetings and always praised him lavishly to reporters. His respect for Walsh increased after the Super Bowl win, and for the next few months, Walsh could do no wrong in Eddie's eyes.

But that started to change as early as 1982, a season that was a nightmare from beginning to end.

Coach and Quarterback

IT'S AXIOMATIC in sports that it's easier to win a championship than to defend one. Part of the problem comes from within; players tend to relax when they've won a championship instead of continuing to drive for another. The awards and attention resulting from a previous year's success can be distracting.

The more important the player, the more attention. Being the leader of a Super Bowl champion, Joe Montana was also the focus of attention, endorsements, and even television shows. Montana took three trips out of town during the season (on the 49ers' off-days) to make appearances to fulfill endorsement contracts. He also was part of a Sunday night television show on KGO-TV, the ABC affiliate, and was part of a Monday night show on the same station.

Walsh said publicly that he thought Montana's television show was a special distraction. "It's taking away from his concentration. He doesn't always have time to learn all the system, so he's going into a game not fully prepared. I'm really concerned that a potentially great career is going to dwindle away."

Montana disagreed, pointing out that he didn't get the game plan until Tuesday, and he didn't work at anything but football for the rest of the week. His play supported his position, because he had the same kind of season he'd had the year before, as shown by his passer rating of 87.9, virtually identical to the 88.2 of the year before. He was one of the very few 49ers who played as well in '82 as he had the year before.

After the season, Montana quit his television work, but it was probably more because he was uncomfortable in front of the camera than because of Walsh's public criticism. Later, when his career had ended, Montana tried television again but left after one year. Montana was a television star when he was on the field, but his playing charisma was not transferable to the booth or studio.

The sniping by Walsh was indicative of a relationship that was already starting to show some strain. Montana's private comments about Walsh were much more derogatory than Walsh's public comments about his quarterback.

"I could never figure out why Joe never gave Bill the respect he deserved," said Guy Benjamin, who roomed with Montana in training camp and on the road. "We talked about Bill all the time, and Joe was adamant, the way he would put Bill down. In meetings, when Bill would go off on one of his tirades, Joe would turn to me and say, 'Your boy's flipped out again.' He called him a 'dumb, stupid motherfucker,' which was a catchall phrase for anybody he didn't like. He told me one time that Bill didn't want him to have the TV show because Bill didn't want competition, as if there was competition on that level.

"There was ego, of course, but it went beyond that. Joe felt a real resentment. Most people in his situation would have praised Bill. It was the smart thing to do, and Bill is good. He knows what he's doing. There should be a respect there.

"Who knows why Joe was this way. Maybe it's because he felt intimidated by Bill, who comes across so different from other football coaches. Joe is just a guy who grew up in a coal-mining town, after all. I think it's a real shame because I think Bill did everything for Joe. Joe had to play, but Bill created him, crafted him."

Now, with Montana's playing days and Walsh's coaching career long since ended, the two are good friends, often golfing together. But when they were together with the 49ers, the tension was almost always there—except, of course, when the games were being played. Given the competitive nature of both men, that was probably inevitable. Walsh wanted people to realize how important his system was and wanted them to think that the system had made Montana—who, in turn, wanted people to think that his play had made Walsh's system.

The 49ers Versus Themselves

MONTANA AND Walsh, and the team as a whole, were already facing a challenge because other teams give a little more effort against a championship team. In the NFL, too, teams can prepare better for a champion because they have more to look at, including the Super Bowl, where teams hold nothing back.

Many other coaches resented the media's christening of Walsh as a "genius," in part because Walsh seemed to go along with the designation. Walsh has always been very conscious—and protective—of his image; although he is quite emotional and went through stomach-churning times on the sidelines when he coached, he liked the professorial look he projected.

> Walsh wanted people . . . to think that the system had made Montana—who, in turn, wanted people to think that his play had made Walsh's system.

That season, though, it really didn't matter what other teams did because the 49ers self-destructed. The team was torn apart by drug use, and one player was even thought to be dealing. Drug abuse was becoming an increasing problem throughout the NFL; but the 49ers probably had more problems than any other team that year. Walsh was especially frustrated because he could not admit the problem and, in fact, denied it when asked, though he thought there might be as many as a dozen players whose play was affected by drug use.

The entire league had another problem—labor strife that cut out two months of the season after the first two weeks. The 49ers had gone 0–2 before the strike, and they weren't much better when play resumed, winning three of seven. Their last game was a bitter loss to the Rams; after leading, 20–7 at halftime, they fell 21–20. With time running out, they attempted a field goal that could have won the game, but it was blocked by the Rams—the only one they had blocked all year.

The distraught Walsh talked briefly after the game with his players, but he failed to show at the traditional day-after meeting, when players come back to the practice facility and get their personal belongings. McVay met with the players, which is normally the coach's function. Later, Walsh would say that he thought at that point that he would step back from coaching and just be the general manager and that he changed his mind only after talking with several friends in football.

Even knowing Walsh's emotional struggles, most of those close to the team believed he would return as coach. He had worked too hard for too long to become a head coach to quit this early. He had won one Super Bowl, but that wouldn't be enough to establish the reputation he wanted within the NFL. He'd have to coach longer and win more Super Bowls for that.

But by going through the very public soul-searching, Walsh accomplished some goals that were essential to his return. One was sending a message to his players that drug abuse would not be tolerated. Some of the offenders either retired or were released before the next season. Others changed their lifestyles and became good players again.

Another goal was to change his coaching staff, because Walsh was not pleased with the performance of his assistants. Instead of firing coaches, he told his assistants that he might not return as head coach, so they were free to accept other jobs, if offered.

Four assistants left. One, Sam Wyche, was offered the job as head coach of Indiana University and left with Walsh's blessing. Another, running-backs coach Billie Matthews, would have been kept by Walsh but left when he got an offer from Philadelphia. But the other two departures—special teams coach Milt Jackson and defensive coordinator Chuck Studley—pleased Walsh, though he was reluctant to ask them to leave on his own.

Walsh had blamed Jackson for the Rams' loss because the coach had not prepared players for the Rams' successful attempt to block a field goal at the end of the last game.

Studley was a different case and a very difficult one for Walsh. In the 1970s, they had been assistant coaches in Cincinnati and used to drive to practice together, bouncing ideas off each other.

Studley had done a good job for the 49ers in '81, but Walsh felt his approach was too conservative, too geared to stopping the run at a time when pass offenses were becoming more sophisticated and dangerous, in part because of Walsh's influence and in part because of rules changes that made it more difficult to defend the pass. Walsh felt a more creative defensive coordinator was needed if the 49ers were to return to the Super Bowl.

> Seifert and Walsh made a perfect team, coordinating their defensive and offensive game plans to produce 49er victories.

It would have been very difficult for Walsh to fire Studley. If Studley had remained, Walsh probably would have given him a title like "assistant head coach," with the defense turned over to George Seifert. That would have been awkward because, though the public might be fooled by titles, Studley wouldn't have been, and he'd have been embarrassed. Walsh's "pause" gave Studley a chance to save face with another job while Walsh was accomplishing his goal.

As usual, Walsh's instincts were correct. Seifert was as imaginative as a defensive coach as Walsh was as an offensive coach. Though other NFL teams were using "nickel" defenses, taking out a linebacker and putting in an extra defensive back in obvious passing situations, Seifert was the first to really go to "situational defenses," making several position changes depending on down-and-distance. He and Walsh made a perfect team, coordinating their defensive and offensive game plans to produce 49er victories.

Walsh's other motive was to get DeBartolo off his back, at least temporarily. Eddie had been asking too many questions that had no answers during the '82 season, as always after he'd been drinking heavily. But when Walsh threatened to walk away from coaching, he called Eddie's bluff.

In his sober moments, Eddie knew he couldn't do as well with another coach as he could with Walsh. He had to face down his father, one of the few times he ever did. Senior was enraged that Walsh was talking about walking away. "He's a quitter," he told his son. "He wants to walk away from a bad situation. That's when he should be at his toughest. You should fire him." But Eddie knew it wouldn't be that easy to get another coach, because the 49ers appeared to be sliding downhill again.

So Walsh went through the motions. He talked to good friends Mike White and John Robinson and said later he'd asked both of them if they'd coach the 49ers, with Walsh as general manager. White preferred to stay at Illinois, where he was the head coach. Robinson stayed in administration at USC, though he later returned to coaching. Both men thought that Walsh should stay as the 49ers' coach, and neither wanted Walsh looking over his shoulder.

Walsh also talked to another friend, UCLA coach Terry Donahue, but Walsh had already made up his mind. He called DeBartolo in Youngstown, and Eddie told him he thought it would be best if Walsh stayed as coach.

For the moment, Walsh had Eddie at bay. But, of course, that happy situation would change as soon as misfortune hit—and Eddie defined that as losing a game.

CHAPTER EIGHT

Another Championship Season

THOUGH THE 49ers won three Super Bowls in Bill Walsh's last eight years as coach, Walsh's job seemed to be on almost a game-to-game tenure with the short-fused Eddie DeBartolo. Several times Eddie vowed to fire Walsh, stopped only by the delaying tactics of Carmen Policy. The first Eddie explosion came after the disappointing end to the 1983 season.

The 49ers had bounced back from the disastrous 1982 season to win their division in '83 but were decided underdogs in the NFC championship against the Redskins at RFK Stadium in Washington, D.C. The Redskins had beaten Miami in the Super Bowl the year before and were still regarded as the best team in the NFL.

Perhaps the 49ers believed that too. For the first three quarters, they played listlessly and ineffectively, trailing 21–0. In the fourth quarter, though, they rallied behind three Joe Montana touchdown passes to tie the 'Skins before the home team bounced back, with the help of a couple of questionable pass-interference penalties, to kick a game-winning field goal.

After the game, Walsh railed at the officials, claiming that on one of the pass-interference calls, the Washington receiver "couldn't have reached the pass with a 10-foot ladder."

Meanwhile, DeBartolo was railing at Walsh, but privately, to Policy. "I should have fired him last year. I want to get rid of him." He told Policy to call Walsh the next day and fire him. Policy, knowing the volatility of his friend, hoped Eddie would calm down and forget what he'd said by the next day. The phone call was never made, and even Walsh never knew that DeBartolo had wanted him fired.

The disappointment lingered with DeBartolo. Eleven years later, as the 49ers were about to start a season that would end with their fifth Super Bowl championship, Eddie wistfully observed to me, "If we'd gotten to that Super Bowl, we'd have won it. We matched up real well with the Raiders." The Redskins did not; they lost, 38–9.

Eddie's disappointment was only with his coach, not with his players, especially his favorites, Montana and Dwight Clark. The two players had been invited back to Eddie's home in Youngstown. Players never turned down those invitations because they knew Eddie would lavish expensive gifts on them, particularly Rolex watches. This time, Eddie went beyond gifts: He tripled the salaries of both Montana and Clark.

There has always been a pecking order in pro football, and the quarterback is at the top. Other players understand that the quarterback is almost always going to be the highest-paid player on the team, so tripling Montana's salary probably wouldn't have made a big difference to other players. But Clark, though an outstanding player, was no more important to the 49ers' success than several other players, and his new contract changed everything.

The next day, Ronnie Lott was in Walsh's office demanding a raise, which Walsh could not deny him. Several other players followed Lott, and the 49ers' payroll shot to the top of the league. That in itself didn't bother Walsh, nor did it bother him in later years that DeBartolo was willing to pay top dollar to get players, even backups. What upset Walsh was that the 49ers quickly got the reputation of buying championships. He pointed out that they had won their first Super Bowl with a payroll that was at the bottom of the league, but nobody paid attention. All they knew was that the 49ers' payroll was at the top of the league, because of Eddie's impetuous move with Montana and Clark.

Even without Eddie's generosity, the 49ers' payroll would soon have been at the top, because Walsh had been putting together a team of very good players whose contracts would inevitably reflect their excellence. It was already beginning to show on the field. The comeback against the Redskins, though it fell short, convinced the 49ers that they belonged in the NFL's elite circle, and they proved it with their 1984 season.

The football world was changing. The AFC/AFL had dominated, winning 12 of the last 16 Super Bowls, but that dominance would come to a crashing end, as the NFC would win the next 16, many of them by lopsided margins.

> What upset Walsh was that the 49ers quickly got the reputation of buying championships.

Perhaps the shift of power would have come sooner, as DeBartolo suggested, if the 49ers had been in the previous Super Bowl. The Redskins were an overrated team, in part because they played in the East, which has the preponderance of population and preponderance of journalists, including sports reporters and columnists. The Redskins had captured the fancy of the football public with their massive offensive linemen, known as the "Hawgs," but their lack of speed doomed them against the Raiders in the Super Bowl.

The 49ers, though, were the real thing. The 1984 team was probably the best of the 49er champions, though a strong argument could also be made for the 1989 team as the best. The 1984 team had tremendous balance, between offense and defense, between running and passing on offense, between run defense and pass defense.

The offensive line had developed into a very strong unit. Montana was in his physical prime and had total command of the offense. Wendell Tyler and Roger Craig were both outstanding running backs, giving the team weapons it had totally lacked in the '81 championship season. Jerry Rice was still a season away from wearing a 49er jersey, but the 49ers had great weapons in receivers Dwight Clark and Fred Solomon and running back Craig, whose 71 receptions led the team. Defensively, the 49ers had great linemen such as Dwaine Board, Michael Carter, and Gary (Big Hands) Johnson and great cornerbacks in Ronnie Lott and Eric Wright. They outscored opponents by more than a 2–1 margin, 475 to 227.

They were one penalty away from a perfect season, losing to Pittsburgh when Eric Wright was called for pass interference, setting up a touchdown in the Steelers' 20–17 win. Of course, Walsh thought it was a bad call; he never saw a penalty against the 49ers that he liked. There were only a couple of close games; and, by the second half of the season, the 49ers were steamrollering teams, 33–0 over the Rams, 41–7 over the Browns, 35–3 over the Saints, 51–7 over the Vikings.

Strangely, the 49ers were not recognized as a great team until after the season, and many observers thought the Chicago Bears would beat them in the NFC championship game in San Francisco. But the 49ers shut the Bears down totally and won 23–0.

No Home Field Advantage

THE 1985 Super Bowl had some historical significance because for only the second time in its history it would be played in the home area of one of the participants. The January 1980 game had been played in Pasadena's Rose Bowl, near the home of the Los

Angeles Rams. This game would be played at Stanford Stadium, about 25 miles south of the 49ers' home at Candlestick Park.

There was virtually no home field advantage for the 49ers, though, because the NFL spreads tickets around to all teams; 49er fans would be less than a fourth of the stadium capacity. And, of course, the 49ers had no familiarity with the Stanford field, never having played there. They might actually have been at a disadvantage because, being home, individual players were besieged by ticket requests. Players soon learned not to answer their phones or to leave their houses except to go to practice.

Walsh . . . never saw a penalty against the 49ers that he liked.

The Dolphins dominated the pregame publicity because of their second-year quarterback, Dan Marino, who had shattered the NFL record for touchdown passes in a season by throwing 48.

The Marino publicity show enraged Montana, though typically he did not say anything publicly, and enraged Lott, who did talk about it. Montana felt that his good season was being overlooked simply because he was in a balanced offense, while Marino was almost the entire Miami offense. Lott bristled when reporters wondered if he were fast enough to cover the Dolphin receivers, Mark Clayton and Mark Duper. "I've covered good receivers before," said Lott.

Because of Marino and Montana, the pregame expectations were for a wide-open offensive show. While we were both being interviewed for a radio show, a Fort Lauderdale reporter predicted a 48–41 Dolphins win. I thought the 49ers would win by something like 35–21, which wasn't far off the mark.

What most reporters didn't realize was that the 49er defense was good enough to at least slow down the Dolphins' lopsided offense, but the Miami defense didn't have a prayer against the 49er offense. The Dolphin defenders were so undersized that

Walsh would be amazed when he walked by them, wondering how Shula had gotten this bunch to the ultimate game.

Even before that, Walsh had been supremely confident, because he knew he could capitalize on the Miami defensive strategy. The Dolphin linebackers covered running backs coming out of the backfield, and Walsh knew none of them could cover Craig, who caught balls with a receiver's skills. Because the linebackers would turn their backs to the line of scrimmage while covering a back, Walsh told Montana to be alert for that and run if he saw an opening.

The Dolphins also inadvertently played into the 49ers' hands. 49er defensive coordinator George Seifert had been very successful with "situation substitution," making defensive replacements based on down-and-distance. To prevent Seifert's substitutions, the Dolphins went to a "no-huddle" offense, which didn't leave enough time between plays for defensive substitutions. Know-ing the Dolphins were more likely to pass, Seifert took out linebackers Dan Bunz and Jack Reynolds and put in better pass defenders, linebacker Keena Turner and Jeff Fuller, who was a combination linebacker–defensive back. That was also his best overall defense.

The 49ers led at halftime, 28–13, and won the game easily, 38–16. Craig caught seven passes for 77 yards, scored three touchdowns, two on receptions, and was the game's Most Valuable Player. Montana ran five times for 59 yards, including a memorable play in which he ran down the sideline behind an unknow-ing Miami linebacker who was chasing Craig. As the clock ran down at the end of the game, Randy Cross shouted gloatingly to the crowd, "Only one offense showed up today."

Trouble Returns

THE DEBARTOLO-Walsh relationship had spectacular ups and downs, depending on whether the 49ers won or lost. The 1984 season, of course, was an up period, but Eddie's memory was a short one. The following two seasons were definitely down, and Eddie's short fuse blew again.

The 49ers couldn't even successfully defend their NFC West title in '85 and lost a wild-card playoff game, 17–3, to the New York Giants in the Meadowlands. (In the winners' dressing room, Giants coach Bill Parcells derisively commented to reporters, "What do you think of the West Coast offense now?" From that point, Walsh's offense, whether used by the 49ers or one of the many other teams that copied it, was referred to as the "West Coast offense," though it was used by teams in all parts of the country. Parcells's comment was typical of many by other coaches, jealous of Walsh's reputation for innovation.)

> The DeBartolo-Walsh relationship had spectacular ups and downs, depending on whether the 49ers won or lost.

The 1986 season was much worse. After opening the season with a win in Tampa Bay, the 49ers got the worst possible news before the next game, against the Rams in Anaheim: Montana would have to undergo back surgery. It seemed unlikely he'd be able to play at all that season, and it was possible his career was over.

Montana's injury was bigger news than what the 49ers were actually doing on the field. His surgery was front-page news, of course, and the *San Francisco Chronicle* ran a banner at the top of the page reporting the first time he ate solid food after his surgery. There were daily, almost hourly, reports of his medical progress.

Meanwhile, the 49ers still had to play out the season. Walsh had traded in the off-season for Jeff Kemp, son of Jack Kemp, who had been a topflight quarterback for the Buffalo Bills in the old AFL and had since gone on to political fame. Jeff Kemp was under six feet but had a very strong arm. Walsh redesigned his offense to have Kemp throwing long, and the 49ers seemed capable of getting to the playoffs with him.

Then Kemp injured his hip, and Walsh was down to his third-string quarterback, Mike Moroski, who had played at UC Davis, a Division II school. Even for the renowned quarterback coach, this was too much. The 49ers actually won the first game they played with Moroski, against the Packers in Green Bay, but then lost to the Saints in New Orleans, 23–10.

Eddie DeBartolo, watching and drinking in the dressing room, was enraged by the loss, throwing his glass at the television monitor at one point. When players came into the dressing room, they saw pieces of glass on the floor. DeBartolo started yelling at them and then at Walsh when he came into the room.

Walsh pulled DeBartolo into the coaches' room and told Eddie not to yell at the players, who were doing their best. All that accomplished was to turn Eddie's fury onto Walsh. He told Walsh to get his attorney and he would get his, and they'd talk in the morning about Walsh's contract.

Walsh returned to San Francisco on the team plane that night, not knowing whether he'd have a job the next morning. He was justified in his concern. DeBartolo and Policy flew back to Youngstown and, when they arrived, Eddie told Policy to call Walsh and tell him he was fired. Policy said it was too late to call, but said he would call in the morning. He didn't, and Eddie didn't remind him, so that storm blew over, but there would be more and worse ones to come.

CHAPTER NINE

A Challenge to Montana

JOE MONTANA courageously returned from his back surgery after only seven weeks in 1986, and Walsh rushed him back into the lineup. Montana had been cleared to play, but even so, it might have been better to keep him out at least another week. Walsh felt he had no choice, with the pressure he was feeling from Eddie DeBartolo to win.

Montana's first game back was a strange one, a tribute to his stature in a very unusual way. He might as well have had on the red jersey quarterbacks wear in practice to remind defenders not to hit them. The St. Louis Cardinal defensive linemen would get right up in Montana's face but not hit him. Nobody wanted to be the one to apply the hit that might paralyze him; and the 49ers won, 43–17. The next week at Washington, Montana threw an incredible 60 passes; Walsh later said it was one of his biggest mistakes to put that much pressure on Montana so soon. The 49ers lost that game but won five of the seven after Montana's return.

It wasn't enough. Montana's seven-week absence had doomed the 49ers' chances of winning the NFC West, so they were sent back to the Meadowlands for another wild-card game against the New York Giants. This one was even worse, a 49–3 humiliation in which, early on, when the game was still close, Jerry Rice fumbled while apparently on his way to a touchdown. Worse, Montana was knocked out of the game with a concussion in the second quarter.

Walsh would not be caught short again. He had always been concerned that injury would cause Montana's career to end prematurely, because Joe was always a fragile-looking player and had battled back problems even before his surgery. By 1986, Walsh thought Montana's career was very close to its end; and the 49ers' main divisional competitor, the Los Angeles Rams, had just traded for Jim Everett, who was supposed to be the quarterback of the future. Walsh felt he had to get a young quarterback who could replace Montana in the near future and battle on even terms with Everett.

So he started talking to Hugh Culverhouse of the Tampa Bay Buccaneers about Steve Young.

Young's career had already taken some strange twists and turns. He was the very first pick of the NFL draft in 1984, taken by Cincinnati, but the Bengals did not come close to what Young's agent, Leigh Steinberg, was seeking in a contract. So Steinberg turned to the Los Angeles Express of the newly formed USFL, who signed Young for what was reported to be a $40 million contract. In fact, it was $5 million up front, with most of the rest of the contract in annuities. However structured, it was still the richest football contract yet.

Young's USFL experience was not a happy one. The league would soon fold, and the Express's owner, William J. Oldenberg, was about to go bankrupt. When injuries hit the Express, Young was shifted to running back.

Young had agreed to go to the USFL because he reasoned that, if it didn't work out, he could become a free agent. The NFL stifled that dream. When the USFL folded, the NFL held a supplemental draft, and he was selected by Tampa Bay.

Young took a beating in Tampa Bay. The Bucs had little talent and no offensive system. "[Coach] Ray Perkins would send me out there and say, 'Make something happen,'" Young noted sardonically many years later. Young would scramble and try to find somebody open, but neither he nor the Bucs were successful.

When Young first arrived in Tampa Bay, Culverhouse told him, "You're my quarterback and you'll always be my quarterback." But that had been when Leeman Bennett was the head coach. Perkins didn't feel the same way. He planned to draft Vinny Testaverde, who was expected to become a great NFL quarterback, and had worked out a tentative deal with the St. Louis Cardinals to trade Young for multiple draft picks.

Young heard about that plan and went to Culverhouse. "I reminded him of what he'd said and told him he should at least give me the chance to go to the team I wanted to be with," said Young. "He asked me where I wanted to go, and I said my first choice was the 49ers. I had heard that Bill Walsh had been asking about me, and I wanted to play for him."

Young's information was correct; Walsh wanted him. Culverhouse was more interested in money than in improving his team. He was willing to give up Young for just a No. 2 draft pick, but he insisted on a $1 million sweetener. When Walsh went to DeBartolo, Eddie swallowed hard and said, "Do you want this guy that much?" Walsh said he did. "OK," said Eddie, "you've got him."

Most people in the NFL thought Walsh was crazy. Young was regarded as a great athlete who might be able to make it as a running back, but he didn't look like a quarterback.

Most people in the NFL thought Walsh was crazy. Young was regarded as a great athlete who might be able to make it as a running back, but he didn't look like a quarterback. By that time, everybody had forgotten what made Young the very first pick in the '84 draft: an NCAA season record for passing accuracy, 70 percent as a senior at BYU.

Walsh remembered, though, and he was certain that he could make Young a topflight quarterback within his offense, though he knew it would take time to break the bad habits Young had developed while playing in the USFL and with the Bucs.

Young was delighted to be with the 49ers, for personal as well as playing reasons. "I couldn't believe it when I got here," he said years later. "At Tampa Bay, there was so much going on—racial fights in the dressing room, guys stabbing each other in the back. If I hadn't been traded, I might have decided it wasn't worth it and just gone to law school.

"When I got here, there was none of that. Everybody was just focused on winning, and they expected to win. I think that was the greatest thing Bill did as a coach. I know Bill passed up some players who were talented because they didn't have the right attitude. You'll notice the 49ers have always had players like Tom Rathman and Mike Walter and Bill Ring. There might have been more talented players, but they had great attitudes."

Walsh was delighted to get Young, and he worked from the beginning to prepare Young to take over for Montana. In normal team practices, the starting quarterback gets most of the snaps (plays), but Walsh changed the 49ers' practice so that Young would get half the snaps.

The Young-Montana Rivalry

THOUGH HE had taken a beating playing for Tampa Bay, Young hadn't lost any self-confidence. When he came in to the first 49er mini-camp, after his trade, he made it clear that he expected to compete for the starting quarterback position. He did not defer to Montana, despite Joe's two Super Bowl rings. Forced to watch from the sidelines most of the time for the next four years, he would come to appreciate Montana for the great quarterback he was, but he had come to the 49ers to play. "I had always played," he said years later, "and I expected to play here. I was forced to learn by watching and I eventually realized how blessed I was to have a quarterback like Joe to emu-late, but it certainly wasn't my choice to just watch."

> "I realized how blessed I was to have a quarterback like Joe to emulate, but it certainly wasn't my choice to just watch."
>
> —Steve Young

In his quiet way, Montana burned with rage. Perhaps because Young acted as if he expected to start, Joe thought the change in the practice schedule was Young's idea. Montana never voiced his complaints publicly; in this case, he went through his good friend, Ronnie Lott, who told writers that Young had demanded to get extra snaps. That version spread quickly because Lott, who was very cooperative and always had something interesting to say, was interviewed frequently.

Lott's remark was the start of what became an intense rivalry, which eventually involved players, the front office, and the fans. Strangely, there was no direct conflict between Montana and Young. "We never had cross words," said Young. "In fact, I remember talking on the sidelines with Joe in a game during the '88 season when everything was going wrong when he said, 'They can't blame this on us.'" But there was no doubt that Montana felt the rivalry on a very basic level. Later, he would break off his rela-tionship with Dwight Clark, from whom he'd been inseparable for many years, because of it. Clark went on to work in the 49ers' front office after he retired as a player and also did announcing on 49er preseason telecasts. On one telecast, he praised Young. Montana did not speak to him for three years.

There were good reasons for Montana to worry about the

competition with Young. Walsh had a well-deserved reputation for replacing veterans, even when they seemed to have some time left in their careers, either benching them or forcing them to retire. Montana had already seen that happen with several players. In 1985, for instance, Walsh benched wide receiver Freddie Solomon and replaced him with Jerry Rice, keeping Rice in the lineup even when he played poorly in early games; at the end of the season, the popular Solomon retired. Montana's close friend and favorite target, Clark, would be forced to retire after the '87 season, though he wanted to keep playing. Walsh's theory was that younger players would improve rapidly if given the chance, while older players would decline rapidly from their peak. His success in bringing in good young players to replace veterans was one of the most important factors in the 49ers' continued success.

Walsh never forced a veteran to the bench or retirement if he didn't have a good young replacement ready. Until 1987, he'd never had a reserve quarterback who could challenge Montana. Guy Benjamin, Matt Cavanaugh, and Jeff Kemp had played well when Montana had been unable to play, but Walsh never regarded any of them as a permanent replacement for Montana. As long as Joe was healthy, he knew he'd be the starter.

When Young arrived, he no longer had that assurance. Young was a long way from mastering the Walsh offense, as Montana had done, and he had picked up bad habits in Tampa Bay, but his physical ability was unmistakable. He had a stronger arm than Montana, making him better able to throw the long ball to Rice, and he was an accurate passer, though he did not have Montana's unparalleled ability to hit a receiver exactly in stride. Montana was an effective scrambler and runner, but Young was an outstanding runner, one of the half dozen best running quarterbacks since the T-formation had become the standard pro offense.

The dramatic differences in their personalities added to the rivalry.

Montana was a classic athlete, for whom sports had been a way of life since he was a youngster. His dad remembers driving Joe to all-star games in Pennsylvania (their home), New York, and New Jersey for Little League and Pop Warner. He was a three-sport star—football, baseball, and basketball—in high school. He was about to accept a basketball scholarship to North Carolina State when Notre Dame offered a football scholarship, which he accepted. Though he got his degree in business administration/marketing from Notre Dame in 1978, the NFL was his career goal.

He also had the confidence of a great athlete. Benjamin roomed with Montana in 1980 and '81, and he was struck by Joe's confidence in '80, when he started the season as a backup. "It was like he never doubted that he'd be a star, and that he'd make a lot of money," said Benjamin. "He never worried about that part of it at all."

Montana came from a working-class background. Young came from an upper-middle-class background. His father was an attorney, and he was born in Salt Lake City but raised in Connecticut; he had an impressive lineage, being the great-great-great grandson of Brigham Young, founder of the Mormon religion.

Young would go on to get a law degree at BYU, working his way through law school in the off-season while playing for the 49ers. He is a personable man with a good, often deprecating sense of humor, which he used to good effect when he gave an address to the graduating class of the University of San Francisco law school in June 1996 (which I heard because my son was a member of the class), noting that his graduating class had the highest per capita income of any that year, not needing to add that it was because of his football salary.

His playing ability brought his salary to the highest level in the NFL, but money is hardly a motivating factor for Young. He spends very little on clothes and drove an old car for years, before his commercial work with Toyota brought an upgrade in his vehicle of choice. After being hounded for years by his agent, Leigh Steinberg, he finally bought a house on the San Francisco Peninsula, but he lived for years in a rented loft.

Did Montana look at Young and think, "This guy could do anything he wanted but he's trying to take away the one thing I want?" Probably. But Young is no less competitive than Montana, and football has always been what drives him. "I like the action, the competition, the hitting," he said in one of our training camp conversations.

Young has always hit people more often than his coaches would like. He's played quarterback with a linebacker's mentality, trying to run over tacklers to get extra yardage instead of running out of bounds. For years, critics said his career would come to a premature end as a result, but Young always disputed that argument. "The serious quarterback injuries usually come when you're in the pocket and not expecting to be hit," he argued. "When I'm running, I expect to be hit, and I prepare for it." Unfortunately, his point would be proved in 1999, when he was knocked out of the lineup with a concussion after being hit by a blitzing linebacker while he was in the pocket.

In his first year with the 49ers, Young was quick to take the ball and run because he did not understand the complexities of the offense. Montana had long since learned to run through as many as five potential receivers, but Young usually looked at no more than two. If they were covered, he ran, because he knew he could pick up yardage running. In part, that was also a carryover from his experience in Tampa Bay, where he was often forced to scramble to avoid losses.

> In his first year with the 49ers, Young was quick to take the ball and run because he did not understand the complexities of the offense.

Tumult in 1987

THE START of the Montana-Young rivalry was just one of the stories in 1987, a season that would eventually blow everybody's emotional circuits.

After an opening-day loss in Pittsburgh, the 49ers seemed on their way to a second straight loss in Cincinnati, trailing by six points with only six seconds left. But Bengals' coach Sam Wyche, a Walsh assistant for the first Super Bowl season, chose not to punt on fourth down, fearing a block. Kevin Fagen broke through to tackle running back James Brook for a loss, and the clock was stopped with just a couple of seconds left. The 49ers quickly took the field, and Walsh called a play that sent three receivers to the left and Rice to the right. Montana faked left and then threw to Rice in the end zone for a touchdown. The ecstatic Walsh actually skipped as he left the field for the locker room.

Then the NFL players struck. After a one-week hiatus, the league resumed the season with teams made up of replacement players, though regular players were invited to come back.

Anticipating the strike, Walsh had put together a strong replacement team. Other teams, including the New York Giants, the 49ers' first opponent when the season resumed, had not.

But, as with all the other teams, there was a split on the 49ers between those who wanted to come back and those who were backing the Players Association, which was trying to convince all the players to stay out. Among those who wanted to come back were Montana, Clark, Russ Francis, and Roger Craig. Probably the most fervent of the union supporters was Lott, despite his friendship with Montana.

Walsh was trying to keep his team from imploding. He also was concerned about pickets and possible violence in New York, directed at players who returned, so he convinced all his players to stay out for the first game. Competitively, it made no difference, because the 49ers' replacement team was so strong. The 49ers won the game, 41–21, and Walsh playfully used the Wishbone in the fourth quarter.

Montana returned for the next game, in Atlanta, but played little, throwing only eight passes in another easy 49er win. By this time, there were players on the lower end of the salary scale who were hurting for money, so Walsh talked with Eddie DeBartolo, and Eddie agreed to "loan" them money, which everybody understood didn't have to be repaid. The Good Eddie had surfaced again.

The strike ended the next week, though not all the players returned in time to play in that week's game. Montana had a very good game, completing 31 of 39 passes, and the 49ers needed all of that to beat the St. Louis Cardinals, 34–28.

The week's high drama, though, came on the practice field, the day after the strike ended, when all the players were back at practice. The players met in the center of the field, far enough removed that writers couldn't hear what was being said, only that most of what was being said was in screams, with Lott and Francis the most vocal. Much of Lott's invective was aimed at Walsh, but the session ended with all emotion spent and the 49ers still together as a team.

There was one more hurdle: Some players who did not get "loans" from DeBartolo resented the fact that they'd been left out, so Walsh and DeBartolo worked out an arrangement for players to get their playoff money doubled, which would give them an extra $10,000. Thanks to the three wins with their replacement team, the 49ers were 4–1 and almost guaranteed a playoff berth.

John McVay had checked with the league office to get approval for DeBartolo's arrangement, but the league later decided the move was not legitimate and fined DeBartolo $50,000. Some players thought they should chip in to pay the fine. "I like Eddie, but not that much," said Keith Fahnhorst, the club's player representative. Eddie had to pay his own fine. He could afford it.

The strike and its aftermath had taken the focus off the

Montana-Young rivalry for the public, but certainly not for the participants. Montana was injured often enough for Young to get some significant playing time, which added to Joe's concern for his future.

Young's first start, when Montana had an injured right hand, came against New Orleans; he completed five of six passes, including a 46-yard touchdown to Rice, and ran four times for 24 yards before being knocked out of the game with a concussion.

When Montana was injured in the first quarter against the Chicago Bears, Young came in to throw four touchdowns. The following week, with Montana still sidelined, he completed just 13 of 30 passes for 216 yards but ran for an additional 83 yards, including a 29-yard touchdown run. Critics still wondered if he could play quarterback, but everybody agreed he would have been a great single wing tailback. "I might have enjoyed that," admitted Young, who always resisted suggestions he should switch to running back.

> The strike and its aftermath had taken the focus off the Montana-Young rivalry for the public, but certainly not for the participants.

The 49ers clinched their division title early that season, eventually finishing with an NFL-best 13–2 record, so Walsh started Young in the first half of the season finale against the Los Angeles Rams. Young had a great half, completing 10 of 13 passes for 174 yards, including a 50-yard touchdown strike to Rice, and the 49ers romped, 48–0.

That set the stage for a playoff game against the Minnesota Vikings, a game that would have repercussions far beyond the playing field.

The 49ers were probably overrated going into this game. Walsh had thought going into the season that he was still building a team that would peak in the 1988 and '89 seasons, but the 13–2 record had seduced everybody. Nobody remembered that one of those wins was the fluke victory over Cincinnati and three wins had come with the replacement team.

The Vikings were a wild-card team that had been just 8–7 during the regular season but had demolished the New Orleans Saints, 44–10, in the wild-card game the week before. CBS commentator Hank Stram, with whom I talked frequently, warned me that the Vikings were on a roll and could beat the 49ers.

Stram was on target. The Vikings came out hot and never let up. The 49ers were flat. Walsh never could explain why, though he thought the emotional final game of the season against the Rams, before which Fahnhorst had talked to the team about this being his last regular season game, might have contributed to it.

Montana, who was generally at his best in postseason games, was far off his game. He even made an uncharacteristic mental mistake in the second quarter. On a play designed to go to Rice, Montana instead threw into double coverage to Clark. The pass was intercepted and returned 45 yards for a touchdown by Reggie Rutland.

Meanwhile, the Vikings' Chris Carter was having as good a game as a receiver could have. Carter caught 10 passes for 227 yards that day, but the statistics alone don't tell the whole story. On most of the plays, Carter was well covered by the 49ers, but he made leaping catches, often changing directions in mid-air. Nobody could have stopped Carter that day.

The 49ers trailed, 20–3, at halftime, and when they started sluggishly in the second half, Walsh replaced Montana with Young. It was the first time since he'd become the starter that Montana had been taken out of a game when he wasn't injured.

Young performed heroically, completing 12 of 17 passes for 158 yards and rushing for a team-high 72 yards and another touchdown. But every time the 49ers scored, the Vikings would counter, and they won the game breezing, 36–24.

Eddie on a Rampage

THE LOSS was devastating, and DeBartolo's reaction to it would bring an early end to Walsh's coaching career with the 49ers.

This time there was no dressing room scene, like the one in New Orleans the year before. There was no scene at all. Eddie didn't even come down to the dressing room, leaving the stadium immediately with Policy. Soon the two were on their way to what was supposed to be a vacation in the Caribbean. Perhaps it was for Eddie, but not for Carmen, who had to listen to constant diatribes by De-Bartolo against Walsh.

Once again, Eddie was determined to fire Walsh. Or so he said. By this time, he must have realized that his directives to fire his coach were not being delivered, but he continued to work indirectly toward his stated goal. Perhaps he didn't want the direct confrontation. Perhaps he realized that his actions were not always rational and was using Policy as a buffer to protect him from himself.

> The loss [to the Vikings] was devastating, and DeBartolo's reaction to it would bring an early end to Walsh's coaching career with the 49ers.

This time, though, he seemed much more determined. Policy steered the conversation in another direction, suggesting that Walsh was trying to do too much. If Walsh could focus on football, he would be more effective, Policy argued. That year, the 49ers were remodeling their old warhorse of a stadium, Candlestick Park, to put in luxury boxes. Walsh was supposed to be overseeing that project, in addition to his other assignments. Policy said it would be best to relieve Walsh of his responsibilities for the remodeling project.

Eddie agreed and told Carmen to talk to Walsh when they

returned from their trip. Policy agreed but didn't schedule anything right away. He felt it was best to let Walsh's wounds heal,
too, before approaching him. To buy time, he told Eddie that he
had talked to Walsh and Walsh agreed to step back.

After thinking about it for some time, though, DeBartolo
decided he had been right the first time: He still wanted to fire
Walsh. He told Policy to make the move, but Policy delayed, giving both DeBartolo and Walsh more time to cool off.

Not until two days before the NFL meetings in Phoenix in
April did Policy and Walsh actually talk. When Policy told Walsh
what De-Bartolo wanted, Walsh was so angry that he threw a glass
at the cabana wall; the glass shattered, and one piece ricocheted and
nicked Policy's ear.

Then Policy told Walsh his contract would be extended, and
he would get a raise. That mollified Walsh.

There was one problem: Policy didn't have the authority to
change Walsh's contract. So he went to DeBartolo and suggested
to Eddie that he extend Walsh's contract and give him a raise. "Are
you nuts?" yelled DeBartolo. "I send you to fire the guy and you
give him a raise?" But Policy reminded his friend of the 49ers' success under Walsh and returned to his earlier argument that Walsh
could get the 49ers back to the Super Bowl if he were focused on
football, without the business-side distractions.

Finally, Eddie acquiesced, but there was one last snag: He
wanted to take away Walsh's title of president, which Eddie had
bestowed in 1983, and give it to Policy. The first part was fine with
Carmen, but he felt that if he became president, the change would
in effect be saying that Walsh hadn't done the job and had to be
replaced. He suggested that Eddie take back the title of president,
which he'd had previously, to spare Walsh's feelings.

This time, though, Policy miscalculated. Walsh did feel his role
was diminished when he lost the president's title, and his simmer-
ing anger would carry over into the contentious 1988 season.

CHAPTER TEN

The Surprising 1988 Season

JOE MONTANA's benching in the playoff loss to Minnesota set up a tense training camp in 1988, and Bill Walsh made it even more contentious at a press conference in London before an exhibition game between the 49ers and Miami Dolphins. After reporters had questioned Miami coach Don Shula, who enumerated various problems with his team, they asked Walsh if his team had any problems. Walsh was generally happy with his team, which he had expected to peak in 1988–89, but he said, "We may have a quarterback controversy." From that point, the battle between Montana and Steve Young became the focal point of stories, even more than whether the 49ers won or lost.

Walsh later claimed he had intended to say only that Young had proven he was a legitimate NFL quarterback but that Montana was still the 49ers' starter. Montana, though, was worried that Walsh's statement meant he was trying to phase Joe out—and he was right.

In fact, Walsh had talked to the San Diego Chargers in the off-season about trading Montana for linebacker Billy Ray Smith. He knew the trade would be a bombshell to 49er fans, but he thought it would help the team; and he wanted to make it while Montana still had trade value.

Walsh had always consulted with others on both his coaching and administrative staff, and he brought this potential trade up in a morning meeting of his coaching staff. He asked for a show of hands from those who thought trading Montana would be a good idea. No hands were raised. Walsh stormed out of the room. In the afternoon, he called another coaches' meeting and brought up the possible Montana trade again. Still, no assistant would raise his hand. Walsh usually stuck with his decisions; but faced with the total opposition of his staff, he ended negotiations with the Chargers.

> By the time Young would be needed as the full-time quarterback, Montana's trade value would have dropped precipitously, and so Walsh considered trading Montana a year early.

The trade talk didn't mean that Walsh undervalued Montana. He knew that Montana ran his offense better than any quarterback he'd ever coached, but he feared that Montana's physical fragility would bring a quick end to his career. He had brought Young in to be ready when Montana could no longer play every game, and he expected that Young would be the starting quarterback no later than the start of the '89 season. This plan was consistent with his philosophy of replacing veteran players with younger players even when it seemed the veteran still had something left. Montana had been a great quarterback for the 49ers, but Walsh thought Young would be a great quarterback, too, and he was preparing to make the switch. By the time Young would be needed as the full-time quarterback, Montana's trade value would have dropped precipitously, and so Walsh considered trading Montana a year early.

Walsh was right about Young, who set team and league records when he got a chance to play; but he was wrong about Montana.

The competition with Young would get Montana's competitive juices flowing faster than ever, and Joe would play two and a half seasons at a higher level than he'd ever played—and probably at the highest level any quarterback has ever played.

It took a half season for Montana to get into that stretch, though, and in the interim, he very nearly lost his job. Only a combination of circumstances beyond Young's control prevented him from putting Montana permanently on the bench in a season that had many bizarre twists and turns.

Quarterback Shuffle

MONTANA STARTED the season opener; but he injured his elbow on the artificial turf of the Superdome in a wild 34–33 win. Young started the next game, against the New York Giants. When Young had trouble moving the team, Walsh put in Montana for the second half. Joe had his problems, too, but he also combined with Jerry Rice for a 78-yard touchdown with just 42 seconds left to win the game.

Montana started the next six games, but Walsh twice replaced him with Young late in two games, both times because of special circumstances.

The first came in a game against Denver on October 9 when the wind was worse than anybody can remember for a football game at Candlestick. Weather conditions for games in San Francisco are often just the reverse of those for the rest of the country. Summer baseball is played in fog and fierce winds, while fall football is often played in weather so warm and calm that men sitting on the west side of the stadium will take off their shirts to catch some sun.

Not this day, though, when the wind was as strong as any ever faced by the baseball Giants. When the game went into overtime, Walsh felt that it was impossible to throw the ball, so he put in

Young, thinking he might be able to create something with his running ability. "I didn't know I was the hurricane quarterback," Young said wryly, years later. He tried to pass but was intercepted, and the Broncos kicked a field goal to win the game.

The next weather problem was icy cold in Chicago on October 24, but a bigger problem was Walsh's unexpected timidity. His success as a coach was based on his ability to make opponents change their game to try to stop his team; but this time, he so feared the Bears' all-out pass rush that he changed his offense, keeping backs Roger Craig and Tom Rathman and tight end John Frank in to block, instead of sending them on pass routes. Late in the game, as Montana tired, he put in Young, again hoping that Young's spontaneity and running ability might disrupt the Bear's defense. It didn't, and the Bears won, 10–9.

Despite the extra protection, Montana had taken a beating in the game. Physically, he was a mess. He'd injured his elbow, his back was a continual problem, and he'd lost weight he couldn't afford to lose in a bout with dysentery. Walsh decided that he would give more playing time to Young for the next game, perhaps even start him.

Unfortunately, he didn't tell Montana before he announced his decision to the press the next day at his weekly luncheon. That wasn't surprising to anybody who knew the two. On the field, the communication between them was perfect; off the field, it was virtually nonexistent. Throughout Montana's career with the 49ers, he and Walsh seldom talked except to discuss plays and game plans.

> Throughout Montana's career with the 49ers, he and Walsh seldom talked except to discuss plays and game plans.

Reporters immediately went to Montana for his reaction. The story was even juicier because the Sunday opponent would be the Minnesota Vikings, who had in a sense started the quarterback controversy with their playoff win the year before. Reporters provoked Montana by exaggerating Walsh's statement to make it seem Young was replacing him—though Walsh had explicitly said that Montana was still the starter, no matter how much Young played in the Minnesota game—and Joe responded with a strong defense of his play.

That forced a meeting between the two that was uncomfortable for both. Walsh tried to soothe Montana's feelings by saying he just wanted Joe to get healthy for the stretch run. Montana wasn't placated; he was still certain that Walsh was trying to replace him. Then, as he started to get up from his chair to leave, his back went into spasms. Dr. Michael Dillingham, the team doctor, told Montana to stay out of practice; 48 hours later, Dr. Dillingham ruled him out of the game.

Somehow, the fact that Montana was ruled out of the game for medical reasons got lost in the excitement of the change to Young; the change was interpreted as a benching of Montana.

Young's play in the Vikings game was a microcosm of his 49er career to that date. He was hyperactive in the first half, and the result was an inconsistent 49er offense that could score only three points, on a Mike Cofer field goal. Young started the second half, though, by directing a 97-yard touchdown drive and then connected with John Taylor on a 73-yard touchdown pass.

The Vikings matched those touchdowns with two of their own and led, 21–17, with just over two minutes to go. Then Young made a brilliant play that would have been inconceivable for any other quarterback in the game; and, typically for his early 49er career, he made it with his feet. Back to pass from the Minnesota 49, he seemed about to be sacked as he disappeared momentarily under the Vikings pass rushers. Then he somehow burst free from the pack and started running to his left. He faked a pass and then headed downfield, breaking through tackles from what seemed like every Minnesota defender, and he finally flopped across the goal line, totally spent, for the touchdown that won the game.

That sensational play—and the announcement from Walsh the following day that Montana would be kept out another week—made the quarterback controversy virtually the only sports story the next week.

It was not the finest hour for sports journalism in the Bay Area, as reporters and columnists consistently misinterpreted comments and actions. Asked whether Young might be the starter for the rest of the season, Walsh answered, "Anything's possible, but none of us anticipate that." A beat reporter quoted the first two words but not the rest of the sentence, an edit that totally changed Walsh's comment. After interviewing Montana, a columnist wrote that Joe thought the 49ers were trying to trade him. Because the trading deadline had passed three weeks earlier, the 49ers could not trade Montana that year, but neither Joe nor the columnist realized that.

The next game, in Phoenix against the Cardinals, became another turning point in a season that had already had almost too much drama even for the participants.

The 49ers completely dominated the first three quarters of the game. With Young playing more consistently than he had before, the 49ers took a 23–0 lead before the Cardinals scored their first touchdown late in the third quarter. Though it was a very hot day and players were tiring, Young felt confident of a victory at that point.

But that Cardinal touchdown, on a pass from Neil Lomax to Roy Green, had exposed the 49ers' Achilles heel: their pass defense. One starting cornerback, Tim McKyer, was injured and didn't play; Darryl Pollard, who had been with the team only a couple of weeks, had replaced him. The other corner, Don Griffin, who was beaten on the Green touchdown, was coming back from an injury and was not at his best.

With a weakened defense, the 49ers should have kept applying offensive pressure, but Walsh became conservative with his play-calling. Perhaps he didn't trust Young enough at this point, but the effect of his conservatism was to allow the Cardinals to creep back into the game with a field goal and another Lomax touchdown pass to bring the Cardinals to within six, at 23–17.

Even so, the 49ers should have won the game and, in fact, were only one play away from the first down that would have enabled them to run out the clock. The Cardinals had called time with the 49ers on their own 21, facing a third-and-four call with 1:38 left. Walsh and Young conferred on the sideline. They agreed that Young should roll to his left and run for the first, as he had done earlier in the game. Young seemed to have the first down when he was run out by defensive end Freddie Joe Dunn, stopping the clock, but the official marked it six inches short. (To this day, Walsh and Young are both convinced that Young had the first down on the play.) If Young had made the first down, the 49ers could have run out the clock. If he had stayed in bounds, the Cardinals probably would have had only about 45 seconds left when they got the ball back. Instead, they had 1:27 left after the 49er punt, and Lomax moved his team 66 yards in seven plays against the weakened 49er defense, throwing a nine-yard touchdown pass to Green over Pollard with just three seconds left.

It was a devastating loss, made worse by the fact that Walsh had two ribs broken when an Arizona running back ran into him on the sidelines. He raged at the team and his coaches in the locker room and then sat in a near-catatonic state on the team plane for the ride home, second-guessing himself for the call on Young's run. When Young rolled out,

The game [against the Cardinals] also put Young's starting career on hold for another three years.

it was usually to his left because, as a left-handed passer, it was easier for him to throw while running in that direction. But Walsh felt that, this time, he should have surprised the Cardinals by having Young roll to his right. For Walsh, always so supremely confident—and rightly so—of his judgment, it was just another bit of evidence of coaching burnout.

The game also put Young's starting career on hold for another three years. "If we'd won the game, Steve would have continued as the starter," said Walsh years later. "He'd played well, and it certainly wasn't his fault that we'd lost that game. But there was just tremendous pressure to start Joe, and I couldn't resist that. I didn't think he was ready, but he started the next game."

Walsh was right. Montana was still weak from the combination of dysentery and his bad back, and he and the 49ers played very poorly the next week, losing to the Raiders in a battle of field goals at Candlestick, 9–3. Montana was 16 of 31 for a paltry 160 yards, but he would remain as the starter.

The Turnaround

A WEEK of meetings followed that game. The players met without coaches and decided that, if the season were lost, the blame would fall on them, so they had better turn it around themselves. It was an emotional meeting, with several players, including the usually quiet Montana, making speeches. The players bonded as a result of the meeting, and it was a different and much better 49er team the rest of the season.

Meanwhile, DeBartolo flew out from Youngstown to meet with Walsh. This time he didn't use Policy as his go-between because he intended to fire Walsh; he wasn't going to let Policy talk him out of his decision. But when they met, Walsh broke down. The combination of the pressure of coaching and his separation from his wife (they later got back together) was crushing. Eddie didn't know how to react, so that meeting ended with an agreement that they'd meet again later in the week. But those meetings ended in much the same fashion. Finally, Eddie told

Walsh to just let the season play out and they'd deal with the situation when the season was over.

As speculation mounted in the media over just what was said in the first Walsh–DeBartolo meeting (nobody knew there were subsequent meetings as well), the players turned their season around. It started with a 37–21 win over the Washington Redskins, another team at the crossroads of a season, and continued for five straight wins. Amazingly, after all their troubles, the 49ers actually clinched their season with a week to go, so Walsh was able to rest many regulars, including Montana, in the second half of the last game, a meaningless 38–16 loss to the Rams.

Again, the 49ers' playoff opponent would be the Vikings, but this game would be nothing like the 1987 disaster. The 49ers were always at an advantage in the '80s when they had already played a playoff team in the regular season, because both Walsh and defensive coordinator George Seifert were adept at coming up with different formations.

This time, Seifert's defense set the tone for the game, holding the potent Minnesota offense to a field goal in the first half and just one touchdown in the game.

Meanwhile, Walsh's offense was turning the Vikings' strength against them. The strength of the Minnesota defense was the great pass rush of Keith Millard inside and Chris Doleman from the outside, but Walsh devised plays that would start one way and then cut back the other; Millard and Doleman couldn't reverse direction quickly and were out of the plays. The most spectacular 49er play was a cutback by Roger Craig, who went 80 yards for the final score in the 34–9 win.

When the 49ers went into Chicago for the NFC championship game, the local media believed the only question was the Bears' victory margin. The 49er offense couldn't match the Bears' defense, especially in the bitter cold of a Chicago winter.

The Bears were a very strong team, though not quite so dominant as the 1985 championship team. Defensive coordinator Buddy Ryan had installed a pressure defense that would be adopted (though not so successfully) by many other teams, just as other teams had copied Walsh's offense. The defense, nicknamed the "46 defense" because that was the uniform number for middle linebacker Mike Singletary, put eight defenders on the line of scrimmage before every snap. At the snap, some defenders would drop back into pass coverage, but the offense never knew which players would rush and which would drop back—or whether all eight of them would go for the quarterback, as happened fairly frequently. The Bears consistently disrupted offenses, which couldn't get into a rhythm.

Walsh had learned his lesson from the regular season game, and he was determined to run his offense, with as many as five possible receivers for Montana's passes. The weather conditions even helped; on a first-quarter play, Jerry Rice took a short pass from Montana and ran past Chicago defenders, who slipped on the icy field, for 61 yards and a touchdown. The 49ers rolled up 406 yards in total offense in a surprisingly easy 28–3 win.

The Super Bowl Again

AFTER THAT, the Super Bowl was expected to be a romp for the 49ers, as the four previous Super Bowls had been for the NFC champion; but this would be a very different Super Bowl, because the pregame focus was on Walsh's intentions. By now, even DeBartolo had changed his mind. The man who wanted to fire Walsh after the '87 season and mid-season in '88 was now telling reporters that he hoped Walsh would continue coaching.

Walsh wasn't talking, saying only that he'd make an announcement after the game. He later said he thought he had defused the issue so his players wouldn't be distracted; but in fact, he had done just the opposite. Because he wasn't talking, reporters constantly asked 49er players what they thought. Some players, especially the emotional Ronnie Lott, were angry that Walsh wouldn't tell them his intentions. The game became secondary.

And the 49ers played that way. After the game, writers would say that this was the most exciting Super Bowl to date, but that was only because they'd forgotten the first three quarters. The 49ers dominated for most of that time but, because of fumbles and penalties, couldn't get anything but two field goals. The Cincinnati Bengals also got just two field goals, so the score was 6–6 with just 50 seconds left in the third quarter. Tense, yes, but hardly exciting.

Cincinnati's Stanford Jennings broke for 93 yards on a kickoff return after Mike Cofer's second field goal, and the Bengals still held a 16–13 lead with 3:20 left in the game and the 49ers pushed back to their own 8.

But the 49ers had Joe Montana. This was always what made Montana so special, his ability to make the big play in the clutch. It wasn't that he raised his level of play but that he was able to sustain it at a time when others were so tense they could hardly move. Montana just kept doing what he had practiced. On this drive, he did get so excited at one point that he hyperventilated, but he just threw the ball to Rice, and everything was all right again in 49er land.

> The Super Bowl was expected to be a romp for the 49ers, as the four previous Super Bowls had been for the NFC champion; but this would be a very different Super Bowl.

This drive was even tougher than the one against Dallas in the '82 NFC championship game that had first made Montana's reputation because he had almost two minutes less to work with. However, he also had the advantage of knowing that a field goal would tie the game and send it into overtime; a field goal wouldn't have been enough against the Cowboys.

When the 49ers got to the Cincinnati 8 with 39 seconds left, though, nobody was thinking field goal. Walsh called a play designed to look like the play that had just been run, a completed pass to Craig. This time, though, Craig was the decoy. While Taylor faked to the outside and then broke to the middle, Craig was cutting across the middle, so the linebacker would cover him instead of dropping back to help against Taylor. Craig actually lined up on the wrong side in the excitement but it made no difference because the linebacker still followed him. Taylor's fake fooled the safety, so he couldn't get back to help in coverage, and Taylor beat the Cincinnati cornerback to take Montana's pass in the end zone. The 49ers had a 20–16 win that really should have been much easier.

Though Taylor caught the winning touchdown, Rice had been the game's dominant player, catching 11 passes for a Super Bowl record 215 yards and winning the Most Valuable Player award. The moment turned sour for Rice, though, when Montana got the "Ride to Disneyland." Rice thought that honor was supposed to go to the game's MVP. In fact, it went to the quarterback of the winning team; but in the years since the award had existed, the MVP had also always been the winning quarterback, so nobody was aware of the distinction. Rice then complained about lack of endorsements for star black players, including himself, of course, and that one petulant episode cast a shadow over his great career for years afterward.

Exit Walsh—For Now

THE STAGE was set for the last bit of drama: Walsh's retirement.

It was obvious to anyone close to Walsh that he could not coach another season. He was an emotional basket case, and the players had in essence coached themselves during the second half of the season. His once-great relationship with the media had deteriorated badly, because most reporters felt he was manipulating them. Instead of being bravura performances by the coach, as they once had been, his press conferences were often confrontational.

Walsh being Walsh, though, he delayed his decision for dramatic effect and also to help push George Seifert as his successor. He was expected to announce after the game whether he would quit or continue coaching, but he flew home with the team without saying a word about it. He was pressuring DeBartolo to hire Seifert as his replacement.

Eddie had another coach in mind: Jimmy Johnson, then the very successful coach of the Miami Hurricanes. Walsh argued that Johnson had no pro experience and that he was using a much less complex system than the 49ers'. The 49ers, he said, had a smooth-running offensive system, and Johnson would upset it. In addition, he said, Johnson's country ways (he was from Arkansas) would not play well in the sophisticated San Francisco Bay Area.

If the 49ers wanted to go outside the system, Walsh said, UCLA coach Terry Donahue would be a good choice, but he felt that it would be best to have Seifert, who knew everything on the defensive side and had a good offensive coordinator Mike Holmgren to keep the offense going. And, of course, Walsh would still be there as general manager and support for Seifert.

> Walsh being Walsh, he delayed his decision for dramatic effect and also to help push George Seifert as his successor.

The scenario became more dramatic than even Walsh wanted. As the top aide on a very successful team, Seifert was in demand; and he was scheduled to interview in Cleveland the week after the Super Bowl. Meanwhile, Walsh was negotiating furiously with DeBartolo, who still wanted Johnson. Seifert, a native of San

Francisco who had grown up as a 49er fan, wanted the 49er job, but he wasn't going to wait around to be asked. He was actually on his way to Cleveland when he got a call at the Dallas–Fort Worth airport from Policy, who told him he should return to San Francisco because he was going to be named as Walsh's successor.

So Walsh got his way, as he usually did. In an emotional press conference in Carmel later that week, he announced his retirement; and DeBartolo announced that Seifert would succeed Walsh.

It didn't work out quite the way Walsh planned. He himself left the organization for television work in the spring. Meanwhile, Seifert suffered all throughout his run as 49ers' head coach because of his attempt to emulate Walsh, who truly was unique in his time. It might have been better for the 49ers if Johnson had been hired, because Johnson proved with the Dallas Cowboys and, later, the Miami Dolphins, that he was an outstanding coach and talent evaluator.

> Seifert suffered all throughout his run as 49ers' head coach because of his attempt to emulate Walsh, who truly was unique in his time.

But in the winter of '89, anything Bill Walsh wanted from Eddie DeBartolo he got. If it had been that way throughout his 49er coaching career, Walsh would probably have had a longer run, but he had done enough to qualify for eventual election to the Pro Football Hall of Fame.

CHAPTER ELEVEN

Team with a Mission

THE 49ER players were on a mission in 1989: They intended to prove that they could win without Bill Walsh.

This would probably have come as a surprise to 49er fans, who venerated Walsh for what he had done as a coach. It certainly came as a surprise to Walsh, who had been totally oblivious to what his players really thought of him. Walsh thought his players respected and liked him; and he envisioned that, in retirement, he would have lunch with former players and golf with them. What he didn't realize was that his players had feared and even, in some cases, hated him. Many former players thought they had been forced into retirement when they still had some playing time left, and they were resentful. Eventually, Walsh realized how they felt and started repairing fences with his former players, calling them to invite them to lunch. He now has a good relationship with most of them, and he and Joe Montana frequently golf together. But it took a while.

It wasn't happening in '89, for sure. As usual, Ronnie Lott was the most vocal, declaring that this was to be the "We'll show Walsh" year. Lott was still fuming because Walsh had not told the players of his impending retirement. (There was one exception.

Walsh and Randy Cross had talked on the plane going to Miami. When Cross told him that he would announce his retirement during Super Bowl week, Walsh hinted broadly that his announcement would follow. But he knew Randy would not say anything, if for no other reason than that Cross didn't want his own retirement announcement to be trumped.)

Lott now says that Walsh's leaving created a "challenge" for the '89 team, but his calm words today mask the great emotion of the time.

Everybody who has ever been close to Ronnie Lott has tremendous respect and admiration for him. As gentle off the field as he was ferocious on it, Lott has always been very active in charity work, especially with youth, starting the "Pros for Kids" program to benefit youth sports groups.

> As usual, Ronnie Lott was the most vocal, declaring that this was to be the "We'll show Walsh" year.

As a rookie, he took a back seat to Dwight Hicks, the only member of the great 1981 backfield who had any NFL experience, but he soon became the acknowledged leader of the defense. When he was moved to safety, he determined play assignments for the defensive backfield, and he was quick to jump on anybody who didn't complete his assignment.

Lott always completed his. He not only covered receivers but also delivered crushing tackles to anyone in his path. As defensive coordinator, George Seifert had often commented on Lott's effect on the defense. "We'll be playing along at one level," said Seifert, "when Ronnie will just level a guy with a tackle, and all of a sudden, our whole effort will step up."

It was also remarkable how Lott's emotions helped him. Most players who play with such emotion are inconsistent, their play reflecting their emotional ups and downs. Lott always played at a fever pitch, and he played at a consistently high level.

He had been angry with Walsh since the 1987 strike, his emotions overcoming his intellect then; contrary to what Lott thought, Walsh had kept the team together by not favoring either the strikers or the players who came back. Their split was inevitable because the two approached life so differently, Lott externalizing everything and Walsh internalizing his problems. If Walsh could have talked openly to Lott, their relationship would have been much better. But Walsh didn't want to show any sign of weakness with players, which was probably wise from a coaching standpoint, and it wasn't his method of operation.

With Lott's anger lifting the team to a high emotional pitch for the season, the 49ers would get past the problem they faced as NFL champions.

Twice, they had failed to repeat. The 1982 team had been torn apart by drug problems. The '85 failure was less understandable, because the 49ers still had most of the players from the team that had swept the board the previous season, and they had Jerry Rice as well. In his rookie season, Rice wasn't the great receiver he would be in the years to come, but he still gave the 49ers an added receiving threat. Yet the team didn't come close to repeating.

This time, though, the 49ers would sweep through the season, and their crushing defeat of the Denver Broncos in the Super Bowl would be the most lopsided game in the history of that series.

Seifert's Good Fortune

THE HAPPY beneficiary of these circumstances was Seifert, who could hardly believe his good fortune. Seifert wasn't the first coach to get the job he'd always dreamed of, but he was certainly the first to be rewarded with a Super Bowl championship in his first season.

As a head coach, Seifert was quite different than he'd been as a defensive coordinator or as a defensive backfield coach before that.

As a position coach, he'd been hands-on, very close to his players, as a good assistant must be. As a coordinator, he'd been a brilliant strategist, as good in his way as Walsh was on offense, though with markedly less publicity. Like Walsh, he was especially good at devising defensive schemes in the postseason, especially if the 49ers had played the team in the regular season. I talked to Seifert frequently in those days, but it had to be early in the week, before he started working on the defensive game plan. At that point, George just retreated from the world, the mad scientist at work.

When he became head coach, he liked to repeat the advice from his wife, who had told him, "Don't screw it up, George." That was good advice. When Seifert acted as caretaker, just staying out of the way, he was fine. When he tried to do more than he was able to, he got himself and the team into trouble.

His most obvious mistakes were made in the draft. At first, he tried to be like Walsh, making the big decisions, until Carmen Policy realized that approach wasn't working and brought others into the decision-making process.

Seifert had inherited Mike Holmgren as offensive coordinator, and as long as he left Holmgren to run the offense, it ran smoothly. But Seifert couldn't stay away, and Holmgren left to become head coach at Green Bay. Seifert's meddling got worse after that, and it wasn't until Mike Shanahan arrived, in '93, that he backed off. Shanahan's offensive mind was nearly the equal of Walsh's; and with Shanahan running the offense, the 49ers got back to the Super Bowl after the '94 season. But when Shanahan left to become head coach of the Denver Broncos, Seifert resumed his meddling in the offense, and the 49ers suffered.

Most coaches get hired because the team is bad; that's why Walsh was hired in 1979. Seifert inherited a championship team, which is certainly an advantage. But he knew when he was hired that he would never get credit for winning because everybody would still regard the 49ers as Walsh's team as long as the players were the ones Walsh had brought in. Even in '94, Seifert's sixth

The Catch: Dwight Clark miraculously pulls down the winning touchdown pass of the 1981 NFC Championship, sending the 49ers to their first Super Bowl in franchise history. (Photo by Fred Larson)

ABOVE: The 49ers' impenetrable defense celebrates its famous goal line stand that sealed the team's first Super Bowl victory. LEFT: Happy Days: Eddie DeBartolo hands off the Vince Lombardi Trophy to Bill Walsh after the 49ers' Super Bowl XVI victory.

Ronnie Lott, elected to the NFL Hall of Fame in 2000, quickly proved to be a valuable leader for the productive 49er defense. (Photos this page by Fred Larson)

ABOVE: Joe Montana eludes defenders as he scrambles for yardage in the 49ers' victorious trip to Super Bowl XIX. (Photo by Mike Maloney) LEFT: Best friends Clark and Montana were the first of the 49ers' famous pass-catch tandems. (Photo by Fred Larson)

An exciting scrambler, Steve Young rushed for a 49-yard touchdown against the Vikings, a breath-taking play dubbed "The Run." (Photo by Deanne Fitzmaurice)

ABOVE: Roger Craig, the first NFL player to surpass 1,000 yards rushing and receiving in a single season, fights for yardage in Super Bowl XXIII. LEFT: Bill Walsh devised the efficient West Coast Offense. (Photos by Fred Larson)

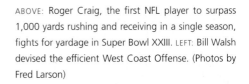

A master defensive strategist, Seifert holds the best win percentage of all coaches in NFL history. (Photo by Deanne Fitzmaurice)

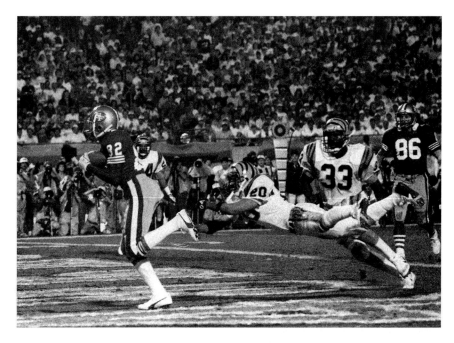

The Drive: John Taylor squeezes a Montana pass to put the 49ers atop the Cincinnati Bengals in the closing seconds of Super Bowl XXIII. (Photo by Deanne Fitzmaurice)

ABOVE LEFT: Montana shows his famous signal of success in the 49ers' Super Bowl XXIV rout of the Denver Broncos. ABOVE RIGHT: A hand injury sidelines Montana in the 1990 NFC Championship game. The 49ers lose the game and their chance at three straight Super Bowls. (Photos by Fred Larson)

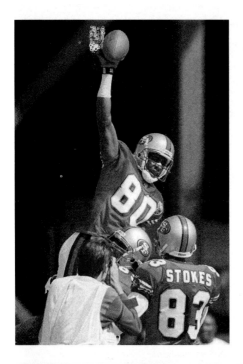

ABOVE: Carmen Policy discusses DeBartolo's resignation amid a Louisiana gambling scandal. (Photo by Fred Larson) LEFT: Jerry Rice celebrates his record-setting catch in 1996, becoming the first NFL receiver with 1,000 career receptions. (Photo by Vince Maggiora)

Ricky Watters high-steps across the goal line in Super Bowl XXIX, the 49ers' fifth world championship. Watters had already set an NFL single-game playoff record with five touchdowns against the New York Giants. (Photo by Deanne Fitzmaurice)

San Francisco Mayor Willie Brown, DeBartolo, and Policy look over a proposed new stadium in 1997. Plans have never gotten past the drawing board. (AP/Wide World Photo)

Five Vince Lombardi Trophies: the 49ers were the first of only two teams to win five Super Bowls. (Photo by Fred Larson)

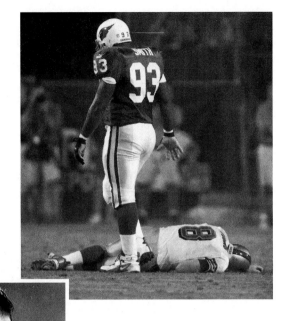

RIGHT: A Cardinals lineman stands over a motionless Young after a hit in the third game of the 1999 season, which gave Young his second concussion in two weeks and effectively ended his career. (Photo by Michael Maloney) BELOW: Steve Mariucci had little to smile about during the devastating 1999 season. (Photo by Michael Macor)

Rice walks off the field in Atlanta after the last game of the 1999 season. Many thought he would not return to the 49ers in 2000, but he re-signed through 2004. (Photo by Fred Larson)

TEAM WITH A MISSION • 117

season, the key players were Steve Young and Jerry Rice; Walsh had traded for Young and drafted Rice.

Seifert faced an impossible task. No coach could have replaced Walsh in the eyes of 49er fans because Walsh had assumed mythic status by the time he left. Seifert would never be a legendary figure. He was, though, a solid coach and a good one for the 49ers at this time in their history because he was able to keep the team on an even keel, not too high after wins, not too low after losses. That trait was extremely valuable because, by the end of the 1980s, the 49ers were expected to win every year, causing tremendous pressure, well beyond the normal in an NFL season. With Seifert at the helm, the 49ers were able to take the pressure in stride.

> No coach could have replaced Walsh in the eyes of 49er fans because Walsh had assumed mythic status by the time he left.

Seifert's calm was especially important that first year because the 49ers were driven hard internally by Lott, whose fierce, vocal competitiveness was a good complement to the quiet leadership of Montana.

As good as Lott was—and he was very good, an All-Pro at both cornerback and safety during his career—it was Montana who was the main man for the 49ers, as he was throughout his career when he was healthy.

Montana at His Best

IN 1989, Montana was in the midst of the finest stretch of his career. Following the miserable 1988 loss to the Raiders that brought the 49ers down to 6–5, Montana played 34 regular season games over the next two and a half years. In that stretch, he completed 67 percent of his passes, averaging about 275 yards a game and 2.2 touchdown passes. His quarterback rating over that period was 108.7, much better than his career rating of 92.3. He was even better in the playoffs, as the 49ers swept the board in '88 and '89; in six games, he threw for 19 touchdowns with only one interception.

Two games in that stretch deserve special mention. One was the third game of the 1989 season, in Philadelphia. The Eagles had a 21–10 lead going into the fourth quarter that day, and they had sacked Montana eight times. But Joe got off the floor to throw four touchdowns in the fourth quarter, as the 49ers won, 38–28.

Montana threw for 428 yards in that game, but he surpassed even that in a December 11 game against the Rams, throwing for 458 yards on 30 completions in 42 attempts.

Montana did not do it alone, of course. He had two great receivers in Jerry Rice and the much underrated John Taylor. Montana's chief asset as a quarterback was his decision-making ability, because he had an unparalleled ability to see the whole field and pick exactly the right receiver, and he was an extremely accurate passer. He not only completed a high percentage of his passes, but also had the ability to hit a receiver right in stride, enabling him to run for extra yardage after the catch. Taylor was especially good at the extra run; in one memorable game against the Rams in '89, he caught two short slant passes and went 92 and 95 yards for touchdowns, the first time in NFL history a receiver had two touchdowns of more than 90 yards in one game.

In addition, Brent Jones had matured into a pass-receiving threat at tight end, with the speed to go deep and the catching ability of a wide receiver. The 49ers' pass offense was truly unstoppable, and Montana had a record-breaking year, including a club record .702 percentage and an NFL-record 112.4 quarterback rating.

Among those who watched the 49ers in the 1980s, there's always been a debate over which team was the best, the '84 championship team or the '89 team. The '84 team had the best season record, 15–1, and it won by a lopsided margin in the Super Bowl, 38–16 over the Miami Dolphins. The 1989 team was just a shade off in the regular season, finishing at 14–2. But in the postseason, that team was as dominating as any team in NFL history.

The Minnesota Vikings were the first playoff opponent in 1989, and they went down easily, 41–3. In the NFC championship game, the Rams scored the first three points of the game and that's all they got, going down 30–3, as Montana completed an improbable 26 of 30 for 262 yards and three touchdowns.

No Chance for the Broncos

THE DENVER Broncos had won the AFC title, and the Denver fans did their celebrating the week before the Super Bowl in New Orleans. At dinner in a Bourbon Street restaurant one night, I watched a conga line of Broncos fans wending their way down the street in serpentine fashion. The fans were wearing orange, often Denver jerseys or sweatshirts, except for one man who was seemingly dressed only in a barrel, having fortified himself with alcohol to keep warm.

Sports fans are eternal optimists, but I had a sense that the Broncos fans were celebrating early because they knew they'd have no chance to do it after the game. There have been many mismatches in Super Bowl history, but none more than that year. The Broncos got to the game strictly on the strength of John Elway's arm. They did not have the 49ers' offensive versatility or their defensive strength, and they didn't even have a very good defensive scheme.

When I talked to Walsh before the game, he analyzed the Denver defense and said there was no way the Broncos could stop Montana. He thought the 49ers would score at least five touchdowns and saw no way the Broncos could get more than two or three. He was conservative. The 49ers led, 27–3, at the half. By the third quarter, former 49er Randy Cross said to me, "If this were a fight, the referee would call a technical knockout." The final score was 55–10, and it wasn't that close. Elway, under tremendous pressure throughout the game, completed only 10 of 26 passes for 108 yards. He was intercepted twice. Nobody questions Elway's reputation as one of the top quarterbacks of all time, which only emphasizes how good the 49er defense was in that game and that season.

> The [team] wanted to be the first team to win three straight Super Bowls, and they made up a word, "three-peat," to symbolize their quest.

As it would turn out, it was Montana's final Super Bowl; and he went out with a flourish, becoming the first player to win three Most Valuable Player awards in the game, as he completed 22 of 29 passes for 297 yards and a then-record five touchdowns. In four Super Bowls, he threw for 11 touchdowns and was never intercepted. There is no better example of how Montana could raise his game to another level when it counted most.

Trying for a Three-peat

THE HARDEST thing in sports is not winning a championship but repeating. The 49ers had not been able to do it after their first two Super Bowl wins. They had done it in the 1989 season and now they set another goal: They wanted to be the first team to win three straight Super Bowls, and they made up a word, "three-peat," to symbolize their quest.

They almost made it, falling just one play short, but 1990 was an agonizing year. The whole organization seemed to feel the pressure. Executives and coaches were wound tight, often snapping at innocuous questions from reporters.

The team was wearing out. Roger Craig, the great warrior, tore a ligament in his knee in the fourth game, but he continued playing. He had his poorest season as a 49er, rushing for just 439 yards and averaging 3.1 yards a carry. As a team, the 49ers gained only 1,718 yards rushing that season, worse than the 1981 team, which was thought to have no running attack but gained 1,941 yards.

Montana started the season as strongly as he'd finished in the Super Bowl, setting a club record that still stands by throwing for 476 yards against Atlanta. He threw for 411 yards against Green Bay and had other games with 398, 390, and 318 yards in the first half of the season.

But Montana, too, was beginning to wear out, and his decline started to show in the second half of the season. The loss of Craig as a running threat was a contributing factor, but Craig had not been able to run well for most of the first half of the season either, and Montana hadn't missed a beat. In the second half, though, he didn't have even one 300-yard game, and he fell below 200 yards three times. Though the fans who expected him to play forever certainly didn't realize it, Montana would never again be a consistent top-level quarterback.

Amazingly, even with Montana's decline and Craig's injury-plagued season, the 49ers kept winning. They were 10–0 when they met the New York Giants, also 10–0, in San Francisco on a Monday night in December.

Though the fans who expected him to play forever certainly didn't realize it, Montana would never again be a consistent top-level quarterback.

The hype for the game was incredible and, as so often happens when a game is promoted that hard, it was a disappointing game for the spectators. Ronnie Lott later said it was the best game in which he'd ever played, but that was because Lott was playing defense. The coaches, Seifert and Bill Parcells, played very conservatively, hoping not to make mistakes on offense and letting their defenses dominate. It was Stone Age football, very physical, very limited. In the end, the 49ers prevailed, 7–3, on a four-yard Montana pass to Taylor.

The 49ers won just three of their next five, but their 14–2 finish and win over the Giants guaranteed them home field advantage in the playoffs. Inevitably, the 49ers and Giants met again in the NFC championship game at Candlestick; and just as inevitably, this was another defensive struggle.

There was one big offensive play, a 61-yard pass play with Montana and Taylor that produced the game's only touchdown. Otherwise, it was all field goals, and the 49ers led, 13–12, with about three minutes to play. There was too much time for the 49ers to sit on their lead, so Montana was trying to pass when Giants defensive end Leonard Marshall broke through to sack him, breaking Montana's right hand, bruising his sternum, and giving him a concussion.

Montana was replaced by Steve Young, who had hardly played that season; in the first 14 games of the season, he threw only one pass. On his first play, Young completed a 25-yard pass. Then the 49ers called a running play, with Craig carrying, hoping to take some time off the clock and perhaps get down to the two-minute warning.

It seemed a safe call. Craig was a reliable back who knew how to protect the ball. He had a clause in his contract that awarded him a bonus if he fumbled fewer than three times in a season, and he'd always earned that bonus. But this time he fumbled, and Lawrence Taylor recovered for the Giants on their own 43. They drove just far enough to give Chris Bahr a chance to kick his fifth field goal of the game, this one from 42 yards out on the last play of the game, giving the Giants a 15–13 victory.

In two games between the teams, 120 minutes, the Giants had not been able to score a touchdown. But they were going to the Super Bowl, and the 49ers were staying home.

The game left Young wondering about his fate. He had almost replaced Montana in the '88 season but had gone back to the bench because of calls and decisions that were not his fault. If Craig had not fumbled, the 49ers would have won this game, and Young would have had a chance to show what he could do in the Super Bowl. As it happened, he would have to wait another four years for that chance, and in the interim he'd take a lot of grief from the fans who loved Montana.

The loss was such a bitter one, after the way the 49ers had fought through a season of adversity, that it had a carryover effect in the off-season and even into the next year.

The organization had hung on to veterans for the push in '90, but after this loss, the team immediately cut Eric Wright, Keena Turner, and Mike Wilson.

At the time, in a futile attempt to put off true free agency, the NFL had what was called Plan B. Teams could protect 37 players but the remainder were free agents. There was some player movement under this plan, but the stars stayed in place, which was what the league wanted.

Often, teams would make high-salaried veterans available, gambling that other teams wouldn't want to take on the salaries. The 49ers tried to do that with Craig and Lott. They weren't concerned about losing Craig, who signed with the Los Angeles Raiders, because they figured he was through as a top-notch running back.

Lott was another matter. The 49ers wanted to re-sign him, at a lower salary, though they figured he had only about one good year left. Because Seifert had been the defensive backfield coach in Lott's rookie year and they'd been close ever since, Carmen Policy asked Seifert to talk to Ronnie and explain that they wanted him back. But when the two sat down, Seifert blurted out, "You've been put on Plan B," without first explaining the reasoning. Lott's pride was stung and he angrily departed without giving Seifert a chance to say anything else. He then signed with the Raiders, and it was years before the breech between Lott and the 49ers was healed.

So it would be a very different 49er team in 1991. It would even be the start of the Steve Young era, though that wouldn't become clear until after Young had actually started for two years.

CHAPTER TWELVE

Replacing Bill Walsh

THE LOPSIDED Super Bowl win after the 1989 season might have made it seem that the 49ers' success would go on indefinitely, but it only helped disguise the problem the organization faced in replacing Bill Walsh.

Note the word: organization. George Seifert was doing a fine job of coaching the team, keeping it on course to the Super Bowl championship in his first year and nearly getting the 49ers there in his second year as well. But Walsh was also a great general manager. Nobody was better on draft day, and he was always adept at judging when a veteran player should be replaced and in anticipating need, as he had done by trading for Steve Young while Joe Montana was still playing. Seifert couldn't replace Walsh in those areas.

The problem was, he tried. He ran the draft as Walsh had, and the results were not good. His first-round draft picks in his first three years were running back Dexter Carter, nose tackle Ted Washington, and defensive back Dana Hall. Nobody else in the draft room wanted Carter, who was a specialty back—a kick returner, a back to bring in on third down to catch a pass. He was not big enough or strong enough to be an every-down back, and he did little for the 49ers. Washington eventually turned into a player, but it was with Buffalo, long after he left the 49ers, for whom he was overweight and underproductive. Hall was simply a bust.

The 49ers always had the disadvantage of drafting low in the first round, because of their success, so the sure-thing picks were long gone when their turn approached, but they still needed to do better than they were doing.

And, of course, he also botched the Plan B maneuverings, losing Ronnie Lott and Roger Craig.

Carmen Policy was appalled as he watched Seifert's less-than-masterful management touch. He had to tread cautiously at first because—although he had been associated with the team since Walsh had been hired in 1979—he had not become president until '91. But he was still determined to make changes. Years later, he would say to me, "People watch Joe Montana and they think that's the only way you can play quarterback. They watch Bill Walsh and think the way he did it is the only way. But there's only one Joe Montana and there's only one Bill Walsh. When you don't have one of those guys, you have to find another way to get the job done."

On the field Steve Young was the answer. In the front office, Policy's answer was to divide responsibilities. It was a way of operating that he was comfortable with. As he often admitted, he knew no more about football than the ordinary fan did, so he needed football people around to make player evaluations. His strength as an administrator was his ability to get the most out of others, to know their strengths and draw from them—and also to form a harmonious group. There would be no more of the one-man rule that had characterized the Walsh years.

Policy's reasoning was simple: It was much better to put in a system and find men with complementary abilities who could fit the system than to find one genius. Walsh had always tried to get input from as many people as possible, coaches and scouts, but the final decision was always his. Policy also sought opinions from as many valid sources as possible, but otherwise his system was much different. When it was time to make a decision, there would be more men around the table and more voices heard.

One of the voices, surprisingly, would be that of Dwight Clark, the one-time star receiver for the team. Clark had been hired originally in 1989 because he was a favorite of Eddie DeBartolo's. He still had the air of a country boy, which made many think he wasn't very bright, but those who talked to him on more than superficial terms knew otherwise. He was a hard worker, a trait that had been perhaps the biggest factor in his athletic success. And with the 49ers, he worked both in coaching (as an assistant in training camp) and in administration. He discovered that he had a talent for evaluating players and decided that he wanted to work in that area. By '91, he was an assistant to Policy, but he was definitely on trial. "He has to prove he can do the job," Policy told me before the season started. "Eddie has agreed to that. If Dwight can't cut it, he won't be kept around just because Eddie likes him."

> Policy's reasoning was simple: It was much better to put in a system and find men with complementary abilities who could fit the system than to find one genius.

Soon, Clark proved he belonged, and he and Policy became not just close on the job but friends away from it as well.

Vinny Cerrato was also brought into the mix, first as head of college scouting and later as player personnel director. Cerrato was a tireless worker, seemingly always on the road, seeking out the unknown small-college player who would become a star. Cerrato was at his best when he was able to uncover a hidden gem, such as Lee Woodall, a sixth-round pick in '94 who became an excellent starting linebacker, or Terrell Owens, a third-round pick in '96 who became the team's franchise player by 1999.

But Cerrato would ultimately undermine the system. The "Council of Equals" approach works only if all those involved are interested in working together. Often, one man with the force of personality to get his way will rise above the others.

And Cerrato was that kind of man. He was forceful and had strong opinions; when Walsh came back to the club as a consultant, he saw that Cerrato overwhelmed others with his arguments. Cerrato wouldn't listen to evaluations by others, but stubbornly advanced his own. Because he often ran with Policy at the 49ers' facility, others in the organization made the mistaken assumption that he was Policy's friend, another reason not to oppose his judgment.

Cerrato's critics said he acted as if he knew everything, but his judgment was erratic; he hit big on some players, totally missed on others.

Problems with the Draft

THE 49ER drafts in the post-Walsh era were all over the map. There were some great picks; in consecutive years, the 49ers picked Dana Stubblefield and Bryant Young, who were the two best defensive tackles in the game when they played together. But they also made some questionable decisions, such as trading away the No. 1 pick in the next draft to pick up wide receiver J. J. Stokes in '95 (apparently, Seifert's idea) and taking defensive end Israel Ifeanyi, an immediate bust, on the second round the next year, reportedly at the urging of defensive coaches Pete Carroll and Bill McPherson. Because the drafts were so hit-or-miss, the 49ers didn't develop the kind of depth they'd had when Walsh was coaching and drafting.

The most controversial pick during this period was the selection of Virginia Tech quarterback Jim Druckenmiller on the first round in 1997. Ever since, the story has been that Walsh recommended Jake Plummer but the 49ers disregarded his advice to take Druckenmiller.

It wasn't quite that simple. I talked to Policy before the draft and Walsh after and they told the same story: Walsh had been given a list of quarterbacks who might be available on the second or third rounds and was asked to evaluate them. Of those quarterbacks, Walsh preferred Plummer. In his report to the 49ers, Walsh listed 19 positives for Plummer in the 26 different categories he was asked to evaluate and wrote, "A perfect fit for the 49er system."

Druckenmiller, who was rated as the top available quarterback in every predraft report, was not on the list, because the 49ers expected him to go in the first 10 picks, long before they had a chance to draft at 26. Just in case, Walsh was given the coaches' film of Druckenmiller to watch, but he concentrated on the quarterbacks on his list. "I like Plummer because I saw some of the same abilities that Joe Montana had," he told me. As usual, of course, Walsh's evaluation was right on target. He added, though, that "He's the kind of quarterback I'd like to coach, but I'm not sure I could recommend him to another coach who might want a different type of quarterback."

The 49ers had gone into the draft thinking they'd take an offensive lineman on the first round and hoping they could get a quarterback for the future on the second. They had lost Elvis Grbac as a free agent, so they wanted to get a young quarterback who might be groomed to eventually succeed Steve Young. Steve Mariucci, who would start his first season as head coach that year, wanted his college quarterback, Pat Barnes, but was told early that Barnes would not be the choice.

Cerrato liked Druckenmiller and had been pushing him for weeks, showing video clips and newspaper stories to others. Despite the opinion of everybody else in the draft room, he was convinced that Druckenmiller wouldn't go until right around the 49ers' pick. Some in the draft room wondered how much Cerrato's opinion was influenced by the fact that both he and Druckenmiller had the same agent, Gary Wichard, but nobody actually asked the question.

As the draft went on, those in the draft room talked more and more about quarterbacks. Walsh spoke up for Plummer, but he agreed that Plummer wasn't really a first-round pick. Arizona was certain to take Plummer, who had played at Arizona State, if he was still there for the Cardinals' high second-round pick. The 49ers debated trading down and taking Plummer with either a very low first-round pick or a second-round pick ahead of Arizona. Plummer was also attractive to Policy because the quarterback was represented by Leigh Steinberg, with whom Policy had often negotiated contracts. Steinberg always got the best possible contract for his clients, but he was not unreasonable, and he always worked very hard to get his clients signed before the beginning of training camp.

Then the 49ers got word that Plummer was facing possible criminal charges for rape (he eventually was charged, but acquitted), so they backed off on him. Shortly afterward, their turn came up and Druckenmiller was available. By then, they were looking at a quarterback who they thought might be Young's successor and who would come at a relatively cheap price and salary cap number because of his low pick in the first round. Druckenmiller had looked good in the Shrine East-West game at Stanford, which further boosted his stock. He had a reputation for being a hard worker, often coming into the Virginia Tech football facility in the evening to look at game films. When the decision was made to pick him, there were no dissenters in the draft room.

A Poor Match

FROM THE start, though, it seemed a poor match. The prototype quarterback for the 49er offense was mobile, as Montana had been, as Young was. Druckenmiller was slow. He had a cannon arm and was very strong; a draft-day video showed him pulling a tractor. For the 49ers, though, accuracy and touch were far more important than arm strength, and there were doubts that Druckenmiller had either. It didn't help that his contract wasn't finalized until midway through training camp, at a time when all the offense had already been put in. Druckenmiller was already behind before he even took a snap in practice.

His intelligence and judgment were suspect too. He got in Mariucci's doghouse early for being late to meetings and even missing a plane. The 49ers had a long-standing practice of forcing rookies to pick up pizzas for veterans. Druckenmiller was supposed to supply the pizzas one day before the 49ers took off on a road trip, but his car got stuck in traffic. He arrived late and had to pay for his own transportation on another plane, as well as a hefty fine. Those were very expensive pizzas.

> For the 49ers, accuracy and touch were far more important than arm strength, and there were doubts that Druckenmiller had either.

Things got worse. Druckenmiller was a big fan of Howard Stern, and he agreed to go on Stern's show. Not surprisingly, Stern's first question was whether players compared penis size in the locker room, though Stern didn't phrase it that delicately. Tapes of that interview were passed around the locker room for weeks.

As a rookie in 1997, Druckenmiller started the second game of the season, against St. Louis, because Young was out with a concussion. Though the 49ers won, it was in spite of him, not because of him, as he threw repeatedly into coverage.

The errors he made would be expected from any rookie quarterback. What bothered the 49ers was that he seemed to make no progress in practice. In his second year, he was still making bad reads, and his throwing had deteriorated. He would go long spells in practice without completing a pass—even though, in practice, pass rushers never hit the quarterback, so he doesn't have game-type pressure. The 49ers had acquired Ty Detmer before the 1998 season, but Mariucci had hoped Druckenmiller would show enough in training camp that he could be the No. 2 quarterback, with Detmer used as the emergency quarterback. When Druckenmiller made no progress, Detmer was moved up to No. 2.

Druckenmiller's lack of judgment was highlighted by his arrest on a rape charge during the off-season in 1999. He was eventually acquitted, but testimony in the case showed that he had had sex with a young woman who was so drunk that she was probably unconscious part of the time and unable to actively participate.

Beating the Salary Cap

IN ANOTHER era, the 49ers would have been done in by their shaky drafts, but they were able to stay in contention in the post-Walsh era, even winning another Super Bowl after the '94 season, because they hit the free-agent market hard.

That wasn't supposed to happen. When the salary cap was installed in 1993, many in the league thought it would bring down the 49ers, whose payroll was at the top because of their many stars. "When I looked at the agreement, it was obvious that it was designed to bring down teams with veteran stars and that the 49ers and Redskins were the main target," said Policy.

But he also saw a loophole that others would eventually recognize as well: Signing bonuses were pro-rated for salary cap purposes over the length of the contract, although they had to be paid in cash up front, so contracts could be written that allowed a team to stay under the cap but actually committed the team to salaries that put them well over the supposed limit.

To Policy, that was the only competitive choice, the only way he could keep his star players. Otherwise, the 49ers would have to cut players and rebuild, with no guarantee they'd ever again approach their championship level.

First, though, he had to sell his idea to the DeBartolos, both Eddie and his father. "That was a period when the corporation was going through some tough economic times," Policy remembered, many years later. "I went back to Youngstown, and both Eddie and Senior listened to me for a long time and then told me to go ahead. I went back to Santa Clara, and we were restructuring contracts right up to the last minute, bringing players in off the practice field to sign in some cases."

By the 1999 season, salary cap problems would force a restructuring of the 49ers that helped bring them to their knees.

There was one further risk to the strategy, which Policy realized: "You can really get in trouble if you sign a player to a long-term contract and he only plays a couple of years. But our stars all played out their contracts. We got lucky."

That luck didn't last forever. By the 1999 season, salary cap problems would force a restructuring of the 49ers that helped bring them to their knees, but there would be a Super Bowl and six playoff seasons before that happened. Without Policy's maneuvering, the 49ers probably would have entered a long stretch of mediocrity.

CHAPTER THIRTEEN

Young's Team?

VETERAN PLAYERS seldom extend themselves in the exhibition season—the preseason in NFL talk—so nobody thought much about it when Joe Montana sat out a game against the Seattle Seahawks in August 1991 because of a twinge in the elbow of his throwing arm. There was no reason for Montana to push himself in a meaningless game.

But Montana's problem was much more than a twinge. Four days after that game, he was put on the injured reserve list. On October 9, the week after the 49ers had played their fifth league game, Montana had surgery on his elbow, which meant he'd be out for the season. It was Steve Young's team.

Or was it? Young didn't know, and neither did his teammates. "Joe had been in there so long, the team didn't know where to go," said Young later. "Players had a loyalty to Joe, naturally, but after a while, they had to respond to a different style. The team wondered, 'Do we look at Steve as a replacement, or do we look at Steve as the quarterback?' That went on all through '91."

There was a special problem with one teammate, Charles Haley, after the fifth game of the season, a dreadful field-goal game in Los Angeles that the Raiders won, 12–6, dropping the 49ers to 2–3.

Haley was a notoriously unstable personality in those days, and something in him snapped in the locker room after the game. The media had not yet been allowed in the dressing room, but even from outside the walls, reporters could hear Haley screaming curses at Young. Soon, Ronnie Lott was summoned from the Raiders' dressing room to come in to calm down Haley.

Bill Walsh had drafted Haley and, perhaps for that reason, had a rapport with him, so—when Walsh was the coach—he was able to deal with Haley's mood swings. Haley also respected Lott, as did everybody, so he listened when Lott talked. But Seifert had no control over Haley; and with Lott gone, there was no player on the roster who could help control Haley's behavior.

After the '91 season, the 49ers traded Haley to the Dallas Cowboys. When Haley played well for the Cowboys' Super Bowl teams, the 49ers were often criticized by writers and fans for trading him, but they had no choice.

Young Takes Over

YOUNG WAS no longer young for an athlete; he would reach his 30th birthday in the 1991 season. Physically, athletes are generally considered to be in their prime between 26 and 28, but Young had spent those years sitting on the bench behind Montana.

Young's agent, Leigh Steinberg, had advised him to ask the 49ers to trade him because Young could have started for almost any other team in the NFL. The 49ers would have agreed if he'd asked because it certainly wasn't Young's fault that he wasn't playing. When he played, he played well enough to be the starter, but the 49ers would have been crazy to bench Montana when he was playing at such a high level.

Steinberg was also concerned about what would happen when Young finally got his chance to play because the expectations for Montana's successor would be impossibly high. Such expectations had doomed Danny White when he replaced Roger Staubach with the Dallas Cowboys and Mark Malone when he followed Terry Bradshaw with the Pittsburgh Steelers.

Young resisted Steinberg's advice, and he welcomed the challenge of following Montana. "There were times watching Joe when I just said, 'Wow, that set a standard for me,'" said Young. "Left to yourself, you might not set the bar so high, but when you see it right in front of you, you know you have to play that way. And I wanted to do it as a 49er. This was my team."

The fans didn't feel that way. Almost without exception, they felt it was still Montana's team, and Young was just keeping his seat warm. "I could understand that," said Young, "because the fans had formed an emotional attachment when the team had won four Super Bowls with Joe as the quarterback. They didn't want to see any change."

It wasn't just the fans, either. Sportswriters set an impossible standard for Young, comparing him to a Montana who had by now reached mythical proportions. As great as he had been, there were times when Montana threw incomplete passes, was sacked, or simply made bad plays, but all these were forgotten when Young started to play. The press box mantra became "Joe would have made the play" any time Young failed. Though he was completing nearly two-thirds of his passes, Young was faulted for not always hitting receivers in stride, a feat that had been Montana's trademark. He was criticized for running too much, though his ability to run for yardage on broken plays made pass rushers slow their chase. If a pass was high, he was faulted for making receivers vulnerable to a hard hit. Though he eventually threw more than twice as many touchdowns as interceptions, a better ratio than Montana the year before, sportswriters explained that away by talking of "near interceptions," a phrase that popped up in almost every story about Young, but a category that has yet to make it into the NFL record book.

It didn't help, either, when Jerry Rice complained that he had problems adjusting to Young. Eventually, Young and Rice would combine for more touchdowns than any other quarterback-receiver combination in NFL history, but Rice was not happy that year with the quarterback change. He said that he and Montana were so attuned to each other that he could change a route and Montana would know instinctively where he was going. It takes time for a quarterback to get to know a receiver that well, but Jerry wasn't inclined to give Young any slack. Because of Rice's stature, his criticism damaged Young's image and probably his ability to lead the team too.

> There were times when Montana threw incomplete passes, was sacked, or simply made bad plays, but all these were forgotten when Young started to play.

Special historical circumstances worked against Young as well. From the first, the 49ers had a tradition of outstanding quarterbacks—from Frankie Albert to Y. A. Tittle to John Brodie—but Brodie had retired after the '73 season. Few of the writers and only the long-time fans had seen him play, so the only point of reference for everybody else was Montana.

And, of course, the 49ers had never won more than a divisional title before Montana's appearance, and they had won four Super Bowls with him. Attendance at 49er games had fluctuated, often dropping into the 30,000 range, before their championship run started. Many of those who jumped on the bandwagon after 1981 had not followed the 49ers before, so they thought Montana's way was the only way. Few of them realized that Montana's style was not typical of most of the great quarterbacks of the past.

As a quarterback, Young was very different from Montana— physically more gifted because of his speed and stronger arm, able to throw the deep ball better than Montana ever had. He did not have Montana's ability to make quick and correct decisions, an ability that set Montana apart from all quarterbacks, not just Young. Nor did Young have Montana's grace or consistency. He made many more bad plays than Montana ever had.

But he also made many good plays, and some great ones. Young, in fact, played very well in that 1991 season, without getting much credit for it. He threw for 348 yards in separate games against San Diego and Atlanta, and he had a near-perfect game against Detroit, 18 of 20 for 237 yards and two touchdowns.

His individual success didn't mean team success, though. The 49ers struggled through his first eight games, winning just half of them. The quarterback change wasn't the only difference. The team missed the defensive leadership of Lott and had little in the way of a running game. Keith Henderson led the team with only 561 yards rushing; Young was second with 415 and the team's highest average, 6.3 yards per carry.

> Young was very different from Montana—physically more gifted because of his speed and stronger arm, able to throw the deep ball better than Montana ever had.

Several times during the season, Young got calls from Bill Walsh, by then an analyst for NBC on NFL and Notre Dame games. The message was basically the same each time, as Walsh offered encouragement. "If you're willing to take the blame," he told Young at one point, "there will be plenty who will be willing to let you take it. But this isn't your fault. You're playing well, and the team should be winning."

IN THE ninth game, Young injured his knee in the first half. Steve Bono replaced him, and Atlanta came back in the second half to win. The 49ers also lost their next game and fell to 4–6, but then rallied behind Bono and won five in a row.

Bono played much more like Montana did, and the two were close friends off the field. Many fans felt that if they couldn't have Montana, they wanted Bono at quarterback; but Seifert didn't hesitate when Young was healthy again, starting him in the final game of the season. Young responded with a magnificent day, completing 21 of 32 passes for 338 yards and three touchdowns, and rushing for 63 yards and another touchdown in a 52–14 rout of the Chicago Bears.

The 49ers' sixth straight win had brought them to 10–6, and many in the NFL thought they were once again the best team in the league; but they had started their run too late and finished out of the playoffs for the first time since 1982. It would be the last time they'd finish out of the playoffs with Young as their starter.

Young had an excellent year, completing 65 percent of his passes, throwing 17 touchdowns and only eight interceptions. His quarterback rating of 101.8 led the NFL.

But for the 1992 season, Joe Montana's picture was on the cover of the 49ers' media guide.

Another Season Without Montana

MONTANA'S SURGERY seemed to have worked, and he threw well in a 49ers' mini-camp in the spring of '92; Seifert, in fact, said Joe was throwing better than ever, which would have been at least a minor medical miracle. In May, he had minor surgery to remove scar tissue, so that he'd be ready for training camp in July.

In training camp, though, his elbow started bothering Montana again and it didn't respond to treatment. He had still another operation on September 12, his third in 11 months. "All we could think of," said Carmen Policy, "was 'here we go again.'" Policy and other 49er executives debated whether to put Montana on injured reserve, which would have ruled him out for the year, but decided against it—partly because they didn't think it would be fair to Joe if he could come back and partly because they still thought Young might falter and Montana would be a nice insurance policy if he came back strong from the latest surgery.

Seifert had already made his own decision, though he didn't announce it: Young was his quarterback. As a coach, Seifert knew the speculation about Montana returning was tearing the team apart, and he also knew that Young was playing better than fans or writers were willing to acknowledge. For the rest of the season, Seifert deliberately kept Montana on the back burner. When Montana was able to throw again, he did it away from the 49ers' practice facility, a Seifert edict. There were constant reports in the newspapers and on radio and TV about Montana's progress, but Joe wasn't around the team, so there was no distraction.

Young also had the advantage of a new offensive coordinator, Mike Shanahan. Mike Holmgren had been the offensive coordinator for the three previous years, and he was certainly a fine coach, as he proved by turning the Green Bay Packers into Super Bowl champions after he left the 49ers. But Holmgren never had total freedom to run the offense because Seifert poked his nose in from time to time, undeterred by his ignorance of offensive football.

Shanahan was different. He agreed to come to the 49ers only if he had complete autonomy, and for the three years he was offensive coordinator, he had it. He also brought a creative mind and a slightly different approach to the 49er offense, which was especially helpful against divisional foes who had seen so much of the Walsh offense. Shanahan made minor changes, but those were enough to make the plays look different and harder to defend.

He also helped Young by making him think more about what the defense was going to do. Young told me one time that Shanahan had an amazing ability to think like a defensive coach and predict what the defense would do in the upcoming game. That gave Young an edge going into the game, and his play that season showed it.

Young had one of the finest seasons a quarterback has ever

had, completing two-thirds of his passes, averaging 8.6 yards a pass, throwing 25 touchdowns and only 7 interceptions, and again leading the NFL quarterbacks with a 107 rating. He was voted the NFL's Most Valuable Player.

The 49ers lost only twice that season, and one of their losses came against Buffalo, 34–31, despite a heroic performance by Young, who threw for 449 yards and rushed for another 50 in the game.

Young didn't have to carry the offensive load as much in subsequent games because the 49ers had a much better balanced offense in 1992 than in 1991, primarily because Ricky Watters stepped up to rush for 1,013 yards and catch 43 passes, giving the 49ers another dangerous receiver to go with Rice (84 catches) and tight end Brent Jones (45 catches)

But as the Buffalo loss showed, the 49ers were vulnerable defensively, and that weakness would catch up with them in the playoffs.

Nothing Young did satisfied the 49er fans (and writers), who still lusted for Montana. At midseason, Shanahan called Young aside and showed him both the statistical breakdown and his own evaluation of Young's performances, game by game. "I don't know what other people are seeing, but here's what I see," he said. "You're playing as well as any quarterback I've ever coached." What Shanahan didn't have to say was that he'd coached John Elway in Denver.

> Nothing Young did satisfied the 49er fans (and writers), who still lusted for Montana.

Meanwhile, Montana's elbow was healing. He probably was able to play by about the 12th game of the season, but Seifert wasn't going to open that can of worms. He had his quarterback, and he didn't want the team divided again by Montana's return.

So Montana didn't play again until the second half of the last game of the season, a meaningless Monday night game (the 49ers had already clinched home-field advantage in the playoffs) against the weak Detroit Lions, who only wanted the season to end.

Despite the cold, wet weather, a capacity crowd was at Candlestick, and the buildup for the game was intense. The fans roared when Montana came onto the field and yelled even louder when he threw two touchdown passes in the fourth quarter.

Montana's performance against the demoralized Lions proved nothing except to show that Seifert had been right to keep the once-great quarterback on the back burner. Despite Young's great season, some writers were suggesting that Montana should be the starter in the playoffs.

He didn't start, and in fact didn't even play. Young started both games, a 20–13 win over the Washington Redskins and a 30–20 loss to the Dallas Cowboys in the NFC championship game.

Young didn't play as well in those games as he had in the regular season, but the main reason for the loss in the championship game was the 49ers' inability to stop the Cowboys. That didn't stop 49er fans from blaming Young for the loss. Montana was still the people's choice. It would be a lively off-season

CHAPTER FOURTEEN

Montana Says Goodbye

BETWEEN THE 1992 and 1993 seasons, radio talk shows in San Francisco were inundated by callers who asked, over and over, "Why didn't George Seifert play the greatest quarterback in history in the playoff games?" The callers admitted that Steve Young had had a fine season but insisted that he couldn't win the big games, ignoring the fact that the 49ers defense had been the main reason they lost to the Dallas Cowboys in the NFC championship game. The callers also insisted that Joe Montana should be the starter in '93, citing the old coach's adage that "you don't lose your starting role because of an injury." Of course, coaches who said that were talking of players who had missed a few games in a season. Montana had missed nearly two full seasons.

The quarterback controversy wasn't the 49ers' only problem. In the first year of free agency, the NFL had passed what was called the Rooney Rule, named for Pittsburgh Steelers owner Dan Rooney, which limited the ability of teams in the playoffs the previous season to sign free agents; those teams could pay only as much for free agents as they lost with players who had left their teams. Though the rule specified playoff teams, there was no doubt that the target was the 49ers, because Rooney and other

NFL owners had long hated the free-spending ways of Eddie DeBartolo.

In the off-season, the 49ers lost tackle Pierce Holt, their best defensive player, and defensive end Tim Harris, a top pass rusher. They signed safety Tim McDonald, a client of Leigh Steinberg's; McDonald and Steinberg were later the models for the main characters in the movie *Jerry Maguire.* Steinberg always tried to steer his players toward the 49ers because of DeBartolo's generosity and the way the 49ers treated their players, and McDonald would be a real plus for the team for the rest of the decade. But when the 49ers tried to sign Reggie White, the great defensive end who was leaving the Philadelphia Eagles, the Rooney Rule kept them from matching Green Bay's offer. Had they signed White instead of the Packers, NFL history in the '90s would have been quite different.

These issues, though, had only a peripheral impact on the fans and, for that matter, the 49ers, who were torn internally over the Montana question. Seifert, the one who was most affected, wanted to keep Young as his quarterback because he was realistic: Montana had been a great quarterback, but he would be 37 before the season started and he had just missed virtually two full seasons. It didn't make sense to bench the league's MVP for a player who, if he wasn't at the end of his career, could see it without looking too far into the distance. But inside the 49ers' executive offices were men who had known great success since Montana had been the quarterback, and they didn't want to let go.

And, of course, neither did Eddie. DeBartolo's defining moment, as club president Carmen Policy noted, had been the 1981 Super Bowl, with Montana leading the way. Eddie had once been very close to the players, but as he got older and a younger

> DeBartolo's defining moment, as club president Carmen Policy noted, had been the 1981 Super Bowl, with Montana leading the way.

group of players came in every year, he had grown apart from them. It was the players from the earlier teams with whom DeBartolo related, and Joe was the only one left. Dwight Clark, another favorite, was in the front office. Ronnie Lott was with the New York Jets. Eddie didn't want to let Montana go.

It might have been different if Bill Walsh were still there. Walsh had often persuaded star players, Clark among them, to quit before they had to be replaced. Perhaps he could have persuaded Montana to walk away, to have a special ceremony honoring him at a game during the season. Of course, Walsh had never had to "retire" as big a star as Montana, and he'd had his own problems with Joe in the contentious 1988 season.

Without Walsh, there was nobody in the 49er organization who could have persuaded Montana to retire at that point. Nobody was even inclined to try, not with DeBartolo in the background hoping Montana would stay. Though Eddie never directly pressured coaches regarding who to play, nobody doubted that he wanted Montana back as the starting quarterback.

So the 49ers' front office deferred to Montana himself. Many 49er fans still think that Montana was forced out, but that's not at all what happened. Montana was told in January that the team would do whatever he chose. If he wanted to stay, he would stay. If he wanted to leave, he was free to talk to other teams and see who wanted him. This was unprecedented. It's common now for players to leave as free agents, but Montana was under contract to the 49ers. If the 49ers had not given their permission, any club whose executives or coaches talked to him would have been penalized by the league office for tampering.

Montana took three months to decide. Perhaps he wanted to see the 49ers squirm. More likely, he just needed the time to make a difficult decision. Obviously, he would have preferred to stay with the 49ers. The players he had been closest to were gone, and he no longer had the bond he'd had with the team because he'd not been a part of it for two years; but he still had a loyalty to the team and its fans because of the glory years. Yet he wanted to play, and he knew he couldn't win the competition with a younger, healthier Young.

The 49ers were getting calls from other teams, wondering what was happening. Tentative trade offers were made, but the 49ers told the other teams that nothing would be done until Montana made his decision. Montana's market value was far less than most 49er fans would have assumed, with clubs not willing to yield more than a third-round draft pick. As good as Joe had been, he was damaged goods.

Then Phoenix owner Bill Bidwill went public with an offer of the Cardinals' first-round draft pick. That was like an overbid at an auction; any other club interested in Montana would have to match that offer. One other club did, the Kansas City Chiefs, who needed a quarterback and thought that Montana could lead them to a championship.

As good as Joe had been, he was damaged goods.

At that point, Seifert announced that if Montana returned to the 49ers, he would go into training camp as the No. 1 quarterback. Everybody assumed that DeBartolo was pulling the strings on that announcement, but Seifert, DeBartolo, and Policy have all insisted since then that it was George's decision. Of course, Seifert knew that it was what his boss wanted to hear, and he may also have figured that it was a way to defuse the controversy—knowing that Young would take the job away from Montana anyway.

It made no difference. Montana had made up his mind to go to the Chiefs, and Policy worked out what turned out to be a good deal for the 49ers because the first-round pick was Dana Stubblefield, who gave the 49ers five good years at defensive tackle before leaving as a free agent.

Before he made a public announcement in April, Montana flew to DeBartolo's home in Youngstown to tell Eddie, and then the two flew out to San Francisco together for the press conference the next day.

"That's the tough part of being close to players," DeBartolo told me later, "because you know the time of reckoning is going to come. Joe came back to tell me that he wanted to move on, and he thought he should do it face to face. I told him that he would be the starter and he didn't say no right away, but when we flew to San Francisco the next day, he told me on the plane that he just couldn't accept it. That was a rotten day. I didn't talk about the press conference. We tried to talk about kids, about the state of Montana . . . everything but the 49ers and Kansas City."

> Montana was realistic about what was happening, but he still couldn't forgive Young for replacing him.

Before the press conference, Montana told Policy he knew the salary cap would be a problem for the team if he stayed. "If I go to Kansas City, I'll be the man. If I get injured, they'll pray for me to get well. If I get hurt here, I'll be pushed out the door."

So Montana was realistic about what was happening, but he still couldn't forgive Young for replacing him. After he retired, Montana was still bitter about not being able to finish his career in San Francisco. He even resisted having his uniform retired, until he finally relented in 1997, giving the 49ers a chance to hold a touching ceremony at halftime of a Monday night game.

Before that, in 1996, the year after he retired, the city of San Francisco held a special program for him at noon in the Justin Herman Plaza by the Embarcadero. Thousands of San Franciscans crowded the area, blocking off traffic in all directions, to pay tribute to their great quarterback.

A prankster had sent a phony invitation to Young asking him to speak. Taking it seriously, Young planned to go and talk graciously about how much he had learned from Montana and how much he admired him. When Montana heard of this, he said, "No way." Event organizers had to call Young and tell him to stay away.

The 1993 Season: Life Without Montana

THERE WAS a conspicuous lack of comment from Young while the drama was playing out. When I was working on this book, I learned why for the first time: Steve didn't know what was happening.

"I went off to law school after the season," he said. "I was studying for finals, literally sleeping in the library, studying around the clock, and I had no idea what was happening with Joe. I came out of my last final and jumped in my car and turned on the radio and heard that Joe had been traded to Kansas City. I had missed the whole thing.

It was a blessing because I missed all that turmoil, but in the end, it probably didn't really make much difference because I was so confident, I knew it would all work out.

"It's very rare for this to happen, very difficult to figure a way to make this kind of transition. I never held any animosity. I had grown through it after those five years. It was a great story for the media because it never ended. It really didn't end for another couple of years."

By the time we talked, in the spring of 1998, Young had the advantage of perspective, five years removed from the event, and he had thought about his decision to fight his way through the years behind Montana instead of leaving the team.

"The easiest thing in the world would have been to say, of course, you can't do this, following Montana. I never let myself think that or say that. I wanted to play long enough to develop my own mark. I knew there would be a lot of mixed emotions, but I used that as a motivational tool. I really am grateful for the experience."

At the time, though, it wasn't easy for Young because he was facing constant comparisons to the mythical Montana, the one who never made a mistake. It didn't help when Young broke his thumb in an exhibition game against the Raiders, which contributed to six interceptions in the first two league games. When the thumb healed, he was back on target and ended the 1993 season with 29 touchdown passes, a club record 4,023 yards passing, and another NFL passing title, with a 101.5 rating.

But the Cowboys again stopped the 49ers in the NFC championship game, a 38–21 defeat that was even more one-sided than the final score. That gave the Montana lovers another chance to claim that Young couldn't win the big game. (Interestingly enough, Montana's team played in the AFC championship game that same weekend, and the Chiefs lost in Buffalo to the Bills, 30–13. Trying to throw into the stiff wind coming off Lake Erie, Montana looked like exactly what he was, a quarterback near the end of his career.)

> Whatever Montana's fans thought, Joe's decision to move on was best for everybody.

Whatever Montana's fans thought, Joe's decision to move on was best for everybody. He got two more years and, as he predicted, the Chiefs were patient with him when he was injured, as he often was. The 49ers were a better team with Young. By January 1995, Montana was retired, and the 49ers, with Young at quarterback, were winning the Super Bowl.

CHAPTER FIFTEEN

Reinventing the 49ers

THE 1994 season seemed to have worked out perfectly for the 49ers. Carmen Policy's plan of strengthening the team with free agents brought in players who helped produce the team's first Super Bowl championship in five years. Steve Young answered his critics with his finest season, setting club and NFL records, and capped it by throwing a record six touchdowns in the Super Bowl.

Yet, even in that success, seeds were being sown for the team's decline and eventual fall into the abyss, though many problems would be hidden for the next four years by the individual brilliance of Young.

With Vinny Cerrato in charge, the 49ers had their best draft since Bill Walsh's bonanza in 1986, which produced eight players who eventually became starters. The 1994 draft didn't quite match that, but the 49ers moved up to the seventh pick in the first round to get defensive tackle Bryant Young, who would become the key to their defense, and they also got fullback William Floyd late in the first round. Floyd was a devastating blocker, a solid runner, and a good receiver out of the backfield; and his emotional approach to the game also made him an inspirational player. The team got an excellent kicker, Doug Brien, on the fourth round, and a real surprise in the sixth round in Lee Woodall; athletic enough to play defensive back in college, Woodall would become an excellent outside linebacker.

That draft strengthened Cerrato's position in the organization, making him the strongest voice in the decision-making process, but he never again had such success in evaluating talent; the next four drafts under his direction produced very little that helped the team.

Eventually, too, the 49ers' reliance on reinventing the team each year with free agents showed itself to be a costly policy, both in terms of building up salary-cap obligations for the future and in slowing the development of young players. But in '94, it was the 49ers' free-agent harvest that made the difference, as they built back up to the championship level.

The 49ers had no choice but to try to beef up their defense after they'd been embarrassed in the NFC championship game the previous season. One of their free-agent choices was an offensive player, center Brad Oates, but the others were all defensive players: linebackers Ken Norton, Jr., and Gary Plummer, linebacker/defensive end Rickey Jackson, defensive end Richard Dent, and cornerback Deion Sanders. All but Dent, who tore knee ligaments in the second game and missed the rest of the season, made significant contributions to the 49ers' success that year.

Neon Deion

THE MOST intriguing story by far was Sanders, the flamboyant "Neon Deion." Sanders was considered the best cornerback of all time by many, an opinion I came to share after watching him that season, because his incredible timing and speed allowed him to play off a receiver and then close so quickly when the pass was thrown that he could either knock it down or intercept it. When he made an interception, he was a very dangerous open field runner; he returned six interceptions for 303 yards and three touch-downs for the 49ers in 1994, one of them for 93 yards. Because he was so dangerous, most teams simply did not throw in his direction, basically giving up half of the field.

Though 49er coach George Seifert chose not to use him in either category, Deion was also a superb kick returner and a big play receiver when he was used that way in four-receiver spreads. He was also a star in baseball and would become the first player ever to start in both the World Series and the Super Bowl.

Given his outstanding talents, the competition for his services was not as spirited as it should have been. Many teams considered Sanders to be more trouble than he was worth. They didn't like his antics on the field; he would sometimes run backwards for the final 10 yards of a touchdown run, and he always did dances in the end zone. He dressed flashily with an excess of costume jewelry, and he traveled with an entourage. He played his first five years for Atlanta, experiencing only one winning season. That wasn't his fault, but it led to the impression that his individual feats didn't advance the team's cause.

> The most intriguing story by far was Sanders, the flamboyant "Neon Deion."

There was one serious bidder for Sanders, the New Orleans Saints, who made an offer that was reported to be a four-year contract for $17 million, at the time a very generous offer for a non-quarterback. But as with all football contracts, it was not quite what it seemed because it wasn't guaranteed. If Sanders were hurt or didn't play well, he could be cut. If he played up to expectations, he would be bound to New Orleans for four years; and the Saints, after a brief period of respectability, were headed back toward the bottom half of the league. The 49ers had been able to sign Jackson because he was tired of playing for the Saints, who had never advanced past the first round of the playoffs. Coming off a loser in Atlanta, Sanders didn't want to take a chance on being stuck with another one for four years.

So, though the 49ers couldn't offer nearly as much money, Deion was drawn to them. He reasoned that he could prove with the 49ers that he was not a troublemaker and that he could help a team win big. After the second game of the season, he signed a one-year contract with the 49ers.

Before he did, he met with Seifert, who had his doubts about how Sanders would fit with a team whose stars, despite their individual accomplishments, had worked so well within a team concept. The interview was insulting in tone because Seifert questioned Sanders openly about his individual antics and told him he couldn't expect to clown around with the 49ers. He didn't object to the end-zone dances, but he didn't want Sanders showboating before he reached the end zone. He wanted Deion to concentrate on defense, where the 49ers really needed him, and forgo kick returning and receiving for this season. Seifert bluntly told Sanders that if he couldn't play by the 49ers' rules, he should move on.

Sanders bit his tongue during the interview because he had his own agenda; and during the year, he abided by Seifert's rules. He sublimated his ego enough to fit in well in the 49ers locker room. There would be one little dustup with Jerry Rice, after Sanders had come in past curfew one night, but that was a minor episode, significant only because it happened during Super Bowl week, when the dearth of hard news forces writers to make more than they should of lesser stories. Some writers have since speculated that the flare-up made it inevitable that Sanders would leave, because there wasn't room in the 49ers' dressing room for two egos like his and Rice's, but that is nonsense. Deion never intended to play more than one year for the 49ers. He moved on to Dallas, which paid him much more and gave him the extra playing time and personal freedom he wanted.

Deion was such a model citizen that Seifert suggested to me one day that he'd be a good role model for youth. "He doesn't drink at all or take drugs," noted Seifert, "and he works very hard to stay in top condition. He puts as much into his game as Jerry or Steve. I can't ask for anything more than that."

Seifert was right. Sanders may have been a 49er only one year, but it was a great one. The 49ers couldn't have won without him.

A Super Bowl Season

THE SEASON opened with a 44–14 rout of the Raiders that was noteworthy not just in itself but also for an individual performance by Rice. Trailing Jim Brown by two in his goal of setting the all-time career touchdown record, Rice said in training camp that he wanted to get the record in the first game. That seemed unlikely, but Young and Rice teamed up for a 69-yard touchdown on the 49ers' first series, and then Jerry tied the record with a 23-yard reverse in the fourth quarter.

> Sanders may have been a 49er only one year, but it was a great one.

The 49ers had a commanding lead at 37–14 when the Raiders tried unsuccessfully for a first down in their own territory, surrendering the ball on their 38 with just 4:05 left in the game. Seifert sent Young and Rice and the entire first unit back into the game to everybody's surprise, but his motive became clear on the first play: Young lofted a pass to Rice, who leaped high into the end zone for the record-setting touchdown.

The next Sunday brought the 49ers back to earth with a thud, as they were downed by the Chiefs in Kansas City, 24–17. It was a particularly humiliating day for Young, because Joe Montana was the winning quarterback. Young had outgained Montana, 288–203, but he had thrown for just one touchdown and had two interceptions; Montana had no interceptions and two touchdowns. Young was gracious in defeat. "I learned at the feet of the master today," he said, but the game added fuel to the fire for the Montana fans who still blamed the 49ers for not keeping their hero.

That game was just a blip. Far more serious was a 40–8 pasting at Candlestick by the Philadelphia Eagles in the fifth game of the season, the worst defeat in nearly 14 years. Trying to protect his quarterback, Seifert took Young out in the third quarter. Young felt he was being made the scapegoat for a team letdown, and he screamed profanities at his coach. It wasn't until the following day, when Seifert sat down with a calmer Young to explain his actions, that normal communication between the two resumed.

There were two problems at this point. The 49ers had been hit hard by injuries, particularly in the offensive line. Defensively, they were less than the sum of their parts because the new players had not been absorbed into the team. Confusion over their roles had caused players to be hesitant in their play when they should have been aggressive. Seifert and defensive coordinator Ray Rhodes had a long meeting with the defense the day after the Philadelphia game, essentially telling them to stop thinking so much and start reacting.

Noting the lack of cohesion, reporters suggested that the wheels were coming off the 49ers' wagon, that the addition of free agents had not improved the team and that the 49ers would be lucky if they even made the playoffs.

It certainly seemed the critics were right when the 49ers fell behind the Lions, 14–0, in the first half in the next game, in Detroit. Then Young ignited the team with his courage. A brutal hit had left him almost motionless on the ground. He gathered the strength to crawl off the field, unable to get to his feet, and he later admitted he didn't think he could return. But he did, and

> Noting the lack of cohesion, reporters suggested that the wheels were coming off the 49ers' wagon.

he led a rally that saw the 49ers score 27 unanswered points to beat the Lions, 27–21, the start of what would become a 10-game winning streak.

As they had been so many times, the Cowboys were directly in the path of the 49ers' road to the Super Bowl when Dallas came to San Francisco for the 10th game of the season, and one of the most memorable in this bitter rivalry. The Dallas pass rush, led by ex-49er Charles Haley, overwhelmed Young early, but then offensive coordinator Mike Shanahan figured out a way to slow down the rush: running Young on the naked bootleg. Behind, 7–0, the 49ers tied the game with a 74-yard scoring drive, all on the ground. At halftime, the game was still tied, though the 49ers had only one yard passing. In the second half, with the Dallas pass rushers more tentative, Young threw for two touchdowns without an interception. For the first time in three years, it was Dallas quarterback Troy Aikman who had to throw on almost every down in a game of catch-up, and Aikman was intercepted three times as the 49ers won, 21–14.

Despite a season-ending loss to the Minnesota Vikings, the 49ers finished with an NFL-best 13–3 record and reaped the individual honors as well. Young was again the league's Most Valuable Player, as he set an NFL record with a passer rating of 112.8, surpassing Montana's 112.4 in 1989. He also won the coveted Len Eshmont Award, given by his teammates, as the most inspirational player.

Sanders was named the NFL's defensive player of the year. Seifert was the NFC coach of the year. Policy was named one of the 100 most influential sports figures by the *Sporting News*.

When the postseason started, the 49ers defeated the Chicago Bears 44–15 in a divisional playoff, and then it was time for the NFC Championship. As everybody expected, the game was a rematch of the 49ers and Cowboys at Candlestick.

This one belonged to the 49er defense and particularly Eric Davis, who had had an excellent year at cornerback, though in the shadow of Sanders. On the third play of the game, Davis stepped in front of Dallas receiver Kevin Williams, intercepting at the Dallas 44 and running to the end zone.

The 49ers had switched their pass defense for this game. Though Michael Irvin was much the better receiver, Alvin Harper had always seemed to make the big catches against the 49ers, so Sanders was put on Harper, effectively taking him out of the game, and Davis on Irvin. When the Cowboys got the ball the next time, Davis stripped Irvin after a pass reception, with Tim McDonald recovering for the Niners. Five plays later, Young hit Ricky Watters for a 29-yard touchdown. The play demonstrated how Young had improved as a quarterback because he had looked first for Rice down the middle and, seeing Rice covered, switched to Watters down the right sideline.

On the ensuing kickoff, Adam Walker jarred the ball loose from Williams, with kicker Brien recovering. When William Floyd scored from the 1 seven plays later, the 49ers had a 21–0 lead; and it was only halfway through the first quarter.

The Cowboys rallied to try to get back in the game, but a 28-yard pass from Young to Rice just before the half made it 31–14. The Cowboys never got closer than the 10 points by which they trailed at game's end, 38–28.

The 49ers were back in the Super Bowl and, just as in their first Super Bowl season, the win over Dallas in the NFC championship game was the *real* Super Bowl. The San Diego Chargers, beaten resoundingly, 38–15, by the 49ers in the regular season were the opponents, and nobody outside the Chargers' locker room expected them to be any more of a challenge for the 49ers than they'd been in the regular season.

The Super Bowl follows form more than any of the other major American sports championships. With two weeks to look at videotapes of the other team, coaches are rarely surprised, so the team that is physically superior will usually win.

In this game, San Diego defensive coordinator Bill Arnsparger tried to surprise the 49ers, but his strategy backfired. In the regular season game, Arnsparger had played his linebackers well off the line of scrimmage, and the 49ers had killed the Chargers with slant passes in front of the linebackers—the receivers then running for extra yardage. So Arnsparger played his linebackers in tight for this game.

But Shanahan, with that ability to anticipate what an opposing defense might do, had anticipated this change, so he prepared Young to look down the field. He also called runs on first down on the first two series, to keep the linebackers anchored and out of the pass coverage on deep throws.

On the third play from scrimmage, Young hit Rice down the middle; the Chargers' safeties were confused in their pass coverage, and Rice cruised 44 yards untouched for the touchdown, just 1:24 into the game, the fastest a team had ever scored in a Super Bowl. The next time the 49ers got the ball, Young hit Watters for a 51-yard touchdown, after Young had faked a handoff so expertly that William Floyd was tackled at the line of scrimmage.

The rout was on. The 49ers led at halftime, 28–10, and by as much as 32 points in the second half, en route to the 49–26 win. Rice suffered a shoulder separation in the second quarter but returned and tied his Super Bowl record with three touchdown receptions. Young, who had gone through the postseason without throwing an interception, was 24 of 36 for 325 yards and a game-record six touchdowns. He also was the game's leading rusher with 49 yards on five carries, keeping two touchdown drives alive with scrambling runs for first downs. "You think you have everything else defensed, and then he breaks loose," said disconsolate San Diego coach Bobby Ross after the game. "You can't defense his running."

And when Young was interviewed after the game, offensive tackle Harris Barton went through an elaborate charade of removing the monkey from Young's back. Joe Montana would never be forgotten, but Young had built his own legion of fans.

No Time to Celebrate

THE 49ERS had very little time to savor their victory before the team started to disintegrate.

As expected, Sanders left. Knowing he had no chance to keep Deion, Policy pretended that he was making a serious bid, forcing Jerry Jones to boost his offer. Eventually, Jones's practice of paying big money to stars like Sanders, Aikman, and Emmitt Smith would make it impossible to keep many other good players, and that brought the Cowboys back to the middle of the league. This fact was scant consolation for the 49ers in 1995, though, because losing Sanders put a serious dent in their defense— and Sanders would also help the Cowboys win one more Super Bowl before they slipped.

> Joe Montana would never be forgotten, but Young had built his own legion of fans.

To compound the problem, the 49ers also lost their other corner, Davis, who had emerged as a topflight player after struggling earlier. The 49ers feared that they'd be overpaying for Davis, and they weren't certain he'd be able to continue playing at his '94 level. They were wrong on both counts, and they've been struggling to find good corners ever since.

The loss of Watters was more understandable, though the 49ers have often been hammered by media critics who didn't understand the whole situation. Watters was an undeniable talent and perfectly suited to the 49er system because he was not only a good runner but also caught passes like the wide receiver he had been one year in college—66 passes in the '94 season. He was also probably the most unpopular player on the team because of his "me-first" attitude; teammates played cruel jokes on him and referred sarcastically to his habit of complaining that he didn't get enough "touches" (runs and catches) in a game, even when the 49ers won.

Despite his personality, the 49ers would have liked to keep Watters, but Ricky wanted out. He wanted to go to a team where he would be the main star, which he would never be on the 49ers. The 49ers had promised Rice years before that they would never pay anybody, other than a starting quarterback, more than he got. So Ricky told his agent to get an offer from another team that would get him more money than Rice. Philadelphia offered him a deal that was front-loaded, which gave Ricky more money in his first year than Rice was getting. The 49ers didn't match it, and Watters was gone. Not until they signed Garrison Hearst in 1997 were the 49ers able to replace Watters, but in the interim, I never heard a 49er player say he missed Ricky.

> I never heard a 49er player say he missed Ricky [Watters].

The team also lost both coordinators, Ray Rhodes and Shanahan. Though Rhodes, who went to the Philadelphia Eagles as head coach, had been an excellent coordinator, the 49ers were able to fill his spot with Pete Carroll, who had been fired as head coach of the New York Jets. If anything, Carroll coached an even more aggressive defense than Rhodes had. In his two years with the team, before he returned to head coaching with the New England Patriots, Carroll did an excellent job, though with less material than Rhodes had had in '94.

The loss on the offensive side of the ball was far more critical, because Shanahan probably had the best offensive mind in the game since Bill Walsh.

Policy certainly knew that, and he knew Shanahan deserved another chance to be a head coach; he had coached the Raiders for little more than a season in the '80s. When Shanahan was invited to an interview for the head-coaching job in Denver, everybody assumed the job was his for the asking.

It was a touchy situation for Policy, not the least because he and Seifert had become close friends; though Carmen is the very definition of "a suit," he had even gone deep-sea fishing with Seifert, who has a passion for the sport. "If George had come to me and said he'd be willing to retire if we'd take care of him financially, I'd have done that and gone to Shanahan immediately," Policy told me later. "But I couldn't do that to George if that wasn't what he wanted."

So Policy tried to sell Shanahan on the idea of continuing as offensive coordinator for two years, with a big pay raise and the guarantee that he'd be head coach after that.

Shanahan wasn't buying. The Denver job was intriguing on its own merits; he had been offensive coordinator for the Broncos before coming to San Francisco, and he had a close relationship with star quarterback John Elway. Nor did he relish the idea of waiting in the wings for two years, knowing how uncomfortable his relationship with Seifert would be.

So Shanahan went to Denver. The 49ers compounded the problem by bringing in Marc Trestman, who had little experience in the pro game, and then hamstringing him with both Seifert's interference and the looming presence of Walsh, brought in as a consultant. It's a moot point whether Trestman was the right man for the job; in those circumstances, nobody could have been successful.

Meanwhile, Seifert's own authority was undermined because Policy's attempt to keep Shanahan on had clearly shown that he was already thinking about the end of Seifert's time as head coach. Policy had become convinced—rightfully so, I think—that a pro coach has no more than 10 years of effectiveness because players quit listening after that. Walsh had had exactly 10 years, and players were tuning him out at the end. Seifert had been head coach for only six years, but he was defensive coordinator for six years before that.

Probably nobody could have prevented the decline the 49ers

started after their last Super Bowl, but Shanahan might have been able to delay some of the problems. Certainly he has demonstrated in Denver that he is a superior coach. But could Policy have replaced Seifert immediately after he'd won the Super Bowl for the second time? Only if he'd had a bomb shelter to hide in when the news became public.

CHAPTER SIXTEEN

Seifert Exits

FOR A time in the '90s, Eddie DeBartolo seemed to be maturing. He was no longer poking his nose into various aspects of the 49ers' operation. He had, he told me, "implicit faith" in Carmen Policy's ability to run the operation. He was involved with the restructuring of the DeBartolo Corporation, which went public in the early part of the decade, and then in the formation of the DeBartolo Entertainment Company. Most of all, he was older—so much so that he could no longer relate to the players. Once he had been very close to the top players, particularly Joe Montana and Dwight Clark, but when I interviewed him in training camp in '94, he struggled to think of players he was close to. He finally mentioned Steve Young and Harris Barton.

But the disastrous 1996 season brought Eddie out of hiding. Just two years removed from winning the Super Bowl, the 49ers lost the NFC West to the expansion Carolina Panthers. Even more embarrassing, they lost their composure in a late-season loss to the Panthers at Candlestick Park, collecting 14 penalties, committing four turnovers, and getting into fights on the field and on the sidelines in a 30–24 loss.

That loss only confirmed what those close to the 49ers already knew: George Seifert had lost control of the team. Dr. Harry Edwards, a sociologist who had been hired by Bill Walsh years before to work with players who had emotional problems, explained over lunch what had happened. "After a few years, the veteran players have heard the same message from the coach so many times that they tune out. In George's case, he'd been here as a defensive coordinator before he became head coach, so his message was really getting old. The younger players take their cue from the older players. If the older players aren't listening, the younger players don't, either."

After the season, Eddie met with a few veteran players in the locker room and became convinced that Seifert had to go, though he had one year left on his contract. Eddie wouldn't be the front man, of course; it had to be Policy. The firing wouldn't be easy because Seifert had a good reputation. He didn't have the charisma of Walsh, but his teams had won two Super Bowls and he had the highest winning percentage of any active coach.

> That loss only confirmed what those close to the 49ers already knew: George Seifert had lost control of the team.

Policy had been watching Steve Mariucci, the head coach at Cal. Mariucci had bounced around. He had been the offensive coordinator at Cal before going to Green Bay as quarterbacks coach, where he tutored Brett Favre as Favre became the best quarterback in the game.

Mariucci had been a head coach for just a year. He was obviously a hot coaching prospect—bright, personable, enthusiastic—but was he ready for the NFL after one year? Policy, Mariucci, and DeBartolo met for dinner at the Hotel Mac in Richmond, to get away from the media scrutiny they would have faced if they'd dined in either San Francisco or near the 49er headquarters in Santa Clara. Carmen tried to persuade

Mariucci to come on for one year as the offensive coordinator to learn the team before taking over as head coach.

Mariucci was not comfortable with the idea of being the coach-in-waiting. An ambitious man, he took the job at Cal intending to prove his ability to be a head coach so that he would get an NFL offer. He showed me, in fact, a list he had compiled during his NFL years of assistants he might choose if he became an NFL head coach. He had not expected an offer to come after just one year, but he told Policy and DeBartolo that the only way he would come to the 49ers would be as the head coach.

Mariucci was only 41, and his year at Cal had been only a qualified success; the Bears had a dynamic offense but very nearly the worst defense in Division 1A. The offense had been good enough to win six games and get to the Aloha Bowl in Hawaii, but the defense cost them that game, and the Bears had ended with a 6–6 record.

Policy thought Mariucci was one of the rising stars of the profession, a coach who had many productive years ahead of him. He saw some of the same things in Mariucci that he had seen in Walsh many years before, especially his quick, imaginative offensive mind and his organizational ability, as well as the enthusiasm and mental energy to deal with the younger players, something Seifert now lacked. He thought that Mariucci was still on a learning curve as a head coach and would make some mistakes that wouldn't be made if he had another year or two of experience as a college head coach; but Policy also knew that if the 49ers waited for him to develop, other NFL teams would be after him too. It was better to grab him now than to wait and possibly lose the opportunity. He told Mariucci to hang tight and wait for his call.

First, Policy had to talk to Seifert, who was out on his fishing boat. He called Seifert and asked him to come to his office. George had been mentally exhausted by the season, too, and had thought, in the solitude of his time on the water, that it might be time for him to retire. But he was also being paid $1.5 million a year to coach the 49ers, and no man walks away from that easily. When he talked to Carmen, he asked just one thing: that he be taken care of financially. Policy assured him that he would be paid his full salary for the year. When the meeting was over, he called Mariucci to tell him he had the job.

It was not a well-kept secret. The news was broken by Brian Murphy of the Santa Rosa *Press Democrat,* who was tipped by a Cal assistant that Mariucci was going to the 49ers. Murphy first wrote that Mariucci was going as the offensive coordinator, because that's what he had heard from his friend, but the full story quickly emerged.

The 49ers held two press conferences a day apart, maintaining the fiction at the first one, announcing Seifert's departure, that his replacement had not been hired; the next day, Mariucci's hiring was made official.

The first press conference, at the same Fairmont Hotel where Eddie had made his ignominious San Francisco debut nearly 20 years earlier, was the most entertaining. Eddie, who had stopped for a couple of pops before entering the room, was uncomfortable. When somebody asked about offensive coordinator Marc Trestman, Eddie blurted out, "He's toast," a particularly ungracious way to announce Trestman's firing. Policy also looked uncomfortable. The only one who seemed to be enjoying himself was Seifert, who pretended that the decision had been his.

Supposedly, Seifert would be a consultant for the team, but everybody knew that wouldn't happen. George himself talked of the places he planned to visit in the next year, and none of them were NFL cities.

The next day, Mariucci's hiring was announced in a press conference at 49ers' headquarters in Santa Clara. The usually exuberant Mariucci was subdued, aware of the responsibility he would be shouldering.

He'd prepared well for his new assignment, learning from

Mike Holmgren when he was at Green Bay and observing other successful coaches as well. He had never backed down from a challenge. He had been offensive coordinator at Cal in '91 when Bruce Snyder left and, only 36 at the time, immediately applied for the job. He was passed over for Keith Gilbertson, not an inspired choice.

> The usually exuberant Mariucci was subdued, aware of the responsibility he would be shouldering.

He was movie-star handsome and looked younger than his age, which may be the reason so many writers focused on his relative youth. In fact, he was not setting any records; Don Shula, Al Davis, and John Madden had all been only 33 when they became head coaches.

Afterward, Mariucci's wife, Gayle, was sitting in Policy's office, waiting for her husband to finish his interviews so they could go to dinner. "Steve just wants to go home and have dinner with the kids," she said, "but I can't face macaroni-and-cheese after this."

She turned to Dwight Clark and asked, "Is there some place around here where we can go for a quiet dinner?"

Clark just looked at her for a moment and then said, "I'm afraid those days are gone forever."

Life for the Mariuccis would never be the same again.

Mariucci's First Season

POLICY'S CONCERN that Mariucci was not yet ready for prime time was unwarranted. In his rookie season, 1997, Mariucci showed a poise under very trying circumstances that would have been admirable in a much older coach, and he kept the team on an even keel that eventually resulted in another divisional championship.

The season started in the worst possible fashion. The 49ers were playing in Tampa Bay against the Buccaneers, who would turn out to be a much better team than expected. In the first quarter, Steve Young was knocked out of the game with a concussion. Young was tackled by Warren Sapp and, as he was going down, Hardy Nickerson's knee hit the back of Young's head, knocking off his helmet. Young came back late in the game but was ineffective, completing only four of eight passes for 30 yards in the game, with one interception.

Then, in the second quarter, Jerry Rice was knocked out with a serious knee injury. Before the 49ers had completed even the first half of their first game, they had lost their two primary offensive players.

Young was still out for the second game of the season, against the Rams in St. Louis, so the 49ers had to start rookie Jim Druckenmiller, the first time a rookie quarterback had started for the 49ers since Joe Montana in '79. Druckenmiller was no Montana; he completed only 10 of 28 for 102 yards, but the 49er defense was strong enough to pull out a 15–12 win.

Amidst speculation that his concussions might force him to retire, Young returned for the next game. Mariucci scaled down the passing offense and emphasized the running game—to protect his quarterback—for the rest of the season. Writers, who had already forgotten that Mariucci originally made his reputation coaching Favre, started referring to Mariucci as a coach who preferred to run the ball.

In a game crackling with excitement, Jerry Rice defied the medical odds and returned for a Monday night game against Denver on December 15. Rice caught a 14-yard touchdown pass in the first quarter but reinjured himself in the second quarter, and his season was over. But his return had inspired his teammates and, with Young completing 22 of 34 for 276 yards, the 49ers beat the Broncos, who would later win the Super Bowl, 34–17.

That pushed the 49ers' season record to 13–2, but it was virtually their last gasp. They had lost Garrison Hearst with a broken collarbone two games earlier, and that short-circuited their running game. Without the passing-running balance, it was obvious they wouldn't make it to the ultimate game.

They got past the Minnesota Vikings, 38–22, in their first playoff game, with Terry Kirby rushing for a career-high 120 yards. But the next weekend, on a cold, rainy day at Candlestick, they fell again to their nemesis, the Green Bay Packers, 23–10. It was no disgrace for Mariucci and the players, who had a much better season than anybody had anticipated after Young and Rice went down in the first game, but it still ended short of what had always been the goal since the 1981 season: the Super Bowl.

The 1998 Season

THERE WAS the usual shuffling of players in the off-season, some going, some coming. Dana Stubblefield, the defensive tackle who had had his best season in 1997, left as a free agent. The 49ers couldn't afford to match the $6 million yearly salary he got with the Washington Redskins, and they weren't convinced Stubblefield would play as hard with a new contract as he had when he was trying to get that contract. In this case, they were right; Stubblefield was a major disappointment for the Redskins.

Rod Woodson, who had been a disappointment in his year with the team, was gone, as were younger players Tyronne Drakeford and Kevin Mitchell, both examples of the 49ers' unwillingness to be patient with younger players. They would regret that impatience in 1998. Antonio Langham, the cornerback signed as a free agent, was an absolute disaster; Drakeford, who went to New Orleans, would certainly have been better. The 49ers signed a New Orleans linebacker, Winfred Tubbs, as a free agent, and Tubbs was an excellent player. But he also was basically the same player as Ken Norton, better on the outside with a chance to use his speed to catch up to plays than plugging the middle, where he was expected to replace Gary Plummer, who had been a rock in the middle of the defense. Mitchell, though not as athletic as Tubbs, would probably have done a better job in the middle.

The Niners also picked up defensive lineman Gabe Wilkins as a free agent, but Wilkins hadn't recovered from knee surgery after an injury with Green Bay; though he eventually played eight games and started four, he was never the important part of the defense he was expected to be.

But the most controversial move, and the most damaging, was the trade of a 1999 second-round draft pick for Denver Bronco offensive tackle Jamie Brown. Though Brown had been a backup in Denver (to Pro Bowl tackle Gary Zimmerman), the 49ers expected Brown to be a starter, replacing the retired Kirk Scrafford. Athletic and big, at 6'8" and 318 pounds, Brown seemed to be capable of fulfilling that role, but he never did.

Brown was injured in the spring, in mini-camp, and he was slow recovering. In training camp, he left briefly and didn't appear at the exhibition game that weekend. When he returned, he had been demoted, though he told writers he expected to be able to win back his spot. He said he had left for "personal reasons" and refused to elaborate.

There was a sad story behind all this. As a youngster, Brown had always sought the approval of his father, a tough man who seldom gave it. As an adult, Brown was still seeking his father's approval. He sent a round-trip plane ticket to his father, who lived in Florida, so that he could come to a 49ers' game, but then Brown was reinjured and couldn't play. When he greeted his father at the airport and told him he wasn't playing, his father said, "You've never been any good and you're no good now," and went back on a return flight. Brown was devastated by his father's coldness—the reason he missed the game.

But the 49ers' front office couldn't reveal that information, and even Brown's teammates didn't know the story. They openly questioned his desire to play, and writers picked up on that feeling. After that, Brown's career with the 49ers was doomed. He played some during the season but did poorly, especially when he was supposed to block Buffalo's Bruce Smith in the fourth game of the season; of course, he was hardly the only lineman bedeviled by Smith during his great career. When Scrafford came out of retirement, Brown's career with the 49ers was essentially over.

Despite the Brown fiasco, the 49ers played very well offensively. With Ty Detmer, signed as a free agent, available as a backup quarterback, Mariucci wasn't so worried about Young's health, so he opened up the offense. Young had perhaps his best season ever, throwing for 36 touchdowns and 4,170 yards, both 49er records, and setting an NFL record with six straight games of more than 300 yards passing, breaking Joe Montana's record of five. Young was perfectly complemented by Hearst, who set a club record with 1,570 yards rushing.

One star was not having a good year: Jerry Rice.

One star was not having a good year: Jerry Rice. Though he had worked hard in the off-season to rehabilitate the double injuries he had suffered in '97, it was obvious that he was not the same dominating receiver he'd been for so long. He could neither separate from defensive backs as he had in earlier years nor get loose downfield for long passes.

Rice had two games reminiscent of his past, both against Atlanta, a team against whom he'd had extraordinary success over the years, even by his standards; he'd caught five touchdown passes in a 1990 game and that was both a 49er and league record. In 1998, he caught eight passes for 162 yards and two touchdowns, one for 66 yards, in the first Atlanta game; 10 passes for 169 yards and a touchdown in the second game.

But in that second game, he'd also dropped an easy pass in the end zone for a touchdown that would have tied the Falcons at halftime. The 49ers had to settle for a field goal and eventually lost the game, 31–19.

In fact, the 49er offense was suffering because Young was looking for Rice as his first option on almost every play, and Rice was either not open or not making the play. The emphasis on Rice started to change with the next game, against New Orleans, when he caught just three passes. Though the 49ers won the game, Rice complained afterward because not enough passes were thrown his way. Rice caught only three passes in the next game, a Monday night win over Washington.

Rice's troubles weren't the story that night, though. Just before the end of the game, defensive tackle Bryant Young suffered a freak injury as teammate Ken Norton was blocked into him and fell across his leg, causing a horrendous fracture that sickened those who saw it up close—or even on the television shots, repeated over and over and over. Young's season had ended, and there was a serious question whether he'd ever play again. It was a devastating turn of events for the player and for the 49ers, because Bryant Young was as important to the 49er defense as Steve Young was to the 49er offense.

> Bryant Young was as important to the 49er defense as Steve Young was to the 49er offense.

The 49ers finished the season at 12–4, the third-best record in the NFC, but that was only good enough for second place in the NFC West behind Atlanta, which finished at 14–2. So the 49ers would have to play Green Bay at Candlestick in the wild-card game, and the Packers had beaten the 49ers the last five times they'd played. Steve Young, in fact, had never played on a team that had beaten the Packers, because Tampa Bay had lost twice to the Packers with Young as quarterback.

It looked like more of the same when the Packers went ahead,

27–23, with just 1:56 remaining on a Brett Favre to Antonio Free-man pass.

But then, after taking over at the San Francisco 24, Young took the 49ers downfield on a drive as memorable as any of the earlier postseason drives by Montana. Still, with eight seconds left and the 49ers no closer than the Green Bay 25, it seemed there would be no happy ending for the 49ers. Then Young dropped back, stumbled on the soggy turf, regained his balance, and threw a per-fect pass to Terrell Owens between two defenders and just past the goal line. Owens grabbed it and the 49ers had an improbable win.

The season would not end on a high note, though. Just six days later in a second-round playoff game in Atlanta, the 49ers suffered a devastating blow on their first play from scrimmage as Hearst broke his ankle. With the defense already hurting from the loss of Bryant Young, the 49ers had no chance without Hearst's running to complement Steve Young's passing. They made it close, nar-rowing the Falcons' lead to 20–18 with 2:57 left, but by the time they got the ball again, there were only 38 seconds left and they were back on their own 4. The game ended as Young's desperation Hail Mary pass was intercepted.

Though most NFL teams would have been delighted to take the 49ers' season, there were some ominous signs. Though he'd had a great year, Steve Young would be 38 in the next season and couldn't be far from the end of his career. Jerry Rice had been reduced to an average receiver. Bryant Young and Garrison Hearst would have to come back from serious injuries, so their futures were uncertain.

But even these problems were taking a back seat to the ques-tion of who would fill the empty executive offices. The 49ers were a rudderless ship.

Eddie Self-Destructs

CARMEN POLICY had always been there for Eddie DeBartolo. He had been Eddie's attorney in Youngstown, and he had done anything Eddie or his father had asked him to do with the 49ers. Help negotiate a contract for Bill Walsh? Sure. Represent the team at league meetings? No problem. Move out to Santa Clara to get the team's finances in order after Eddie's spending sprees in the '80s? It's done.

His biggest job, though, was keeping Eddie out of trouble— whether caused by drinking, gambling, womanizing, or any combination of the three. He often served as the buffer between Walsh and DeBartolo in the '80s. He got Eddie out of any number of scrapes, many of them below the public radar, but not all. There was the sexual assault charge against Eddie that disappeared; there was the punching of a Green Bay Packer fan after a playoff loss that was reduced to a misdemeanor.

Policy also became the front man for Eddie when groups wanted a 49er presence. Eddie never became a part of San Francisco, even though he was a very popular figure because of the success of his team. At home games, his luxury box would be filled with the Youngstown cronies he had flown out, with only an occasional San Franciscan in attendance.

Not realizing his disinclination to be part of San Francisco, various groups tried to get him to make an appearance. He wanted no part of public appearances, so Carmen apologized for him and offered to take his place. At first, he even joked about being Eddie DeBartolo because the two have a superficial physical resemblance. Policy is a warm, outgoing man, a good public speaker with an ingratiating personality in small groups or one-on-one. Organizations were delighted to have him and didn't miss Eddie at all. Before long, they even stopped inviting Eddie and went to Carmen instead.

> Policy was probably more concerned about keeping Eddie out of trouble than enjoying himself. It wasn't easy.

What started as a professional relationship quickly evolved into a friendship—not a surprising development because Eddie is only comfortable working with men he regards as friends. The two were often seen together and even partied together, though Policy was probably more concerned about keeping Eddie out of trouble than enjoying himself. It wasn't easy. One observer, who was invited to a dinner party that Policy did not attend, was astounded at the amount of drinking. "There was just bottle after bottle. I finally had to stop drinking because I couldn't function, but Eddie and his buddies just kept going."

There was always more to the DeBartolo–Policy relationship than appeared on the surface, though; one observer noted that Eddie seemed to go back and forth, treating Policy sometimes as a butler and sometimes as a father-confessor. Nonetheless, the two continued to work together because of Policy's accommodations.

The relationship started to deteriorate after the death of Ed DeBartolo, Sr., in 1994. Senior always had a high regard for Policy, and he expected Carmen to watch Eddie when he was on the West Coast. When Eddie was in Youngstown, Senior watched him himself. As long as his father was alive, Eddie spent most of his time in Youngstown, maintaining a condo on the Peninsula south of San Francisco for his visits there. As soon as his father died in 1994, though, Eddie moved out of Youngstown and bought a home in Atherton, roughly halfway between the 49ers' practice facility in Santa Clara and Candlestick Park, where they played their games.

And psychologically, he started moving away from Carmen. He told Policy that he was going to start the DeBartolo Entertainment Company, which would be involved in various gambling operations. "I tried to tell him that the NFL would be very unhappy with this because of the association with gambling," Policy remembered, speaking before he left the 49ers. "I tried to get him to at least not put his name on the company, but he went ahead."

> There probably was another factor involved in the separation of the one-time buddies: Policy had become too important to the franchise.

DeBartolo's father had been active in various gambling ventures, from a riverboat casino in New Orleans, on which he had reportedly made a profit of nearly $90 million when he sold it, to racetracks in Louisiana, Texas, and Ohio. Eddie thought he could be successful in the gaming field, too, and he was eager to make his name in an independent venture. But he lacked the business acumen of his father.

In one of Eddie's ventures with his new company, he worked to get a card room in South San Francisco, and he wanted to use 49er players in the campaign for the ballot measure. Policy warned him that the league would not allow players to be used in such a role and that commissioner Paul Tagliabue would probably suspend him. Eddie backed off on his campaign strategy; we'll never know what he would have done with the card room because the measure failed.

Because he didn't like Policy's advice, Eddie was listening to another advisor, Ed Muransky, a giant of a man who had once played for the Raiders and who also acted as Eddie's bodyguard. (He didn't always do a good job; it was Muransky who started the fight with Packer fans after the playoff loss in Green Bay in January 1997, and Eddie then joined in.) Muransky fit the mold as a friend of the family; his father had been an insurance broker for the DeBartolos in Youngstown. Whether due to Muransky's advice or Eddie's decisions, the attempts to get gambling projects going for the company all failed.

There probably was another factor involved in the separation of the one-time buddies: Policy had become too important to the franchise. Because he had represented the team for so many years at league meetings, he was on good terms with almost all the owners (Al Davis was a conspicuous exception, and Carmen and Jerry Jones weren't exactly bosom buddies, either); and he was very close to Tagliabue, with whom he'd gone to law school at Georgetown. After years of taking Eddie's place at civic functions, Policy was synonymous with the 49ers to many in the San Francisco area. He had become a close friend of San Francisco mayor Willie Brown.

Eddie's identity was wrapped up in the 49ers; on his 40th birthday, his family had taken out a full-page ad in *USA Today* with his picture and the headline, "The No. 1 49er turns 40." He no doubt thought that when he moved to the Bay Area, his stature would be recognized. But when the media wanted a comment on a 49ers' story, Policy was asked, not DeBartolo. It was Carmen who was going to the best parties and dining with the mayor or Warriors owner Chris Cohan or Carl Pascarelli, CEO of Visa.

Policy was also very accessible to the media, and Eddie never had been. Story after story appeared praising Carmen, and Eddie thought, "Hey, who's the owner?"

Policy had his own grievances. He felt he had worked hard for the team, and DeBartolo hadn't followed through on his frequent promises to give him an equity position in the franchise.

Meanwhile, Muransky was apparently telling Eddie that Policy was trying to put together a group to buy the 49ers. Carmen's protests to the contrary were in vain. Eddie would believe what he wanted to believe. By this time, he was stockpiling grievances against his one-time buddy, thinking that Policy was spending too much time on league business, not the 49ers.

It didn't help, either, that the wives didn't get along. Candy DeBartolo had been good friends with Policy's first wife and resented his second one, Gail, who was young, pretty, and worked hard on physical conditioning. Because of the animosity between their wives, Eddie and Carmen stopped socializing.

Eventually, they stopped talking, and there was little hope of patching the relationship because each got information about the other secondhand, most of it distorted.

The split between the two didn't become public for a couple of years, and it had no immediate effect on the team. Eddie was spending his time at the office of the DeBartolo Entertainment Company in San Mateo, but he had never spent much time at the 49ers' practice facility, anyway, so his absence wasn't noteworthy. Meanwhile, Policy was there every day, as he had been for several years, involved in every area of the operation. Life went on.

A New Stadium

A VERY important issue was looming. For years, there had been talk of building a new stadium. Candlestick Park had originally been built for baseball and expanded in 1971 to house the 49ers. Though the 49ers didn't often face the awful weather that made Giants games so miserable in the summer, the stadium was showing its age. Concession stands were inadequate and bathrooms too small and too few; when luxury suites were added, the second-deck bathrooms were blocked off for use only by luxury suite occupants, so ordinary fans on the second deck had to trek down to a lower level. Because the stadium had not been built for football, sight lines were often bad.

The stadium also suffered from deferred maintenance. The 49ers' contract, which went through the 2006 season, had an out five years earlier if the city did not properly maintain the stadium. If the team exercised that demand, the city would have to pay more than $100 million to repair it.

Policy and the mayor huddled and agreed that it made more sense to build a new stadium than repair the old one, even though that meant passing on a Super Bowl that was scheduled to be played at Candlestick. Willie Brown came up with a complicated plan, under which the city would contribute $100 million in bond money, which he proposed would be repaid from taxes on a mall–entertainment center that would be built adjacent to the stadium. Unemployment is high in the Bay View/ Hunters Point area immediately to the west of Candlestick Point, so Brown thought the plan could be sold because residents in those areas would presumably get work with the stadium project and the mall.

> Eddie was being Eddie, avoiding the work of the campaign while depending on Policy to do all the heavy lifting, which Carmen resented.

Eddie wasn't pleased with the idea because other franchises had been able to get their cities to contribute at least half the cost of the stadium and, in some cases, foot the entire bill. "I think this deal is too good for San Francisco," he said in an interview late in the campaign. Brown and Policy were more realistic because they knew that San Francisco voters didn't believe sports stadiums should be publicly financed. Even deals proposing a partial public input had been rejected. After losing four elections in San Francisco and Santa Clara County, the Giants had decided to finance their new park privately. In that atmosphere, even the $100 million bond issue would be a tough sell.

The election campaign widened the split between Policy and DeBartolo. Eddie was being Eddie, avoiding the work of the campaign while depending on Policy to do all the heavy lifting, which Carmen resented. While Policy worked tirelessly on the campaign, speaking before civic groups night and day, talking to newspaper editors and interviewing on radio and television, Eddie was . . . well, nobody quite knew where Eddie was.

The campaign was in trouble from the start. Because the measure was rushed to get on the June 1997 ballot, precise numbers were unavailable. It didn't help that the George Seifert firing came as the 49ers were preparing the plan. Then, shortly after the plan was released, budget analyst Harvey Rose said he questioned the mayor's assertion that money from the city's general fund wouldn't be touched for the financing. The mayor, emotionally distraught because of the death of his friend, *San Francisco Chronicle* columnist Herb Caen, snarled at reporters who tried to question him about Rose's report and gave them no information.

Even the usually smooth Policy stumbled, telling a group of *Chronicle* reporters and editors that if the stadium initiative didn't pass, the voters would be "kicking us out." Even supporters like State Senator John Burton felt the 49ers were putting a gun to the head of voters, though Policy's statement was simply the unvarnished truth. Even though other NFL teams had been moving around the country, as if in a giant game of checkers, to get lucrative stadium deals in other cities, San Franciscans preferred to think the 49ers would stay put, no matter what.

Policy persuaded DeBartolo to make one campaigning trip, through North Beach. Eddie was reluctant, but he soon loosened up as he and Carmen went from bar to bar and, at each one, he was offered a drink. This was his kind of campaign.

The stadium drive never did get much momentum. Even a heralded visit by Tagliabue was a dud. Policy had hoped to get the commissioner to promise that San Francisco would get at least three Super Bowls with a new stadium, but Tagliabue, who takes caution to a new level, would promise only one. Since there had already been speculation about multiple Super Bowls, Tagliabue's cautious assessment took the air out of the balloon.

> San Franciscans preferred to think the 49ers would stay put, no matter what.

Then, the infamous Jack Davis birthday party threatened to totally derail the campaign. Davis, the political consultant who had been hired by the 49ers to run the campaign, was well known for over-the-top parties, but this one, celebrating his fiftieth birthday before a crowd that included the city's top politicians and representatives from civic groups and the city's professional teams, was outrageous even by his standards.

As party-goers entered the ballroom at the San Francisco Mart, they saw one young man being tattooed and another having bells and fetishes sewn to his back and chest. On the stage, male and female strippers were gyrating to hard rock. For the "main event" a bound man on the stage had a satanic star carved in his back; as the blood flowed, he was urinated on by a leather-clad woman. Supervisor Barbara Kaufman left the ballroom, gagging and yelling, "Gross, gross." Many others had the same reaction, and when news of the party was printed, the 49ers' campaign headquarters was inundated with letters that blasted the party and the 49ers' connection with it.

Davis offered to resign, but the disgusted Policy decided not to accept his offer. "The damage is done," he said. "He's got all the campaign plans in his head. We're lost without that."

At that point, just three weeks before the election, the stadium issue seemed lost no matter what happened with Davis. But minutes after Tagliabue gave his lackluster performance at the earlier press conference, Mayor Brown outlined his campaign strategy. Campaign workers made plans to ensure that voters in the Hunters Point/Bayview areas got to the polls. On election day, those voters turned out in great numbers, and the overwhelming percentage of them favored the stadium. It was just enough to win the election by a few hundred votes, overcoming opposition from most other areas of the city.

The Beginning of the End for Eddie

THE EUPHORIA of winning the election didn't last long. Soon Policy was telling reporters that he thought Eddie might fire him; it was the first hint that there was trouble between the two.

Then, in December 1997, a bombshell struck: DeBartolo received a letter saying he was likely to be asked to appear before a Louisiana grand jury regarding a gambling probe in the state. The target of the probe was former Louisiana governor Edwin Edwards, a long-time friend of the DeBartolo family. FBI agents had wiretapped Edwards's phones and recorded a conversation between Edwards and DeBartolo in which Eddie agreed to pay the former governor $400,000 in cash to help him get a license for an offshore gambling casino in Louisiana.

Shortly afterward, the 49ers officially retired Joe Montana's jersey and had a halftime ceremony at a Monday night game with Denver at Candlestick. Eddie spoke briefly and received a warm welcome from the fans.

That would be the last good news he would get for some time. The NFL was pressuring him to step down as owner until he could clear his name in Louisiana. Policy worked out an agreement with Eddie and his sister, Denise DeBartolo York, for Mrs. York to take over operating control until Eddie's legal battle was concluded. As part of the deal, Policy was supposed to get 5 percent of the team, taken equally out of the shares held by Eddie and his sister. (The DeBartolo Corporation owns 90 percent of the 49ers; as equal partners in the corporation, Eddie and his sister each had 45 percent of the 49ers. It was the only voting stock. Franklin Mieuli owned 5 percent and Rick Morabito owned the other 5 percent.)

Policy never got the 5 percent. Eddie refused to honor that part of the agreement, saying he had been coerced while drinking. By this time, he was convinced that Policy was trying to put together a group to buy the 49ers, although Policy repeatedly pointed out, "You can't buy something that's not for sale." Even if his sister wanted to sell the team, Eddie wouldn't.

Mrs. York, a smart businesswoman, had no interest in football, but she had full confidence in Policy: She sent a letter to Tagliabue to tell him that Policy would be running the team at least through the '98 season.

It wouldn't be that long after all, because Carmen was tired of fighting off allegations. "I've gone from best friend and confidant and advisor to a Judas," he said, bitterly, one day in his office.

As a gourmet and wine connoisseur, Policy had thoroughly enjoyed living in the Bay Area, and he was in one of the nicest areas, Palo Alto, where the year-round sunshine was a pleasant contrast to the years he had spent in Youngstown. But none of that was enough to compensate for the constant animosity from his one-time friend, nor the realization that his job would disappear if Eddie ever regained control.

Meanwhile, the NFL would soon entertain bids for an expansion franchise in Cleveland, and three groups were competing for it. Al Lerner, an extremely wealthy businessman who was one of those seeking the franchise, talked to Policy about heading up his group, with the understanding that Carmen would get 10 percent of the franchise if it were awarded to Lerner. The money meant little to Lerner, and he knew that Policy's league contacts would give him an advantage in knowing how much money to bid and how to approach the owners.

As the 49ers opened training camp on the University of the Pacific campus in Stockton, Policy announced his resignation and his role with Lerner's expansion group. It was a good time to leave because the major player moves for an NFL club are always made between the end of the season and the start of training camp. And it was definitely time for him to move on.

For Eddie, it was a Pyrrhic victory. It gave him personal satisfaction, but it weakened the organization, and even his personal satisfaction would be dimmed in the months ahead as he slowly realized that his return to power would be blocked by the commissioner. And by his sister as well.

CHAPTER EIGHTEEN

A Family Feud

ED DEBARTOLO, Jr., stood at a hotel podium on April 16, 1999, and, his voice shaking with emotion, announced a $150 million suit against his sister, Denise DeBartolo York, for allegedly reneging on a deal to turn the team over to him for $350 million in corporate assets. The San Francisco 49ers were in very public disarray.

There were problems everywhere. Team president Carmen Policy and general manager Dwight Clark had left to run the expansion Cleveland Browns. Legendary coach Bill Walsh had returned as the team's general manager, but he faced a daunting task because the 49ers were so far over the salary cap that they had to release or trade productive players to reduce their payroll. Plans for a badly needed new stadium were on hold, and a proposed Super Bowl for 2003 had been moved from San Francisco to San Diego.

Now the DeBartolo family feud was front and center, the once very private dealings of the family on very public display, the result of a split between Eddie and his sister that went back to childhood.

Ed DeBartolo, Sr., had been a successful and innovative businessman. Thanks to the shopping malls he created, he might be considered the one individual most responsible for changing American shopping habits. He built so many that, when the 49ers played in the Super Bowl in Miami in January 1989, the DeBartolo Corporation took out a full-page ad showing symbols for its more than 50 malls.

Senior dressed in black suits, worked virtually every day up to the time he died, and avoided the spotlight. His marriage was a traditional one: His wife stayed home and raised their two children. Hardly anybody outside their circle of friends even knew his wife's name until her son dedicated the 49ers' practice facility to her memory in 1987; the Santa Clara facility is officially the Marie P. DeBartolo building.

The shopping malls and associated businesses made the DeBartolos immensely wealthy. The natural heir was, of course, the son, who was also the firstborn. The daughter was expected to follow the example of her mother, staying home to raise her children.

Neither of the DeBartolo children fulfilled their roles. Eddie, given every advantage, including a Notre Dame education, was a wild, impetuous youth, and his personality never really changed as he got older. He never settled into the role his father intended him for: the solid businessman who would continue the family business and even expand it.

The daughter fulfilled part of her role, raising four children, two sons and twin daughters, but she also went into business and became almost a clone of her father, a hard worker with good judgment. Even more than her father, she shunned the spotlight.

But even though the daughter was the one who emulated her father, when the wild son came home, he was greeted so warmly that it was obvious he remained the favorite. It was the biblical parable of the prodigal son come to life. Did Denise resent the attention paid Eddie? She'd have been less than human if she hadn't.

As adults, they went separate ways in business. Because they both lived in Youngstown, Ohio, they still socialized, though those moments were often tense because Denise's husband, John York, detested Eddie. Denise worked within the corporation, though she also became president of the Pittsburgh Penguins of the National Hockey League when the DeBartolo Corporation owned the Penguins in the 1981–91 period. Eddie was an executive and on the board of the DeBartolo Corporation, but he spent very little time on company business, especially after the purchase of the 49ers.

Ownership of the 49ers

ORIGINALLY, THE 49ers were in Eddie's name because NFL rules prohibited corporate ownership of a team. In December 1986, the corporation officially bought the team, defying the NFL office; the DeBartolos were fined $50,000.

Of course, Eddie had run up big bills when he started boosting the 49ers' payroll so dramatically in the 1980s. With the corporation now owning the team, the debts Eddie ran up were paid by the corporation, and he was no longer personally responsible for the ones he would run up in subsequent years. For Eddie, it was the best of all possible worlds. He still thought of himself as the owner, and he spent freely in bringing in players, not just starters but expensive backups as well. At one time, the 49ers had Joe Montana, Steve Young, and Steve Bono under contract at quarterback. It was like play money for Eddie because the corporation was paying the bills. The corporation was making so much money on other ventures that nobody seemed to care that the 49ers were losing as much as $20 million a year despite selling out every game.

> Nobody seemed to care that the 49ers were losing as much as $20 million a year despite selling out every game.

Then the corporation got caught in the recession of the late

'80s, and the 49ers' losses were no longer tolerable. There was a debate within the corporation: Would it be best just to get rid of the team? Eddie was enraged. They were talking about his toy, and he thought his sister was one of those who wanted to sell the team, which further divided them. Eventually the corporation decided that the team would be kept but only if expenses were cut back. The team didn't have to make money but it wasn't supposed to lose money, either, so Carmen Policy was sent to the Bay Area to watch the finances. That solution didn't make Eddie happy; living within his means had never been an option for him.

From that point on, Eddie had an "us against them" mentality. When he visited the 49er offices, he told top-level executives not to tell "them" (DeBartolo Corporation officers in Youngstown) what the 49er executives were doing.

In the early 1990s, the DeBartolo Corporation went public, which solved its cash-flow problems and eased the pressure on the 49ers' economics. At about the same time, though, the NFL adopted a salary cap, which prevented DeBartolo from spending money as he had in the '80s; that, of course, was one of the primary reasons for the cap. Neither of these events diminished Eddie's resentment that he had been forced to cut back on his spending by others in the corporation, including his sister.

> The NFL adopted a salary cap, which prevented DeBartolo from spending money as he had in the '80s.

Eddie had never cut back his personal spending. He was running up enormous debts, only hinted at by public disclosures. His excessive gambling and drinking habits were costing him millions, but one friend from those days described that as "chump change." The big losses were coming from bad investments. Eddie had always wanted to prove he could make it financially on his own, independent from the corporation, but he was throwing good money after bad in a vain attempt to recoup losses. To improve his own bottom line, he was charging many of his personal expenses to the team.

His sister was growing increasingly resentful of Eddie's profligate ways with company money, but as long as Senior was alive, neither sibling would move against the other. Some who observed the situation thought Senior should have set up strict rules about who was responsible for Eddie's losses, but he could not come down on his prodigal son.

After Senior

SO THE situation festered. When Senior died in 1994, it was inevitable that the dispute would come to a boil. The only surprise is that it took as long as it did.

Ed DeBartolo, Sr., had arranged that after his death the DeBartolo Corporation interests would be split equally between Eddie and his sister. Denise DeBartolo York's interests were in the corporation, not the 49ers, and she was chairman of the board of the company. She eased Eddie out of an executive role within the company and off the board as well.

> Denise had no interest in football and even less interest in the media attention that most owners (including Eddie) loved.

Eddie had moved to the Bay Area, which physically separated the siblings and contributed even more to his feeling that the 49ers were his. To make that official, Eddie proposed that he exchange his half of the corporation for his sister's half of the 49ers, so he could regain control of the team. But the two could not agree on the value of the 49ers, and no deal could be struck.

Then the bombshell of the Louisiana gambling probe hit, which meant that Denise had to take over as the operating owner of the team, with Policy as president. Denise had no interest in football and even less interest in the media attention that most owners (including Eddie) loved. She was ridiculed in the media because at one game, when the TV cameras focused on the owner's box, she climbed almost frantically up the steps in the back of the box to get out of view. "Nissie's never going to like the spotlight," John York told me later.

Even though Eddie was not in control and could not officially be in control without being reinstated by the NFL, he and his sister were still trying to work out a deal that would make him sole owner of the club, except for the 10 percent of nonvoting stock owned by Rick Morabito and Franklin Mieuli. There were tax complications in the deal, though, and there were also Eddie complications. "Every time we think we have a deal, Eddie blows up and walks out," York told me.

Denise was getting hammered in the press by writers who had been close to Eddie. She was portrayed as a woman who was interested only in the bottom line, someone whose penurious tendencies would bring the 49ers down. That was pure fiction. Both Policy and general manager Dwight Clark assured me that there was no change in the 49ers' practices. "She wants to know where the money's going and whether the expenses are justified," said Clark, "but once we do that, she approves it." In fact, shortly after she took over, the 49ers restructured contracts for Steve Young and Jerry Rice that involved sizeable "signing bonuses."

For the next year, Eddie's friends in the media consistently reported that it was only a matter of time before he got back into operating control of the 49ers. In fact, though, Eddie's chances of returning were always slim, and they went down when he pleaded guilty to a felony charge of not reporting a bribe and was fined $1 million.

I had been talking to the league offices and was told, as background, that Eddie would not be reinstated as long as he was in the middle of the gambling probe. NFL commissioner Paul Tagliabue could not reinstate Eddie before he testified in the trial of former Louisiana governor Edwin Edwards because the league couldn't know what he would say. The NFL is extremely cautious about gambling, as it has to be. Many millions of dollars are bet on NFL games, most of it illegally, so there can be no suspicion that anybody involved with the league and its teams is involved.

Tagliabue was not being pressured by owners to reinstate DeBartolo, either, because Eddie had only two friends among the owners, Jerry Jones in Dallas and Al Davis in Oakland, and both were outlaws in the NFL community. Eddie had alienated other owners by his free spending in the '80s; and because he had no interest in league meetings, sending Policy as the club representative, he had not forged any bonds with other owners. Even if Tagliabue were willing to reinstate Eddie, some owners thought the decision would have to come before the owners for a vote, just as if DeBartolo were buying the club. Eddie's chances of getting approval from the owners were not good.

So, when Tagliabue made the annual commissioner's speech before the Super Bowl in January 1999, he announced that DeBartolo was still under suspension.

"I think that for the foreseeable future, which means at least the 1999 season, Eddie's sister is going to be the person who is principally responsible for managing the 49ers," said Tagliabue. "Eddie has been divorced from the team first by his own decision, secondly by my direction, and I think the likelihood is that that will continue."

Eddie Is Out

MEANWHILE, DENISE was trying to exercise control over her brother's spending. She sold the company plane, which Eddie used to fly to games. On February 24, 1999, she issued a memo to 49er employees saying Eddie would no longer be allowed to charge the team for expenses, such as chartering a plane to fly to games, and that they were not to answer any questions he might have about the operation of the franchise. Those questions were to be directed to the corporation's Youngstown headquarters.

After reviewing the DeBartolo Corporation position and her own and expressing her faith in Bill Walsh's football operations, Denise advised employees:

> We also need your help in monitoring the operations of the team. We realize that the team has long been operated based on certain assumptions as to ownership and management, and it is difficult to disrupt the momentum of these long-standing practices. We hope that you understand that we are still in the process of learning what these practices are and only then can we evaluate whether we might change them or improve on them for the ultimate benefit of the team.
>
> I hope that you can appreciate my efforts to provide you clear direction and to assure compliance with NFL directives. I have formulated these guidelines after giving careful consideration to both the Commissioner's public statements as well as the fact that Eddie is neither an officer nor a director of The Edward J. DeBartolo Corporation or any of its subsidiaries, including the San Francisco Forty Niners, Inc. Accordingly, please be guided as follow:
>
> 1. Eddie and his representatives have been directed to communicate in writing, exclusively through John McVay with copies to me, when he requires information from the team. If you have any concerns about inquiries from Eddie or his representatives, please direct Eddie and his representatives to John McVay. You can be assured that Eddie will understand that you are only doing so because of the corporation's directive in this regard.
>
> 2. Eddie's requests for reimbursement of expenses, further advancement of team funds or use of team assets must be

directed to me for approval before payment or use. When Eddie was involved in the direct management of this team, he enjoyed many of the benefits which are earned when undertaking such responsibility. He no longer functions in that capacity or any other corporate capacity; therefore, we must carefully monitor these records for purposes of compliance with both NFL directives and IRS regulations. . . .

This message was followed by an April 1999 suit filed on behalf of the corporation to recover $94 million in debts owed by Eddie; it accused him of cutting a side deal on the stadium-mall proposal with the mall developer, the Mills Corporation of Arlington, Virginia, claiming that the deal would have paid him $10 million and given him a 22 percent interest in the mall.

So Eddie fired back with his own lawsuit, for $150 million, a week later.

"I placed my trust and my family's financial future in Denise's hands, and that trust has been betrayed," he said, reading from a prepared statement at his press conference, attended by 49er legends Joe Montana, Jerry Rice, and Roger Craig.

"As you all know, there has been a great deal of media activity surrounding my situation—some factual, most just innuendo or speculation. I am far from perfect, and yes, I've made mistakes. But I've faced up to those mistakes [his guilty plea on the felony charge] and am paying the price."

He said he had been stunned by his sister's suit, which left him with no choice but to proceed with his own claim. "I always believed that we could resolve our differences in private, as families should—as my father would have wanted."

The countersuits intensified the need for a settlement. Denise's views were clear: Whatever their personal relationship might be in the future, she wanted their business relationship to be completely severed. She had already removed Eddie from the corporate structure. Now, she wanted him out of the 49ers' operation too. Eddie's

love for the 49ers was still strong, though, and he had been working behind the scenes even while officially not in control. Now,
whenever he and his sister and their representatives met to discuss
the sale of his interest, Eddie's volatility would surface.

The matter had gone to a judge in Cleveland, but John York
despaired of its ever being settled. He could not discuss the details
of the settlement discussions, but he shared his frustration with me
in a telephone conversation.

"Time after time we've met with Eddie and thought we had an
agreement, but then he walks out and tells reporters that we sabo-
taged the meeting," he said. "We don't mind the responsibility. We
took over the racetracks in Louisiana, Ohio, and Oklahoma [after the death of Ed DeBartolo, Sr.] and straight-
ened them out, but we need to know who's responsible.

> Whenever he and his sister and their representatives met to discuss the sale of his interest, Eddie's volatility would surface.

"For three years, our lives have been dictated by Eddie's actions. We're sick of that."

But Eddie's money was running out, and so was his resolve. He had already sold his home on the San Francisco Peninsula and moved to
Florida, where real estate values were much lower and the tax
structure was much friendlier to wealthy men.

In August 1999, a settlement was reached. Though many
details had yet to be filled in, the broad strokes removed Eddie
from the 49ers ownership, giving him possession of one of the corporation's subsidiaries, the Simon DeBartolo Corporation, with
the provision that he could not sell it, protecting him from himself.
His huge debt to the corporation could be paid off on his own
schedule, which in essence meant it was forgiven.

So Eddie was out. His time with the 49ers had been a tumultuous one, full of great highs but also full of an almost unabated tension.

The Yorks in Charge

> So Eddie was out. His time with the 49ers had been a tumultuous one, full of great highs but also full of an almost unabated tension.

NOBODY COULD be quite sure what would happen with York in control, though he had officially taken over in February 1999. There was media speculation that the Yorks would sell the club once the court-decided settlement was final; but if they sold the 49ers in less than two years, the corporation's tax debt would be much higher, making it unlikely that a sale would be immediate.

Meanwhile, York was enjoying his new position. The NFL owners' club is a very exclusive one, and it offers its members a very high profile. York, a pathologist before leaving the profession to get into business, had not had such a heady experience before. Nobody knew whether he could handle it, though York himself seemed to have no doubts.

When I talked to York, I saw a man who displayed both arrogance and an inferiority complex because of the treatment he'd received from the DeBartolo family. When he'd started a pathology clinic in Youngstown, it initially lost a great deal of money. "Then I was the dumb son-in-law," he told me, obviously still bitter.

York had recovered from that early disaster and eventually had three pathology clinics that he sold for a profit. Then he became involved with the DeBartolo-owned racetracks, in New Orleans, Cleveland, and Oklahoma City, first helping Ed DeBartolo, Sr., and eventually taking over full management when Senior died.

"My dad took me to race tracks when I was a kid," explained York. "I knew how to bet the horses when I was eight years old. I was the only one who would go to the track with Mr. DeBartolo, so he turned to me when he needed help with them.

"The tracks were losing money. We wanted to sell them, but nobody would come near them with a 10-foot pole because horse racing was in trouble everywhere in the country, but I got them turned around and eventually sold them all for a profit." (York didn't mention that two of them, Thistledown in Cleveland and Remington Park in Oklahoma City, were bought by Frank Stronach, a multimillionaire who loves horse racing and was buying tracks, including the fabled Santa Anita, to keep them going, not worrying whether they were good investments.)

When I asked York whether he missed the practice of medicine, he had an interesting response. "When I wrote a letter saying why I wanted to go to medical school, I said I looked on it as an intellectual challenge," he said. "I never went into medicine with the idea of saving lives. I had a good mind and I thought this was a way I could use it.

"I've looked at the business operations I've been involved in the same way, so, no, I don't miss medicine. I look at the 49ers as the same kind of challenge. I don't think a football team is anywhere near as complicated an operation as a horse racing track, so I think I can handle this."

York would need all his arrogance because taking over the 49ers at this particular moment in history was about to become comparable to assuming command of the *Titanic* as it approached the iceberg.

CHAPTER NINETEEN

Walsh's Return

WHEN CARMEN Policy left for Cleveland in July 1998, he left a policy vacuum in the 49ers' front office. Eddie DeBartolo filled it. Before long, he had pushed Dwight Clark out the door, fiddled with Steve Mariucci's mind, and then brought back the man who had started the 49ers' great run, Bill Walsh.

Technically, Larry Thrailkill was the new 49er president, but Thrailkill was wearing three hats; he was also chief operating officer of the DeBartolo Corporation and a senior partner in a Nashville, Tennessee, law firm. In his spare time, he taught a Sunday school class.

Obviously, Thrailkill was not going to be able to spend much time on 49er business, so Eddie was able to work through him and office employees who knew him to pull strings. For the time being, his sister didn't interfere with Eddie's manipulations. That changed in February 1999, when Denise's husband, John York, replaced Thrailkill and she sent her explicit memo to 49er employees.

The first evidence of Eddie's work was the failure to give Clark a new contract as general manager.

As a player, Clark had been one of Eddie's favorites, behind only Joe Montana. When Clark's playing career ended, Eddie insisted that he be given a job in the organization. Now, though, he was caught in the middle of the battle between Policy and DeBartolo. Eddie saw him as Carmen's friend—as he was—and so Dwight went from the "us" to the "them" column. Eddie was determined to get rid of Clark as soon as Policy was gone.

Policy tried to protect Clark by giving him a new contract with a pay raise; but when Thrailkill came in, he said he would have to approve it. He never did. There was always a reason. Thrailkill couldn't make a meeting or a complication had surfaced.

But it was really Eddie.

When it became obvious that Clark was not going to get that contract, he decided that he wanted to go to Cleveland to be general manager of the expansion Browns, reunited with Policy. NFL club executives are not usually permitted to change clubs within a season, but there were special circumstances in Clark's case. Cleveland wouldn't field a team until the 1999 season, but there was a tremendous amount of startup work and preparation to be done. And Clark was working without a contract with the 49ers. So NFL commissioner Paul Tagliabue allowed him to go to Cleveland.

Even the Clark situation didn't show the quixotic, mercurial workings of Eddie's mind as well as did the convoluted negotiations for the extension of coach Steve Mariucci's contract.

The idea of the extension was Eddie's in the beginning. Mariucci had not sought an extension—he was, after all, only in his second year—but was happy to have his agent talk with the 49ers about it. One reason: He thought he might like to be more involved in player selection.

Mariucci's extension was supposed to be done in early October, but it dragged on and on. It was embarrassing to Mariucci, who was asked about it at each weekly press conference. His explanation usually was that it was hard for Thrailkill to find the time to meet with his agents, and lawyers were bringing up different points, and so on.

But again, it was Eddie. After starting the ball rolling, he had come to think he could do better.

Eddie first had his eye on Matt Millen, who had played for both the 49ers and Raiders before going into television work, but Millen was a close friend of Mariucci's. The last thing he wanted to do was shove Mariucci out of his job.

Then, Eddie started thinking about Mike Holmgren. The 49er job seemed to be a good fit for Holmgren, who had an out in his Green Bay contract if he were offered a job as general manager. By this time, Clark was gone, so the 49er GM job was open. Holmgren was a San Francisco native and had been a 49er assistant under Bill Walsh in the '80s, before being named head coach in Green Bay.

Of course, Mariucci still had two years left on his original contract, but Eddie had shown when he jettisoned George Seifert that contracts didn't interfere with his decisions. He continued to toy with the Holmgren idea.

Wooing Walsh

MEANWHILE, EDDIE was leaking another idea: that the 49ers would bring back Walsh as general manager. It would be a public relations coup for Eddie, who was under barrage for shoving the popular Policy out the door. Bringing Walsh back would make it all right again.

It was fine with Mariucci, too, because, for personal reasons, he had given up on his idea of more control. A devoted family man, he was bothered by the fact that he had so little time for his family. "I get home and they're already asleep," he told me. He had scheduled "family days" to allow his children and those of other coaches and 49er employees to watch practice, but that was only an occasional thing. He complained that he had no time for anything but coaching. "I haven't even been able to take the time to get a haircut. What would I do if I had more responsibility?"

He was also, he said, looking forward to working with Walsh, if it came to that. "I've never even met him," he said. "I'd really like to talk to him, to bounce some ideas off him."

Mariucci did eventually get his contract extension, though only when Eddie realized he had no other alternatives. Many in the media thought Mariucci's job was on the line when the 49ers hosted the Green Bay Packers in the first round of the playoffs, but even when the 49ers won that game with the miraculous touchdown pass from Steve Young to Terrell Owens in the closing seconds, Mariucci's extension was delayed. Eddie was still talking to Holmgren's agent.

> "I haven't even been able to take the time to get a haircut. What would I do if I had more responsibility?"
>
> —Steve Mariucci

Holmgren ended the speculation shortly afterward by taking the coach/general manager position with the Seattle Seahawks. Holmgren had never commented publicly on the 49er job, but there were several good reasons for going to Seattle instead. It would have been messy for him to join the 49ers, because Mariucci would have to be fired; in Seattle, the twin job was open. The 49ers had been successful for so long that the best Holmgren could do was continue the success. If the team fell short, he would be blamed. In Seattle, by contrast, the Seahawks had been mired in mediocrity, with a .500 record for the past four seasons, though they had good talent. Holmgren had a chance to look very good, and there was little chance he would do worse than his immediate predecessors.

It's likely that, despite the speculation, Holmgren never considered the 49ers. We'll never know, but once Holmgren was out of the picture, Mariucci got his extension, and the focus returned to Walsh.

It had been almost 10 years since Walsh had last coached the

49ers, with his win in the January 1989 Super Bowl his swan song. Yet, he was still a looming presence. The team was still using the offense he had designed, though it had been modified, particularly by Mike Shanahan when he was the offensive coordinator. Though Policy had changed the decision-making process to bring in several voices, replacing the one-man rule of Walsh's era, the organization generally still adhered to the guidelines drawn up by Walsh. The team had won a Super Bowl the first year he was gone, with the players he had brought in and with the coach, Seifert, he had handpicked as his successor. Probably the biggest reason for the 49ers' continued success was the fact that one great quarterback followed another, Steve Young after Joe Montana, and it was Walsh who had brought them both in.

Though he always prefaced any comments on the team with something like "I'm not really following them that closely," in fact, Walsh was very aware of what was happening with the team. He talked to former assistants who were still with the team, Bobb McKittrick and Bill McPherson, and he talked to players, too, particularly Young.

He had tried to divorce himself from the team shortly after he had resigned as coach. He remained on for a short time as the general manager, but was clearly uncomfortable. He didn't want to impinge on anything Seifert did, but his reduced role was frustrating. "I'm keeping busy by researching the best restaurants on the road," he said, sarcastically, one time when we talked. His chief responsibility was the draft, but it was

> It had been almost 10 years since Walsh had last coached the 49ers, with his win in the January 1989 Super Bowl his swan song. Yet, he was still a looming presence.

his worst since he'd come to the team, with not one player who ever made a significant contribution to the team. (The No. 2 pick, tight end Wesley Walls, became a Pro Bowl player, but only after he'd left the 49ers.) "I thought I'd be able to do better because I would have more time to spend on the draft," he told me, "but in fact, I wound up having less, because I was doing so many interviews. In the past, I'd always had an excuse to turn them down, but I couldn't this time."

Shortly after that, NBC-TV offered Walsh a job as an analyst on AFC games (and Notre Dame, as well), and Walsh took it, thinking it would be a way for him to stay close to the game while cutting his ties to the 49ers, so he wouldn't seem to be looking over Seifert's shoulder.

Some coaches take well to announcing; John Madden is the obvious example. Walsh did not. He gave viewers more information than they got from other analysts because he was able to break down a play immediately, not having to wait for the replay to study it, but he did not have the dynamic style of Madden. NBC executives didn't like his voice and had him take voice lessons. It bothered him that executives would tell him, "You're doing a great job," and then he'd hear from friends in the business that they were criticizing him behind his back. The final straw came when he was told by executive producer Terry O'Neil that he would not be the lead analyst the next season. (O'Neil later changed his mind, but it was too late to keep Walsh.)

At dinner one night, Eddie broached to Walsh the idea of returning to the organization, but it was Policy who set the wheels in motion, meeting with Walsh several times. Though some have written that it wasn't certain whether Walsh would return as a full-time operative or as a part-time consultant, Walsh always thought he was being promised the job of director of football operations. Policy and I were talking off the record during this time, and he always spoke to me of Walsh coming back in that role, so I'm certain that was what he was offering Walsh.

The week after the two league championship games in January 1992, Policy told me that he and Walsh had agreed to terms and that a press conference to announce it would be held later that week. But when I talked to Walsh in his Menlo Park office, which had been his base since he'd left the 49ers, he was strangely evasive, unwilling to commit himself beyond a vague statement that it "might happen."

I soon learned why: He feared that his return would be devastating to the organization.

Policy and Walsh had always met outside the 49er office, usually at Walsh's office but sometimes in nearby restaurants. They had been able to keep their negotiations secret. Nobody else in the 49er organization knew about it. Amazingly, even Eddie wasn't talking.

But Walsh blew that cover himself. At the AFC championship game in Buffalo the previous weekend, he had talked to Ira Miller of the *San Francisco Chronicle* about the changes that needed to be made if the 49ers, who had missed the playoffs that season for the first time since '82, were to get back to the championship level. He said nothing about returning to the 49ers himself, but within the organization, Seifert and Clark realized what was about to happen.

Neither wanted Walsh back. Clark actually feared Walsh, a carryover from Dwight's playing days. Walsh had talked Clark into retiring a year earlier than Dwight wanted, and Clark still didn't think he could deal with Walsh on an equal basis. He lobbied Policy not to bring Walsh back.

Seifert approached Walsh directly and asked if Walsh wanted his coaching job back. He didn't, but Seifert, who was under pressure from De-Bartolo for not making the playoffs, didn't want Walsh looking over his shoulder. He worried that his coaching authority would be eroded just

> Seifert, who was under pressure from DeBartolo for not making the playoffs, didn't want Walsh looking over his shoulder.

by Walsh's presence, and he was probably right. After talking to Walsh, Seifert lobbied Policy, just as Clark had, to keep Walsh away.

Knowing this, Walsh was talking to Tom Ford, a very generous donor to Stanford (where a campus building is named after him) and the owner of the building where Walsh had an office. Stanford was looking for a football coach because Denny Green, one of Walsh's many coaching disciples, had left to become head coach of the Minnesota Vikings. Walsh let Ford know he might be interested, and Ford called Stanford athletic director Ted Leland, who had his job primarily because Walsh had campaigned for him. It was a no-brainer for Leland; the leading candidate for the coaching job was an assistant, Ron Turner. If Walsh wanted the job, he had it. Very quickly, he decided he did. There was a press conference for Walsh that week, but it was at Stanford, not Santa Clara. DeBartolo, Policy, and Seifert sat in the front row with big smiles; Seifert's was genuine, but the other two were forced.

Walsh's first team won the Blockbuster Bowl, and he recruited some outstanding players because of his reputation, but his second stint at Stanford was nothing like the triumphant success of his first. He no longer had the physical or mental energy for college coaching. Recruiting was especially arduous. He went the wrong way on a road in rural Nebraska, while recruiting Scott Frost, and missed his plane, forcing him to stay over another night. He even got lost in the hills of Oakland and had to ask directions from a cop who stopped when he saw Walsh's parked car. He hired former players and thought he would coach them to be coaches; but by his third season, he lost interest even in that. He would call a coaches' meeting and then forget about it; his assistants would be sitting in the room wondering what was happening while Walsh was playing tennis.

At the end of the third season, Walsh quit. The experience had taught him that coaching was no longer an option, but he wasn't sure what he wanted to do. Financially, he was secure, largely because of the million-dollar contracts from his last years as 49er coach and his three years at NBC, and he was in demand as a speaker to business groups, at $25,000 an appearance.

His life was certainly more comfortable than it had been when he was with the 49ers. He and his wife, Geri, had taken a Woodside home that had been built in 1929 and gutted it, then rebuilt it with modern conveniences. He had a small vineyard in the backyard and made some wine. He was playing tennis and golfing with friends on a regular basis, even playing in an occasional tournament. He and Geri also had a home in Pacific Grove and often spent weekends there.

But football had been his life since he played college ball at San Jose State in the early '50s, and now he was out of that. He had offers. He could have gone to Tampa Bay and run that franchise, but his wife wouldn't move to Florida. The Seattle Seahawks also talked to him about a position in the front office that would not have required his full-time presence, so he could have spent part of his time in Seattle and part of his time in Woodside.

Walsh listened to both offers. He never rejected an overture immediately, because he was flattered that people still wanted him. Though he had fought his way through rejections in his early career to a success that brought him election to the Pro Football Hall of Fame in 1993, the doubts from those years apparently still lingered, and he needed constant reassurances.

The Consultant

HE WAS never close to accepting either offer, though. After Stanford, he felt drained, not ready to take on the responsibility of a full-time position. When Policy came to him again in 1996 and offered him a consulting position, with the cumbersome title of "administrative assistant to the coaching staff," he accepted.

"I know I'll never coach again," he said, "so I had to decide what role I could fill. I decided I either wanted to come in at the very top, as the head of football operations, or at the bottom, as a consultant. I didn't want anything in between. The more I thought about it, the more I realized that I no longer have the desire to put the time and effort into doing the job at the top that is necessary, so I thought I'd give this a try."

Once again, though, it was a bad fit. Walsh's presence overwhelmed new offensive coordinator Marc Trestman, who already had the unenviable job of replacing Mike Shanahan, who had done a brilliant job and would go on to coach the Denver Broncos to two Super Bowl championships.

At every game, the TV cameras found Walsh. First, he sat in back of Trestman in the coaches' box, and on TV, it appeared he was looking over Trestman's shoulder, as if he were grading him. Then he showed up on the sidelines. Policy blamed Walsh—"Bill always has to be the center of attention"—but it was probably more Walsh's reputation. He was always going to be the big story. On one occasion, the story was amusing: In Green Bay before the Packers game, he lost his copy of the game plan. It showed up on the desk of Packers coach Mike Holmgren, who denied that he used it in the game. Perhaps, perhaps not. Certainly, the Packers had an answer for everything the 49ers did, but because that was only one loss in what became a five-game 49er losing streak to the Packers, it's hard to blame that one on Walsh.

It didn't help that Trestman was also having to fight off advice from Seifert, whose offensive imagination is very limited. The 49ers had returned to the Super Bowl because Seifert had let Shanahan run the offense, but he poked his nose back in when Trestman got the job. Angry because he was being blamed by fans and media who didn't understand the problems he faced, Trestman started rejecting all advice, including notes passed to him by Walsh.

After a year, Walsh had had enough. "When you're a consultant, unless they pay you a huge fee, they don't listen to you," Walsh complained to me. In fact, there was more to it than that.

His attorney, Steve Kay, who probably knows this complex man better than anybody, said privately at the start of the season that Walsh would either be running the team by the end of the year or he'd be gone. When Seifert was forced out after the season, Walsh thought that Policy would put him in charge of the football operations. When that didn't happen, Walsh quit.

That seemed to be that until the Policy–DeBartolo feud became public. Researching an article for *Inside Sports,* I talked to Walsh about it.

"I don't have much respect for either man in this situation," he said. "Eddie has often acted recklessly, but Carmen forgot who was the owner. He was going to the owners' meetings and people were talking to him as if he were the owner."

Nor did Walsh think much of the way Policy was running the 49ers. "You have to have a football man at the top of the operation," he said. "Otherwise the operation gets mired down."

The year he spent as a consultant had convinced Walsh that Policy's system of having several voices in decision making wasn't working, largely because of the strong personality of personnel director Vinny Cerrato. "Vinny just runs over everybody," said Walsh. "Nobody dares stand up to him."

There had been reports, obviously leaks from DeBartolo's advisor/bodyguard Ed Muransky, that Eddie would hire Walsh to run the football operations if Policy were forced out. Walsh said he and Eddie had talked but only in generalities. "He didn't mention any specifics," said Walsh, when we talked.

But when Policy left, Eddie started getting specific about the job. By January 1999, it was only a question of when, not if. Walsh had already talked to John McVay, who had returned on a temporary basis to help the previous fall, to make certain he would stay around. He had talked Terry Donahue into coming on as the personnel director, with the thought that he would take over for Walsh eventually. Cerrato was fired by McVay, but it was obvious that Walsh had been the one who had passed the order.

In late January, the 49ers made it official, with a press conference announcing Walsh's return. By official NFL edict, Eddie couldn't be there, but his presence was felt.

Walsh's Show

THERE WERE many reasons for Walsh not to come back. He had nothing to prove, certainly, and his wife had health problems. His tennis and golf games would have to be put on hold.

Why, then? Part of it was ego. He was tired of hearing people talk about Carmen Policy and the 49ers, and he wanted to remind everybody who was chiefly responsible for the 49ers' success. It was a shame he felt that way. Indeed, the success of the 49ers since his departure was a tribute to him because he had left the organization in great shape.

Walsh also had a genuine concern about the direction the team was taking. For years, the 49ers had been circumventing the salary cap by extending the contracts of veterans, probably beyond the time they'd be playing, especially in the cases of Steve Young and Jerry Rice. They would pay "signing bonuses," which were prorated over the length of the contract, and lower yearly salaries, to lower the cap number.

Other teams were doing the same, of course, but the 49ers were among the most aggressive. Each January, they'd be well over the salary cap and would have to cut players and do more renegotiating of contracts to get back under. This year was the worst ever; the 49ers were $28 million over.

Walsh decided that there would be a minimum of renegotiating and a maximum of slashing. He traded guard Kevin Gogan, a two-year Pro Bowler for the 49ers, to the Miami Dolphins for a fifth-round draft pick. He released defensive end Roy Barker, and Chris Doleman retired, though he later came out of retirement to go back to his original team, the Minnesota Vikings.

Walsh released backup tight end Irv Smith and got Cleveland to take cornerback Antonio Langham, a free-agent bust, in the expansion draft. He also sent them backup quarterback Ty Detmer. At first, the two deals were supposed to be one, but the Detmer part of the deal stalled because Detmer wasn't happy about going to Cleveland and Walsh wanted more compensation than the Browns were willing to give. After Langham had been drafted, Walsh called the Browns and said he'd worked out a new contract with Detmer so he was willing to be traded, and then that deal was made.

Walsh's coach wasn't happy. In his office, Mariucci showed me a roster from the last game with names of departed players crossed out. "I know we have to make some hard decisions," he said, "but we're going to have to start getting bodies in here."

It was the closest Mariucci would come to criticizing Walsh. For the next few months, he would try another tactic, virtually disappearing from the radar screen. There were no Mariucci quotes in the newspapers, just those from Walsh. There were no Mariucci interviews on TV; it was all Walsh.

For those who were close to the scene, there were some disturbing signs. One was that Walsh was not spending much time on the draft or even in the building. He had to spend time with his ailing wife, of course, but even when he was at the 49ers' facility, he didn't show the interest he'd had before. He wasn't taking the time to look at reports himself, and he often dismissed reports from others. In the 1980s, he had made a point of getting input from every assistant and every scout, but not now. He was listening only to those who had been with him in the successful '80s—John

McVay, Bill McPherson, and offensive line coach Bobb Mc-Kittrick, who was seriously ill with liver cancer.

Predraft meetings with the media in the recent past had included the head coach and executives, but this year, it was just Walsh, who was deriding quarterback Jim Druckenmiller but otherwise unable to give much information. Walsh joked sarcastically about the draft-day videos from two years before that had shown Druckenmiller pulling a tractor and made derisive comments about Druckenmiller's arm strength. "Scouts make judgments on how hard a quarterback can throw the ball, but that's the least important factor," he said.

Walsh was frustrated because he had no second-round pick. Though there was talk that he might trade up, he had no leverage with only a low first-round pick.

The draft was a quiet affair for the 49ers. Walsh liked Tulane quarterback Shaun King, but he didn't think King was worth a first-round pick, and King went to the Tampa Bay Buccaneers on the second round.

Walsh took defensive tackle Reggie McGrew on the first round and defensive end Chike Okeafor on the third. He traded fullback Marc Edwards to get an extra pick on the fourth round and took two cornerbacks, Anthony Parker and Pierson Prioleau. With his two fifth-round picks, he took tackle Tyronne Hopson and running back Terry Jackson.

His selections seemed almost whimsical. He picked McGrew though the tackle had had knee problems and refused to work out at the scouting combine, where teams measure and evaluate players. That sent up a red flag with Mariucci and Donahue but not Walsh. (Walsh later said he didn't know about McGrew's bad knee, though the information had been in draft reports by Joel Buchsbaum and Mel Kiper, Jr.) McGrew's knee kept him out of training camp early, and when he seemed finally to be on the mend from that injury, he hurt his elbow and required surgery that sidelined him for the season.

Walsh overrode recommendations by Mariucci and Donahue to pick Parker, who reminded him of former defensive back Eric Wright, who was a real find in the 1981 draft.

On draft day, no comments came from Mariucci. Some wondered if he were even there. He was, but he didn't want to take responsibility for decisions that were not his. It was Walsh's show, for better or for worse.

CHAPTER TWENTY

The Shoulders of Steve Young

BEFORE THE 1999 draft, Bill Walsh held a lunch meeting with a few writers and radio-TV personalities. No great secrets were revealed, but he made one memorable statement: "This franchise is all riding on the shoulders of Steve Young. If something happened to Steve, it would all come tumbling down."

That would prove to be devastatingly accurate.

In the era of the salary cap, all teams are thin, because nobody can stockpile players as the 49ers once did, and the 49ers were now especially vulnerable because their defense had been weakened by injuries and losses in free agency. Their only chance to contend was with their high-powered offense, and Young was the indispensable part of that.

Young on Football

THAT KIND of pressure didn't bother Young, who had worked so hard to get to where he was. He was quite philosophical when I talked to him the next week at mini-camp.

"The older I get, the more I enjoy this game. I realize how

lucky I am to be doing this. When you're younger, you kind of take things for granted. I'm much more aware of what's going on now. I don't mean just in the game but what's happening on the practice field, what's happening in the locker room. I guess you could say I'm just more appreciative of everything."

Young is a very unusual player because of his background, his intelligence, and his education. He took his law education seriously; he was hoping at the time we talked to get time off during training camp to take the bar exam, though he doubted that he would ever practice law.

But despite his intellectual accomplishments, Young was as competitive an athlete as I've known. In training camp after the 49ers had last won the Super Bowl, I asked him why he kept playing, always risking an injury that could affect him the rest of his life, when he had other, less dangerous options.

> Young is a very unusual player because of his background, his intelligence, and his education.

"I love this game and I love competing," he said. "I love it when I get hit and when I hit back. I see kids playing video football games and I want to scream at them, 'No, no, that's not football. It's not the same.'"

He'd had a couple of tough years, with concussions as well as rib and arm injuries that cut into his playing time and hurt his effectiveness at others, but he was coming off a relatively injury-free season and arguably his best in 1998. He was not ready to say '99 would be his last year.

"I'm playing it one year at a time now," he said. "I've taken very good care of myself over the years and I'm trying to conserve myself on the field." He paused and laughed. "I've learned to slide and run out of bounds, which makes the coaches happy. I've never thought it was that big a deal. The bad hits for a quarterback come when it's a surprise, when you're blindsided by a lineman and don't have time to protect yourself. When I'm running and get hit, I'm prepared, and I think I probably give a little punishment myself."

> "One of the things I learned was that you can learn from watching, although that wasn't a lesson I wanted to learn."
>
> —Steve Young

With the passage of time, Young could also be philosophical about his battle with Montana, as well as his battle to gain the support and affection of 49er fans after Joe had left.

"I would have loved to have been playing those four years I sat, but there's a definite reward with staying with this team. I could have forced a trade, but I sensed that in the long run, it would be best for me to stay. That was against all the advice I was getting from my agent, Leigh Steinberg, and my family, but it really has worked out the way I thought it would.

"I look back at some very, very hard times, but I think I grew up a lot. One of the things I learned was that you can learn from watching, although that wasn't a lesson I wanted to learn.

"I was blessed because I followed two quarterbacks I could copy, Jim McMahon in college and Joe Montana. I could do the things they did, not exactly but close enough. I could watch them and repeat it. There were qualities they had that I didn't have that I could learn from. If I was going to be a great quarterback, this might have been the way to do it, though I wouldn't wish it on anybody."

Following Montana was tough, as he could admit now.

"The easiest thing in the world to say was, 'Of course you can't do this, following Montana.' I never let myself think that or say that. I wanted to play long enough to develop my own mark, and I thrived on the idea that I was going to use this as a motivational tool. Now, I feel as indoctrinated in the 49er way of life, the 49er heritage, as anybody can be."

When Young took over for the injured Montana in '91, it was a shock to everybody, players and fans alike.

"It's very difficult to figure a way to make this kind of transition. I never took it personally to the point where I held a grudge, or held any animosity. Fans had an emotional attachment. People who had developed an attachment to Joe in the '80s weren't going to change, but people who developed it in the '90s went to the quarterback at that time. And winning the Super Bowl made a tremendous difference. That's the way you create emotional attachments.

"I loved the fans for their loyalty. They're very intense, very opinionated, very sophisticated. I really appreciate the people who loved the '80s but can also say, 'You know what, I love the '90s, too.'"

He was also pleased at what was happening within the 49er organization. "Look up there," he said, gesturing at the second-floor windows of the 49ers' facility. "Last fall, there was nobody behind those windows. We tried to say that didn't make any difference to us on the field, but we had to wonder what was happening. Now, Bill is back, Terry Donahue is there, John McVay. We can take care of things on the field when we know we've got support from real football people."

Back to Football

THE 49ERS' facility was light years removed from the ramshackle building in Redwood City that had been used when Walsh first came to the team. The building was completed in August 1987 and sat on 11 acres adjacent to the Great America amusement park in Santa Clara.

The two-story, 52,000-square-foot building (more than three times as large as the former headquarters) has marble floors, spacious locker rooms, large workout areas, and two practice fields.

The head coach's office is on the northeastern corner of the build-ing, overlooking the practice fields, and a balcony runs along that side of the building. There is a huge desk, an overstuffed couch and chairs around a coffee table, and a conference table in the spa-cious room. It also has a small refrigerator and a bathroom.

Walsh, who always needed something to fret over, had worried when the team first moved into the facility that its size would cre-ate a psychological distance between coaches because they weren't as physically close as they had been at Redwood City. That hadn't happened, and the coaches now had the advantage of working with the best technological facilities when they were breaking down films and putting together game plans.

Steve Mariucci now had the big corner office that Walsh had been the first to occupy, and Walsh was down the hall in the less spacious but still quite comfortable office that had been used by Carmen Policy. It, too, had a conference table. When I'd talked to Policy, it had always been at that table, and Walsh directed me there, too, when I visited him one day.

"The emphasis is back on football now," he said, and in case I missed the reference, he added, "Carmen had gotten quite in-volved in league matters the last few years. John York will be rep-resenting us at league meetings, and we have others who can take care of the community concerns. We need to get back to football.

"I think we've got a good group here. I told John McVay that I wouldn't come back unless he did. Terry is working out very well. He's just a very fine football administrator. He ran a top-notch program at UCLA for 20 years. He knows what he's doing."

It was his relationship with the current 49er coach that con-cerned me, though, and I asked him how he and Mariucci were working together.

"I think we've got a good relationship," he said. "Steve gets along with everybody and I think I get along well with people."

Many around the 49ers, though, doubted that Walsh would

be able to resist doing some actual coaching, whether it was advice to quarterbacks or advice on game plans, but he insisted he'd do neither.

"I'll be on the practice field at times, of course, but the most I would do would be to visit with an assistant about a technique," he said.

"I'll be in regular contact with the coaches to make sure we're on the same page, but I'm not going to make suggestions on game plans. I don't even want to know what kind of strategy they have. I think Steve and (offensive coordinator) Marty Mornhinweg have certainly proved they can run an offense and I'm confident Jim Mora [the new defensive coordinator] will do well with the defense. He's on the fast track to be a head coach."

Walsh said he might be able to help in the area of veteran players with problematic personalities, such as Charles Haley, who was about to be signed, or the always-temperamental Jerry Rice, over whom Mariucci had little control. "I might be able to help Jerry adjust to his new [reduced] role," said Walsh. "I think I can probably say some things to him that the coaches might not be able to."

Publicly, Mariucci was also saying he and Walsh could work together, but I had my doubts. I had heard from players that Mariucci spoke frequently of having three former coaches in the front office (though McVay hadn't coached in 20 years), second-guessing his moves. I had no doubt that Walsh, despite his words, would be questioning Mariucci during the season.

> For 20 years, Walsh had been insistent that the coach should be the one with ultimate control of the operation. . . . Now, he was talking differently.

For 20 years, Walsh had been insistent that the coach should be the one with ultimate control of the operation. I had been in his office when he had advised friends not to take jobs where they didn't have control. Now, though he had reiterated that same principle when he was brought back to the 49ers, he was talking differently.

"The general manager and coach are always going to have some differences," he said, "because the coach is necessarily thinking of winning the next game while the general manager has to make some long-range plans."

Didn't sound like the coach would have the final word this time. Walsh, in fact, admitted that they had clashed in at least one instance: the trading of fullback Marc Edwards to get an additional pick in the fourth round. "Steve didn't want to trade Edwards, but we needed cornerbacks," he said. "We only had two cornerbacks signed at the time, and with our cap problems, we couldn't go after a high-priced free agent. [The 49ers took two corners on the fourth round, Anthony Parker and Pierson Prioleau.] I wouldn't have traded Edwards, though, if I didn't know we could pick up Tommy Vardell, who's a little faster and as good a blocker, though he is older."

There were other differences of opinion. Mariucci would have preferred to keep backup quarterback Ty Detmer, whom Walsh had traded to the Cleveland Browns.

Walsh raved about the quarterback he had signed, Jeff Garcia, a former San Jose State quarterback who had starred in the Canadian Football League; Walsh remembered Garcia from his games against Walsh's Stanford team earlier in the decade. "He's got the ability to make a play when the regular offense breaks down," he said. "I'm not saying he's the equal of Steve and Joe, but it's the same type of ability they've shown. That's especially important for a backup because he doesn't get a chance to take many snaps in practice, so he doesn't have the command of the whole offense that the starter has, [and] he has to be able to free-lance." For his part, Mariucci was still reserving judgment because he hadn't seen Garcia in a game.

So, there was obviously some tension, but Walsh had reportedly been deferential to Mariucci in staff meetings and had emphasized the head coach's importance to
the assistants.

For his part, Mariucci didn't seem
to have the desire to have total control that many NFL coaches want;
and, as with Dwight Clark in his first
two years, he was accustomed to
dealing with a general manager who
had control of player deals. On occasion, Clark had had to tell Mariucci
that a player the coach wanted to
bring in for a tryout wouldn't be
brought in, either because of his salary or personality problems, so
it was not that Mariucci had always had his way before.

> The *Chronicle's* Ira
> Miller told Mariucci
> that if Walsh decided
> to stay beyond 1999,
> the coach should hide
> Walsh's old Stanford
> media guides.

The situation now was more extreme, though. Clark had never
gone public with disagreements. With Walsh, everybody knew the
moves he was making, and players became identified as his players, not Mariucci's. Tommy Vardell even went into Mariucci's
office and said, "I know Bill wanted me and you didn't, but please
give me a chance." Mariucci did, but Vardell didn't have much left;
he spent most of the season on the inactive list.

Walsh was bringing back players with whom he had a history.
Mariucci talked of keeping defensive end Chris Doleman, who'd
had 15 sacks the year before, but Walsh didn't listen; he brought
back Haley, who had been a Walsh draft pick in the '80s. Like
Vardell, Haley had very little left. Mariucci tried to rest him—he
even told Haley he didn't have to come to training camp, and
Haley showed up late—but he was almost a total washout.

Even more telling were the former Stanford players Walsh
brought back, including reserve quarterback Steve Stenstrom. The
Chronicle's Ira Miller told Mariucci that if Walsh decided to stay

beyond 1999, the coach should hide Walsh's old Stanford media guides.

The mounting friction between Walsh and Mariucci was shoved into the background that week when the 49ers learned that running back Garrison Hearst, slowly rehabbing from his broken ankle in the playoff game in December, might have a bone disease similar to the one that had ended Bo Jackson's career. The 49ers were looking at the possibility of their two top runners being gone, because Terry Kirby had been an earlier salary cap cut.

Quickly, the team brought in four running back candidates: Lawrence Phillips, Terry Allen, Harvey Williams, and Charlie Garner. Allen and Williams were quickly dismissed. Garner was signed, but he came with a big question mark. He was an excellent broken field runner but he wasn't big, no more than 185 pounds, and he had often been injured. The 49ers doubted that he could be an every-down back. Walsh wanted protection in case Garner joined Hearst on the injured list, so he took a long look at Phillips.

Phillips had been an All-American at Nebraska and highly touted in the draft of 1996; he went to the St. Louis Rams with the sixth pick. But he had been out of shape and ineffective, and the Rams cut him the next year.

Phillips got another chance in 1998 with the Miami Dolphins, but again he showed little, and he was cut by the Dolphins.

From there, Phillips had gone to the NFL Europe League and played very well in the spring of '99. Were that and his collegiate success an indication of his ability, or was he just the kind of player who looked good against inferior players? Opinion was sharply divided around the league, but Walsh was impressed by a Phillips workout at the 49ers' facility, saying he was definitely the best of the backs they had brought in.

In the Bay Area, though, Phillips's ability wasn't as big a question as his character. At Nebraska, he had become enraged because a former girlfriend was with another man, and he dragged her down two flights of stairs by her hair. In Miami, he was accused of punching a woman on the dance floor when she resisted his advances.

This was a player the 49ers wanted to sign in probably the most politically correct area in the country? In the background, you could hear the feminist groups in the Bay Area sharpening their knives, in case Phillips was signed. It looked like a long season ahead.

CHAPTER TWENTY-ONE

Goodbye, Eddie

L<small>AWRENCE</small> P<small>HILLIPS</small> was signed and, before him, Charles Haley. It was a startling departure for Bill Walsh, who had always stressed character in signing players. Phillips and Haley weren't poster boys for character, unless it was bad.

Walsh, who had been ahead of other coaches in so many areas, had brought in Dr. Harry Edwards, a sociologist from the UC Berkeley faculty, to test potential draft choices in the mid-1980s. Edwards's tests revealed character traits, enabling the team to draft players who fit the 49ers' mode.

Sometimes, players slipped through the cracks. Though he had played a key role in the 49ers' last Super Bowl win, running back Ricky Watters had such a "me-first" attitude that the 49ers allowed him to leave in free agency. Tim McKyer, a cornerback with the same attitude, was traded. And Haley, whose volatile temperament went totally out of control in '91, was traded to the Dallas Cowboys; perhaps because his personality fit the Cowboys profile so well, he played an important role in their Super Bowl championships.

Walsh consulted with Edwards, who talked to both Phillips and Haley and assured Walsh they would not be a problem to the team. Nonetheless, Walsh was taking a risk that the two players would upset the team chemistry, a more fragile element than it had been when he coached. In Walsh's time, not only did stars like Joe Montana, Steve Young, Roger Craig, and Jerry Rice set the tone with their work ethic and competitiveness, but a nucleus of only slightly less talented players, with the 49ers for several years, also helped mold team attitude. In the era of free agency, though, rosters turned over so frequently that it was hard keeping a nucleus together.

At the press conference announcing Phillips's signing, Walsh praised Phillips's attitude but added that he had no margin for error: If Phillips skipped a meeting or missed practice without a good excuse, he would be cut immediately. But, said Walsh, the 49ers were not going to watch every move Phillips made. "We're not going to baby-sit him," Walsh insisted.

Funny thing, though—after a couple of days in camp, Craig showed up as Phillips's shadow, going everywhere that Phillips went. Walsh explained that Craig was doing it because he liked being around camp and wanted to make sure that Phillips made it, since the two had both been star backs for the Nebraska Cornhuskers in college. Former 'Huskers stuck together, Walsh said. "We're not paying Roger to do this," he said. That wasn't Craig's understanding, though. "I'm sure something will be worked out," he said.

> In the era of free agency, . . . rosters turned over so frequently that it was hard keeping a nucleus together.

Even with these signings, the 49ers were hardly the bad boys of the NFL, where most teams overlooked player transgressions if the player was good enough to contribute. With Jimmy Johnson as coach, the Miami Dolphins had signed free-agent wide receiver Tony Martin, who was facing a felony charge for dealing drugs (he was convicted in the late spring of '99) and had so many legal problems that one of the coaches said, only half jokingly, that their offense was dependent on keeping their receivers out of jail.

But the year before, Johnson had released Phillips, not because of his off-field problems but because he wasn't a very good back. Many observers thought that Walsh was taking a risk on a back who wouldn't be much help, but Walsh insisted Phillips would be a star with the 49ers.

In the first week of camp, Phillips had another problem: His weight was down to 208. "We think he's too light to be effective," said Mariucci in a post-practice meeting with writers. "He's basically on a fish-and-vegetables diet, and he's lost a lot of weight. That's not good for a football player. I might go on it, though."

Mariucci's banter couldn't hide a real concern: that Phillips was no longer the back who had been a star in college. He had been a slashing runner, not an elusive one. His weight loss had improved his speed, but he had no real moves and he was no longer strong enough to break tackles.

> Eddie was a beloved figure to 49er players in the 1980s, before the salary cap cut into his free-spending ways.

The Phillips controversy was shoved aside the first weekend in camp when word came from Cleveland that a settlement had been reached in the DeBartolo family feud that would end Eddie DeBartolo's role as 49ers' owner.

Ten years earlier, that news would have hit the team hard. Eddie was a beloved figure to 49er players in the 1980s, before the salary cap cut into his free-spending ways. He had spent money not just on salaries but also on operational items that are not obvious to fans: The 49ers always traveled on chartered planes and stayed in first-class hotels, and players all had single rooms. DeBartolo had elaborate ring ceremonies (when players got their

Super Bowl rings) in Hawaii and the Broadmoor Springs resort in Colorado. He often invited favorite players back to Youngstown for charitable events that involved the DeBartolo family, and they returned home with expensive gifts. He would take players with him to the casinos in Nevada and give them thousands in gambling money.

Sports attorney Leigh Steinberg was close to the 49ers throughout the DeBartolo years because there was a mutual trust on both sides. Steinberg's office even gave salary cap tips to Carmen Policy, based on the work of Scott Parker, who runs Steinberg's Berkeley office. "Eddie DeBartolo brought a unique spirit to the franchise because he truly loved the players," Steinberg told me after the DeBartolo deal had been made. "A lot of owners aren't comfortable around players or they're jealous of them, but Eddie loved talking to them. When he stood in the hallway of the dressing room to greet each one individually as they came in, that really meant something to them.

"The great contrast came in the '89 Super Bowl in Miami. Eddie paid for a charter flight for the players and another plane for the families. He put the players up in rooms by themselves and had rooms in another hotel for their families. Cincinnati came down in one plane, and the players all had roommates. That kind of thing makes a big difference to players. Players heard about that on other teams, and everybody wanted to play for the 49ers."

That was the '80s. In the '90s, the salary cap—and financial problems within the DeBartolo Corporation early in the decade—put a brake on Eddie's free-spending approach. As he aged, he was less inclined to spend time around the players, and his ill-fated gambling ventures took him further from the team, so he was almost never at the practice facility at Santa Clara and not often in the dressing room after games, either. The only ones who remembered DeBartolo as an active owner were Steve Young and Jerry Rice.

Young was visibly affected by the news. After a long pause, he said, "Too bad. He's one of the good guys. When I came here in '87 and he greeted me, you just got the sense that something very, very cool was happening. He'll go down as one of the great owners in sports history."

Walsh's response was much more measured. "I could see this coming," he said. "All of us could. I don't think there's any surprise here. I wish Eddie well. He's always going to be a good friend of mine. And in the meantime, the Yorks have control, and I'm certainly prepared to work with them."

And so, Eddie was gone, brought down by his own excesses. The show would go on.

CHAPTER TWENTY-TWO

Who's in Charge Here?

BOTH BILL Walsh and Steve Mariucci hid the friction between them, but it existed.

A good part of it came from the quarterback situation. They agreed that Steve Young was a great quarterback, but they were far apart on the other quarterbacks.

Though Mariucci kept quiet publicly, those close to him knew that he was seething because he had been put in such an awkward position with Jim Druckenmiller, and all because of Walsh's ego.

By the time Walsh came back to the 49ers as general manager, he was firmly identified as the champion of Jake Plummer, who had been an almost instant success with the Arizona Cardinals. Never mind that Walsh had seen Plummer as a good second-round pick, not first round. He certainly wasn't going to remind anybody of that. Meanwhile, the Druckenmiller pick was blamed on those surrounding Carmen Policy.

In that circumstance, trying as he was to erase any of Policy's connection to the team, Walsh could not resist bashing Druckenmiller. If he'd kept quiet, he might have been able to trade Druckenmiller before the draft to get an additional pick, perhaps even one in the second round. But it was obvious to the football world that he wanted to dump Druckenmiller, so the quarterback's trade value was virtually nil.

Mariucci, though, was the one who had to try to find playing time in the exhibition season for Druckenmiller, who had fallen to fourth on the depth chart behind Young, Jeff Garcia, and Steve Stenstrom.

Walsh was finally able to trade Druckenmiller to Miami just before the 1999 season started for a sixth-round draft pick. It was a good trade for Druckenmiller, who went to a team with a drop-back offense—a good fit for him. But it was nowhere near the trade the 49ers could have made if Walsh had just kept his mouth shut. (Walsh had a disingenuous explanation after I wrote about the Druckenmiller fiasco in the *Chronicle:* He claimed he was trying to run down Druckenmiller so thoroughly that nobody would claim him when he was put on waivers; if he cleared waivers, then the 49ers would not be stuck with his salary cap number.)

> "I woke up in the night before the game in a cold sweat, wondering what we'd do if Steve got hurt in this game."
>
> —Steve Mariucci

Meanwhile, Mariucci worried because the 49ers were back to where they had been two years earlier, when they had no proven quarterback behind Young. Ty Detmer's presence had given the 49ers a safety net in the 1998 season because he was an experienced NFL quarterback, but now Mariucci was worrying again about Young's health. He kept the quarterback out of the final preseason game against Denver. "I woke up in the night before the game in a cold sweat, wondering what we'd do if Steve got hurt in this game," said Mariucci. "There was no way I was going to play him."

In the first game of the season, Young had probably his worst game as a 49ers' starter, as the 49ers were humiliated by

Jacksonville, 41–3. Was it rust, or was he showing his age? "I don't think we looked this bad on offense even in '79," said Walsh. Rumors were flying that Walsh had brought in Terry Donahue as a possible replacement for Mariucci. I doubted that, but it was obvious it was not a happy time for the 49ers.

It reminded me of George Seifert's fears in 1992 that, if Walsh came back, he would be such a strong presence that he would overwhelm the coach. That's what was happening to Mariucci. The year before, there had been no question that the 49ers were Mariucci's team. Now players were saying privately that they didn't know who was in charge, Mariucci or Walsh.

Walsh didn't help matters when he went on the field one day to do a little individual coaching of players. He later denied that he was actually coaching, but there were writers who saw it. That only confused the players more. They still liked Mariucci, whose main strength as a coach had always been his ability to get his players to give their best for him, but they wondered.

It got worse. In their next game, the 49ers pulled out a win over New Orleans, but Young took a ferocious pounding, as the 49ers' pass protection broke down completely. The offensive line was still a work in progress with guard Kevin Gogan gone and tackle Kirk Scrafford retired. Second-year player Jeremy Newberry, who had been injured for most of the '98 season, had been shifted from guard to right tackle, Young's blind side. Newberry had played well in the exhibition season and looked good in practice, but he had a terrible game against the Saints, who seemed to be blitzing on nearly every down.

When the blitzers broke through, the 49er backs seldom picked them up. The departed Marc Edwards had been a very good blocker, much better than his replacement, Tommy Vardell. Charlie Garner was too small to be much of a blocker, and Lawrence Phillips was worse.

Then, in the next game, on Monday night in Arizona against

the Cardinals, the worst happened: Just before halftime, a blitz by cornerback Aneas Williams was not picked up by Phillips, and Young was hit and knocked to the turf. His head hit the helmet of teammate Dave Fiore, and he was knocked out for about 30 seconds.

Garcia came on to preserve the victory as Mariucci held Young out for the rest of that game. Garcia played very well in the 49ers' next game, a two-point win over Tennessee, and as well as could be expected when the Rams snapped a 17-game 49er winning streak in the 49ers–Rams series with a resounding 42–20 win in St. Louis.

The Niners Without Young

BUT THE big news was Young, who was consulting doctors about his future. The outlook was worse than the public knew because the 49ers were not forthright about Young's condition. In fact, the concussion in the Arizona game was the second he had suffered; his first one had come in the New Orleans game when he was hit by blitzing safety Chris Hewitt, who hit Young helmet-to-helmet. The closest the 49ers would ever come to acknowledging the first concussion was Walsh's comment two weeks after the fact that he had thought Young sounded as if he were suffering from the after-effects of a concussion when they talked on the phone the Monday morning after the New Orleans game.

After that conversation, Walsh summoned the team doctors to look at the video of the Saints game, especially a play on which Young was knocked flat on his back and didn't get up immediately. When the doctors told Walsh that Young was only "resting," Walsh angrily told them Young had been knocked out and that if anything like that happened again, he was to be taken out of the game immediately—as he was in the game against the Cardinals, of course.

The double concussion was significant because the danger to the player expands exponentially when there are back-to-back concussions. There was even concern by the doctor Young consulted, Dr. Gary Steinberg of the Stanford Medical School, that a third concussion might be fatal. It would take at least two months away from football for Young to be out of danger. Dr. Steinberg recommended that he sit out the rest of the season.

> The team would soon take a nose dive that made it pointless to even think of bringing [Young] back during the '99 season.

For different reasons, this information was not revealed by either the 49ers or Young. The 49ers said only that Young would miss the next game, and the announcements after that made it seem that it was a week-to-week decision for Young. Perhaps they were hoping he would be available for the stretch run, but the team would soon take a nose dive that made it pointless to even think of bringing him back during the '99 season.

Meanwhile, Young's family and friends were advising him to retire, but it was a tough decision for him to make. He had had a great season the year before, perhaps his best, and he had no reason to think he couldn't play at least two more years at a top level. Every moment was golden to Young because he'd had to sit on the bench behind Joe Montana for four years in the middle of his career. He had come into the season thinking Super Bowl, and now he was having to think about retirement.

Walsh again took center stage, telling writers that he might have to decide that Young couldn't play any more, for his own good. No doubt about who was in charge here.

At the same time, those close to Walsh thought he might walk away at the end of the year and that Donahue (and, of course, John McVay) would go with him, because they couldn't work with John York. Privately, Walsh was saying that York was driving him crazy with constant questions about the operation and niggling criticisms. Just one big happy family.

Walsh seemed to be distancing himself from the team already when he embraced St. Louis coach Dick Vermeil in the dressing room after the Rams' win and told him, "You're going all the way, baby!" Walsh and Vermeil had been friends since both were assistants on the Stanford staff in the '60s, and Walsh had pushed hard to get Vermeil the job in St. Louis. Still, it seemed odd for Walsh to be in a congratulatory mood when his team had just been thrashed. Later he explained that he didn't realize his remarks would be so public, though there were TV cameras in the dressing room, along with several reporters. It was a ludicrous statement for a man who had always known exactly how his actions and comments would be taken by the media.

Meanwhile, York was clearly enjoying his role with the 49ers. First a successful doctor, York then moved into the corporate business world and did well; but within the corporation and in Youngstown generally, he was inevitably seen primarily as Denise DeBartolo's husband, and so he was seeking to make his mark with the 49ers. He talked about wanting to know every aspect of the operation, and it was obvious he wanted to be involved in the whole operation, not just the business side.

Though York didn't comment publicly about his brother-in-law, Eddie DeBartolo, his actions spoke loudly. Pictures of Eddie celebrating the Super Bowl wins with Walsh and George Seifert disappeared from the lobby of the 49ers' facility in Santa Clara. After stories made the disappearance public, the pictures reappeared. An employee explained that they had been out for cleaning, but York said there had just been a miscommunication within the office and the pictures should not have been removed, an explanation that only those still clinging to the tooth fairy myth believed.

Sharp-eyed writers also noticed a change in the 49ers' media guide: Lisa DeBartolo, Eddie's oldest daughter, was no longer a vice-president for the club, though she remained in charge of the DeBartolo Foundation. Her vice-president title had been merely an honorary one, in deference to her father. With Eddie gone, the rationale for Lisa's title had disappeared, too, but that only added to the tension felt by Lisa and her younger sister, Nikki, who worked with her on the foundation. By the end of the season, both of Eddie's daughters would leave the organization, moving to Florida to be near their father.

On the field, it got worse, as Young remained on the sidelines and the 49ers suffered an embarrassing loss to the Carolina Panthers, with former 49ers' coach George Seifert getting his 100th win. Seifert earned his 100 wins in fewer games, just 134, than had any other coach in history; the previous record was Don Shula, in 136 games.

Young's value to the team was shown almost more by his absence than by his presence. As long as he was there, the weaknesses of the team weren't so apparent. His brilliance, along with the record-breaking running of Garrison Hearst, allowed the 49ers to overcome their defensive problems well enough to finish 12–4 the year before. With neither Young nor Hearst available, the 49ers were in trouble.

Though not so consistent a runner as Hearst, Charlie Garner was having a good season, but there was no way the 49ers could replace Young. Garcia was not so accurate a passer, and he lacked Young's ability to scramble and still make a big throw downfield. Garcia could throw on the run when the play was designed that way, but when he started scrambling, he kept running. That destroyed the continuity of the offense.

Far from the Glory Days

THE 49ERS of 1999 were a far cry from the team that had dominated the '80s, as could be seen graphically in a comparison of rosters with the 1989 team that had won two straight Super Bowls.

The 1989 team had Jerry Rice, then the best in NFL history, and the underrated John Taylor at wide receiver, with Brent Jones, who caught 40 passes for 500 yards as a tight end that year. The '99 team had nobody the equal of any of the three; Terrell Owens, the best receiver, would have been no more than a backup in '89.

The offensive line in '89 had tackles Harris Barton and Steve Wallace, guard Guy McIntyre, and center Jesse Sapolu. Guard Ray Brown was the only one from the '99 team who could have broken into that unit.

Joe Montana was the quarterback in '89, backed up by Young and Steve Bono. Nobody had ever been better than the Montana of '89, and what depth! Roger Craig and Tom Rathman were the backs; a healthy Hearst was better than Craig, but Rathman was far superior to the 49er fullbacks in '98 and '99.

Defensively, the earlier team had linemen Pierce Holt, Jeff Stover, and a young Charles Haley. Only Bryant Young on the '99 team compared to that group. The '99 linebacking crew of Ken Norton, Winfred Tubbs, and Lee Woodall was good, but the '89 group—Keena Turner, Mike Walters, and Bill Romanowski—was better.

The secondary wasn't close. The '89 team had Ronnie Lott at safety and cornerbacks Don Griffin, Tim McKyer, and Eric Wright. Until he suffered a midseason injury that left him partially paralyzed, Jeff Fuller played the kind of linebacker/strong safety position that Tim McDonald played for the '99 group. McDonald and second-year safety Lance Schulters, who would make the Pro Bowl, were the only defensive backs who could have made the team in '89.

Yet, as long as Young was playing, the 49ers could still think they had a chance to get to the Super Bowl. Without him, it was obvious they'd be scrambling to finish at .500. It was getting ugly, and not just on the field. In the front office, Walsh was scrambling to make sure he didn't get the blame for the disaster in the making.

Not the Walsh of Old

WALSH WAS contradicting his lifelong principle that the coach should be the master of his fate; but, of course, he had held onto that principle when he was the coach. Now that he was the general manager, he was undermining Mariucci, consciously or not.

Part of his interference took place behind closed doors as he talked directly to the team on at least two occasions, usurping the coach's responsibility.

He also went public with some implied criticism of Mariucci and his staff in an interview that appeared the morning of the Carolina game, saying it was up to the coaching staff to figure ways to protect the quarterback, whether it was Young or Garcia. He defended his acquisition of Phillips, though he had been a virtual nonentity. In fact, Phillips's biggest contribution was a negative: the missed block that resulted in Young's concussion.

In an interview with the *Chronicle*'s Ira Miller, Walsh tried to lay the blame for what had happened on salary-cap problems, the obvious implication being that Carmen Policy and Dwight Clark had created the problems, leaving him helpless.

Miller himself had been critical of Policy and Clark, but he noted that at least they'd had a plan: Each year, they tried to bring in free agents to give Young enough support to give him a chance to get to the Super Bowl. They hadn't made any pretense of building for the future. When Eddie DeBartolo was the owner in charge, they couldn't. Eddie demanded immediate success; after the first Super Bowl, he'd never been satisfied with anything less.

With Eddie gone—and it had been obvious before Walsh came

back that he was on the way out—Walsh was no longer under that kind of pressure. Yet, aside from all the players he'd either traded or released to lower the cap pressure, he hadn't changed very much. As Miller noted, the 49ers would still have $18 million to trim in cap obligations before the next season, and they had $60 million in bonus money due the next season, more even than the $52 million in '99.

Few of Walsh's moves had paid off. Haley and Marvin Washington had been brought in to help at defensive end, but Haley had done nothing and Washington had not been a factor before he was knocked out for the year with an injury in the St. Louis game. Tommy Vardell had been replaced at fullback by second-year back Fred Beasley. Cornerback Mark McMillian was released after the Carolina game, on the day of the trading deadline; he had been the worst player in a pathetic secondary.

Probably nobody better symbolized the 49ers' mistakes on player evaluation than wide receiver J. J. Stokes.

In 1995, the 49ers had traded away their No. 1 pick for the next year to move up to the sixth slot in the draft to grab Stokes. If you make that kind of move, you have to get a player who will be a standout for years to come, but wide receiver is usually the easiest position to fill; each year, there are several good players available in the draft at that position. Stokes had been an excellent player at UCLA, using his size (6'4") to make catches against taller defenders. But he had only average speed for a receiver; and with the 49ers, he had been only an average receiver.

In retrospect, the puzzling aspect was that the 49ers already had a very similar receiver on their roster, 6'6" Ed McCaffrey, a former Stanford player. They let McCaffrey get away and drafted Stokes, but in the four seasons Stokes played for the Niners and McCaffrey played for the Denver Broncos, McCaffrey had more catches, yardage, and touchdowns.

In effect, Stokes had cost the 49ers two first-round picks. If they'd kept McCaffrey and passed on Stokes, they'd have had first-round picks in '95 and '96 that they could presumably have used to get more productive players.

Then Walsh compounded the error after he came back by re-signing Stokes, paying him a $4.5 million signing bonus. Walsh hoped to keep the receiving corps together for Young, reasoning that the 49ers' only chance was for their offense to be so productive that it would make up for their defensive weaknesses. It would have been better, though, if the Niners had gone with Mark Harris, who was probably 90 percent of the receiver that Stokes was, and used the money to get help in the secondary or the offensive line.

When he came back, Walsh spoke of the importance of the draft and the need to rebuild the team with young talent, but his draft was still a huge question mark. His No. 1 pick, defensive tackle Reggie McGrew, and fourth-round pick Anthony Parker, for whom he had high hopes, were injured and out for the season. Defensive end Chike Okeafor (No. 3) had been injured in the off-season and had hardly played. None of the drafted players had made a noticeable contribution in the first six games of the season.

Walsh spoke glowingly of Jeff Garcia when he had been signed in the spring, but now that Garcia was playing, Walsh backed off, saying that he had thought of Garcia only as the perfect backup for Young and that he wasn't sure Garcia would be the long-term answer for the 49ers.

The 49ers had made what seemed a surprisingly good pickup with rookie free agent Damon Griffin, a wide receiver who had the speed to stretch defenses that other 49er receivers lacked. But Griffin was cut before the start of the season, caught up in the numbers game because Druckenmiller was still on the roster. Mariucci told me shortly after Griffin was cut that he had wanted to keep the young receiver and would have if the Druckenmiller trade had been made a few days earlier. Griffin was claimed by Cincinnati and played well for the Bengals in the early season.

It would have been unfair to blame Walsh for all the 49er problems because nobody could have stepped into the situation he inherited and turned it around immediately. But his moves hadn't improved the team, and he wasn't even following the strategy he had outlined; in effect, he'd delayed the necessary rebuilding program by a year.

> It would have been unfair to blame Walsh for all the 49er problems because nobody could have stepped into the situation he inherited and turned it around immediately.

Two things were obvious: (1) Walsh was no longer the innovative thinker and decisive administrator he had been in the '80s; and (2) he was determined to find a scapegoat for the team's problems, whether it was the departed Policy or Mariucci, or both. It was not pretty, and it was saddening to those of us who had admired Walsh so extravagantly over the years.

CHAPTER TWENTY-THREE

Could Things
Be Any Worse?

STEVE YOUNG was in denial. Though he was still suffering some post-concussion symptoms, including headaches, a month after being knocked unconscious in the Arizona game, he still harbored hopes of resuming his career in the last part of the season.

Privately, Young was being advised by his family and friends to retire. (His agent, Leigh Steinberg, had actually advised him to retire in '97 because he feared for his health. Steinberg was always concerned about the health of his football clients because he had seen what could happen to those who continued playing after serious injuries. One client, Ken Easley, a defensive back who had played for the Seattle Seahawks, suffered kidney damage when he took excessive pain medication for his injuries.)

Publicly, Young was also being told he should retire by newspaper columnists and even the editorial writer for the *San Francisco Chronicle,* who took time off from advising voters whom they should choose for mayor.

The harshest advice came from *Chronicle* columnist C. W. Nevius, who accused Young of being selfish. "He is starting to look like someone who cannot bear to leave the spotlight," wrote Nevius. "What other motivation can he have?"

Nevius went on to criticize Young for the example he was setting for young players. A 15-year-old high school player, Joseph Barajas, who had suffered previous concussions, had just died from a concussion received in a game. "Would Barajas have returned to football after a concussion if the biggest star in local football hadn't done so?" asked Nevius.

Young was not ready to take anybody's advice to retire.

Young was not ready to take anybody's advice to retire, as he showed when he met with writers at the Santa Clara facility in October 1999. He described the memory tests that doctors were asking him to perform, and he refused to say that he was ready to pull the curtain on the season or his career.

Young said he wanted to take more time to evaluate his condition. "It's a function of time," he said. "It's October, not December. There's time, and every doctor will say that time is the major factor in recovering."

None of us at the press conference thought that Young would be able to return. We weren't happy about that. Even those who had originally been critical of Young's play, when he first took over for the injured Joe Montana, had come to appreciate both his accomplishments and the enthusiasm with which he played, as well as his cooperation with the media. Young would talk to those who criticized him as well as those who praised him, a marked contrast to Joe Montana, who didn't talk to any writer who criticized him. Montana hadn't talked to me since 1986. (Young finally made an exception to his pattern three weeks later. Speaking to writers before a game with the Saints in New Orleans, he pointedly ignored questions from Nevius. When the writer asked why, Young said, "You're asking that after the column you wrote?")

After the Santa Clara press conference, Rich Walcoff, color man for the KGO radio broadcasts of 49er games, told me of a conversation he'd had with Young the day after he'd been knocked out in the Arizona game. "I asked him how he was," said Walcoff, "and he insisted, 'I'm all right, I'm all right. I can play.' I knew he couldn't, but he was absolutely insistent that he get back in there to help the team. He's a real warrior."

Steve Mariucci didn't expect Young to return. Speaking for the team, as Bill Walsh took a temporary backseat, Mariucci said, "We would all love to have him healthy and playing again, but realistically, that's a long shot."

Young wasn't being realistic about either himself or the team. He was such an important player and team leader that he obviously felt his return would make a big difference. Nobody else thought so. The 49ers simply had too many problems.

After his concussion, Young watched from the 49er sidelines. Spotting him during the lopsided loss to the Minnesota Vikings, I thought he had to be thinking that there was no way he could go back on the field behind that offensive line, which simply could not pass-protect. But Young felt he was letting his team down by not playing, and he was willing to go out there when (or if) he got medical clearance.

> Young felt he was letting his team down by not playing, and he was willing to go out there when (or if) he got medical clearance.

It seemed unlikely the 49ers would allow him to play in '99 even if he did get a clearance. Walsh had second-guessed himself many times for allowing Joe Montana to come back early from back surgery in 1986. At the time, of course, Walsh was operating under the coach's mentality of needing to win the next game. Now, as general manager, he could afford to take the long view, and he wasn't going to risk Young's health, no matter how eager the quarterback was to return.

Neither was Mariucci, who had spoken many times of his

concern for Young's health. Mariucci truly cared about his players, in a way I hadn't seen since John Madden was coaching the
Raiders in the '70s.

Privately, Mariucci wondered whether Garcia would even last
the season. Nine years younger than Young, Garcia was better able
to absorb the punishment, but the first-year quarterback had
taken a terrible beating in the loss to Minnesota. Mariucci took
him out in the fourth quarter and put in Steve Stenstrom, to keep
Garcia from absorbing any more hits.

Medical Snafus

OTHER INJURIES raised questions about the 49ers medical staff.
Garrison Hearst's absence was critical, because his running had
taken the pressure off Young. Why did it take so long to recognize
that Hearst wasn't recovering from the broken ankle suffered
in the January playoff game against Atlanta? By the time the
problems were spotted, Hearst had to have another operation, effectively knocking him out for the '99 season. Aside from his running, he was also an effective blocker. Unlike Lawrence Phillips,
he wouldn't have missed the blitzing linebacker who hit Young in
the Arizona game.

When tight end Greg Clark was injured in an August 19 exhibition game, he was first diagnosed by the 49er medical staff as
having bruised ribs. Then, it was decided he had one cracked rib.
Finally, it was discovered he actually had five cracked ribs, and he
missed the first three games of the season, a critical loss for the
49ers because Clark was the best blocking tight end in the league
and also an underrated receiver; he had been a junior college All-
American because of his receiving skills. As both a blocker and a
receiver, Clark was far superior to any other tight end on the 49er
roster.

When Clark returned to action, he was encased in a light body cast; but in the Minnesota game, he was injured again and rushed to a Minneapolis hospital late in the game. Dr. Robert Gamburd, a 49er physician, told the media after the game that Clark's injury, which was life-threatening at the time, was a punctured lung, caused by a fragment from his fractured rib.

At the hospital, doctors told Clark a different story: the needle with which Dr. Gamburd had administered a pain-blocking shot (requested by Clark) penetrated the lung tissue, causing a small hole. During the game, air had escaped through the hole, and the lung collapsed.

Hospital doctors also told Clark that he had not suffered any further injury to his ribs during the game, which also contradicted Dr. Gamburd's theory.

Shortly after getting the injection, Clark had complained to Young that something was wrong. In the second quarter, he told teammate Mark Harris that the Vikings must be spiking the water "because it tastes like kerosene." That apparently was the result of pain medication coming up in Clark's throat.

Clark remained in the Minneapolis hospital for four days after the game. He and his agent, Steve Baker, did not divulge any details of his injury and hospital stay to the media, not wanting to be critical of the 49er medical staff.

The next week was a bye week for the 49ers; and on that Monday, Dr. Gamburd repeated his assertion that a rib fragment had caused the punctured lung, saying, "Greg had previously cracked ribs, and the ribs that he cracked are now broken or displaced. In the CT scan, you can clearly see blood in the lung right around the pointed edge of the displaced rib. While there was one doctor there (at the Minneapolis hospital) that said, 'It had to be the injection,' another, a thoracic surgeon, said it couldn't be. To me, the CT scan showed the cause—a displaced rib. So, it's clearly a matter of opinion."

Walsh, who had already talked to Clark about what the hospital doctors said, was upset at what had happened, but he didn't

want to be in the position of criticizing a doctor who was working for the team. So he asked Clark to tell the media what he had
been told, and Clark did so in the locker room at the 49ers' Santa
Clara facility during the lunch break on Wednesday, with reporters gathered around his locker.

Clark blamed himself in part for what had happened, because
he insisted on playing even though he didn't feel right. "The thing
that's hard for an athlete is, sometimes you get so used to playing
with pain and dealing with pain that sometimes, personally, you're
not sure where to draw the line. You build up this pain tolerance
where you don't know.

"I did express my symptoms throughout the game, and I was
monitored during the game. The important thing was that (at the
hospital), they were able to detect what it was and they got in and
got that straight." Clark was soon back on the playing field, making the fractured rib story even more improbable.

It Gets Worse

THE BAD news just kept coming. On the Friday before the New
Orleans game, the 49ers were having a light practice before their
flight. Running-backs coach Tom Rathman told Lawrence Phillips
to go in for a play. Phillips refused. "Why should I practice when
I'm not going to play?" he said.

Rathman went ballistic because this wasn't the first time Phillips had refused to run plays in practice. Steve Mariucci backed up
his assistant, immediately suspending Phillips.

Mariucci then called a meeting with John McVay, Bill Walsh's
assistant, to explain what had happened. Rathman said, "If Phillips
gets on the plane (to New Orleans) I won't." It wasn't an ultima-
tum so much as an expression of how strongly he felt. It made no
difference. Phillips's 49ers' career was over; the 49ers waited only
to find out all the salary-cap implications from the league office

before officially releasing him. Signing him had been a big mistake. Phillips was not an NFL back. The only ability he'd shown was speed; he wasn't elusive, and he went down immediately upon contact. The only good news for the 49ers was that Phillips didn't get into any off-field problems while he was with the team.

But the 49ers were flirting with another huge mistake. When neither Jeff Garcia nor Steve Stenstrom played well at quarterback, a story broke that the 49ers were considering signing Jeff Hostetler. Having seen

> Once again, there was a split between the coach and the one-time genius in the front office.

Hostetler with the Raiders three years earlier, when he was clearly at the end of his career, I couldn't believe it; but when Ira Miller and I talked to Mariucci that Monday, he said Hostetler would be coming in for a workout that week.

Mariucci was clearly uncomfortable when I told him it would be a mistake. Once again, there was a split between the coach and the one-time genius in the front office. Mariucci said he wanted to find a veteran quarterback who could play for several years, rather than looking for a quarterback in the draft. When Hostetler came in, Walsh said he thought Hostetler could play for a couple of years while they developed a quarterback from the draft. Once again, Walsh seemed to be reaching into the past, thinking of how he had played Steve DeBerg while developing Joe Montana. Hostetler, who had been retired for two years, saved him from that mistake by saying he would spend the rest of the year with his family, not on a football field.

Meanwhile, on the player front, Jerry Rice was making noise again. When the listless 49ers lost to the hapless Saints in New Orleans, probably the worst effort of the season by the Niners, Rice exploded at his teammates in the dressing room.

The frustration was caused by his own problems. Rice had

become no more than an average receiver, unable to get off the line, dropping passes, going down on contact; his average gain was only nine yards. It wasn't his fault. His surgically repaired left knee had recovered, but he had lingering ligament damage behind his right knee. After still another loss, this time to the Rams at Candlestick, he told reporters he had not lost anything physically. The problem was with the "predictable" offense.

Rice had always been good for at least a couple of complaining sessions a season, but when he was producing at such a high level, his teammates and coaches had shrugged off his outbursts. Now he was part of the problem, not the solution.

CHAPTER TWENTY-FOUR

No Way to End the Millennium

THE LOSSES kept piling up, week after week. It was hardest on the veterans, who had been around for the good years and never thought the team would come to this. I talked to one of them, strong safety Tim McDonald, about it.

"This season has been a challenge," he said. "I'm not sleeping well the night after games. But I have to stay focused. I still enjoy playing, even in a season like this."

McDonald was in the middle of the biggest 49er problem: the defense in general, and the secondary in particular. He and free safety Lance Schulters were playing well, but there had been a revolving door at cornerback. Mark McMillian and Darnell Walker had been the original starters, but Walker had been benched and McMillian released after a combination of poor play and surly attitude. Second-year back R. W. McQuarters, who was shaping up as another 49er first-round bust, was tried at corner and failed.

The 49ers had picked up Craig Newsome, Monty Montgomery, and Ramos McDonald from other teams, and McDonald was pleased by what he had seen of the latter two in the second game against the Rams, which had just been played. Though the 49ers lost, the defense had played well, an encouraging sign.

"We stopped the deep ball for the first time in two years, really," said McDonald. "They didn't complete a pass over 20 yards. When that happens, I can be much more effective because I can come up to the line or back off, whatever works best, because I don't have to worry about covering for somebody else."

The respite was short-lived, though. Montgomery and Mc-Quarters were both injured and lost for the year in the next game, an ugly Monday night loss to Green Bay, and the secondary disintegrated.

On December 3 in Cincinnati, the losing streak reached eight, and this loss was probably the worst yet. The 49er offense had a great day, rolling up 542 yards. Jeff Garcia had his best day by far, completing 33 of 49 passes for 437 yards and three touchdowns. Jerry Rice caught nine passes for 157 yards, by far his best game of the season.

And the 49ers lost, 44–30, to the Bengals. "That was the worst secondary play, on both sides of the line of scrimmage, that I've ever seen," said Steve Mariucci.

On the way home, Bill Walsh tried to console his coach. He could sympathize with Mariucci because he, too, had had an eight-game losing streak in 1980 and he knew what agony it was for a coach. "I'm not sleeping nights," Mariucci admitted to me. "I keep thinking there must be something more I could do. You have to be careful talking to the players because you don't want to say the same things every week or they'll start to tune you out, but I want to keep them focused, keep them working. We can't just give up."

Friction at the Top

AT LEAST when they compared losing streaks, Mariucci and Walsh could find common ground. There wasn't much otherwise.

Mariucci was tired of playing the role of the good soldier, pretending that he agreed with Walsh's player decisions. When I asked him if he would want more input into personnel decisions next season, he replied with an emphatic yes, prefacing his remarks by saying they had to remain off the record for the moment.

"I'm the one who has to coach the players," he said, "so I have to be able to say these are the players I want. I know there are a lot of decisions that have to be made because of salary-cap considerations, but aside from that, I'm going to have to have more input, whoever's in charge. This year has been ridiculous."

Though he was the coach caught in the cross-hairs when the team was forced to deal with the deferred payments that had been promised to keep the team nucleus together, Mariucci didn't question Carmen Policy's plan.

> Mariucci was tired of playing the role of the good soldier, pretending that he agreed with Walsh's player decisions.

"If Carmen hadn't done that, this team would have lost most of its stars and just dropped out of contention. If you asked fans if they'd have wanted that instead of what we've had, several years of success and now this, they would say yes to Carmen's way. This was the only way this team could have gone. Nobody's to blame here. We need to just accept what's happening and go on with our lives."

Mariucci questioned Walsh's commitment to the job, because he had to spend time at home with his wife, who was recovering from a stroke. "He's not here today, and he's not here a lot of days. Terry Donahue and I worked our asses off preparing for the draft last spring and then Bill came in and basically ignored all our recommendations.

"Now, we don't know what we're going to do. If Bill is going to come back, we have to work these things out. I don't even know what Terry Donahue's role is. Is he going to replace Bill? He's supposed to be the personnel guy, but he hasn't been out on the road scouting college players the way you'd think somebody in that position would be. And his family is still in southern California. Terry and I work together fine, so I can certainly deal with him being in charge, but I'd sure like to know where we're going."

The bleeding stopped momentarily with a 26–7 defeat of the Atlanta Falcons at Candlestick that was impressive mainly for the effort of the 49er players, who were determined not to tie the franchise record of nine straight losses set by the 1978 team in Joe Thomas's last year. The defense held the Falcons to 105 total yards, and the offense operated efficiently. "For the first time in weeks, I can walk out of the dressing room with a smile on my face," said Tim McDonald, who had made a key end-zone interception in the second quarter.

That did nothing to answer the more important question: What would the organizational chart look like for the 2000 season?

The task ahead was daunting. "If we just released everybody on the roster, we'd be over the salary cap," said Mariucci. "There would be more than $57 million that we owed. Obviously that won't happen because we won't just get rid of everybody, so those obligations will be spread out over several years, but it won't be easy, however we do it."

Walsh was saying publicly that he could give Mariucci and Donahue more input, but he had never been comfortable in anything but an authoritarian role.

Matt Millen told reporters he might be interested in a job in the 49ers' organization, and the idea that he might come in as general manager made sense. He had played for the 49ers and was well-liked by those in the organization. He was intelligent and had been sought for the GM job with the Detroit Lions the previous season. He would have the energy the job required, and he was close to Mariucci, so the two could work together much better than Mariucci and Walsh did. Asked about the story, Mariucci said he had talked with Millen recently but not about that job. "I'm not sure he'd want to leave his current job (as analyst on NFL telecasts). It's a good job and he's very good at it."

Meanwhile, Walsh declared in a newspaper column that he intended to return in 2000 and fulfill his three-year contract, though he had hinted to me in the spring that he'd probably only work a year.

Walsh sent another message in the column, with a long rambling discussion of why Jerry Rice should retire. That only highlighted the difference between Walsh in his first run with the 49ers and Walsh now. A younger Walsh would have called Rice into his office and given him the message directly. In fact, Walsh had said privately the previous November that Rice should either retire or take a much reduced role at a lower salary, but he didn't have the nerve to tell Rice when he was in a position to do it a couple of months later.

York was in Mariucci's corner in his struggle with Walsh, and he told Walsh that he would have to share power if he returned. Walsh was saying publicly that he could give Mariucci and Donahue more input, but he had never been comfortable in anything but an authoritarian role.

Walsh's Public Evaluations

THE NIGHT after the 49ers lost to the Washington Redskins in overtime in their next-to-last game, Walsh was interviewed on television and repeated his belief that Rice should retire. He also said he was convinced that Jeff Garcia would never be better than a backup quarterback, so the 49ers needed to develop another quarterback.

The interview further irritated Mariucci, who believed those evaluations should wait until after the season. He was trying to keep his team together in very trying circumstances, and Walsh's comments were undercutting him again.

Walsh's comments on Garcia were ironic, too, because he had been an early champion of the quarterback and Mariucci an early critic. Now their roles were reversed because Mariucci had been pleasantly surprised by Garcia's play in the last third of the schedule.

Garcia was an intriguing story, largely because of the quarterbacks he had followed—Doug Flutie with the Calgary Stampeders of the Canadian Football League and now Young.

"Flutie was considered the greatest quarterback in Canadian history, so that wasn't easy," he had told me when we talked early in the season, "but this is a bigger deal here because of the fans and the team's success and the fact I'm filling in for a future Hall of Fame quarterback. This team has been quarterbacked by Joe Montana and Steve Young for the last 20 years, so there's naturally going to be a lot of focus on the quarterback. I didn't try to make people forget Doug Flutie, and I'm not trying to make people forget Steve Young. My focus is on finding a way to win with this team."

Garcia had insisted that his CFL experiences had taught him how to handle pressure, but he bent under the pressure of trying to win with a suddenly bad team; and Mariucci replaced him for four games with Steve Stenstrom. At the time, it seemed a questionable move because Stenstrom's limitations were obvious, while Garcia had at least some upside. But Mariucci knew what he was doing. The time off helped Garcia regain his confidence, and when Mariucci put him back in the lineup, it was in the best possible situation, against Cincinnati's porous secondary. Garcia had a great day and went on to finish strong down the stretch. Mariucci and offensive coordinator Marty Mornhinweg helped him by changing the offense to allow him to roll out and throw underneath the coverage to backs and tight end Greg Clark; but by the end of the season, Garcia was also throwing deep to wide receivers.

He had also learned to shrug off comments by others, even Walsh. "There are a lot of crazy things being said," he said. "I believe that Bill believes in my talents and skills but his comments don't surprise me. I've been underestimated throughout my life."

Season's End

THE SEASON ended for the 49ers in Atlanta in a Monday night game that had ABC executives contemplating a jump from a high building. When the schedule was announced, it seemed a game likely to decide the NFC West title and perhaps the eventual NFC champion, but now it was a battle of bottom feeders, with both teams at 4–11. Ratings for the game would be the second lowest of any Monday night game in history.

Garcia threw for 373 yards in a game that showed both the strengths and weaknesses of the 49ers. The Falcons started with the usual strategy of 49er opponents—exploit the secondary—and held as much as a 24-point lead in the third quarter. Then the Falcons relaxed and let the 49ers get back into the game, and Atlanta defenders had to knock down a Hail Mary pass in the closing seconds to seal a 34–29 victory.

Jerry Rice also had an excellent game, catching six passes for 143 yards, including a 62-yard touchdown. Rice was not the great receiver he had once been, but in the last month, he had recovered sufficiently from his leg problems to once again be an effective

receiver; and he said again after this game that he intended to
return for the 2000 season.

In the week before the game, Steve Young told the *Chronicle*'s
Nancy Gay that he also intended to return. "I'll deal with the doctors and get it finalized," he said. Because he would have had nearly
a year off before coming back to football, the immediate danger
that could result from a concussion would no longer be there. The
problem would be this: Would he risk long-term damage by continuing to play?

It would make sense for the 49ers
to bring back Young and Rice if they
were going to help ease a transition—
but the 49ers were not a team in transition. They had fallen to the bottom
of the league and had, in fact, been
beaten by New Orleans and Cincinnati, probably the league's
worst teams except for the expansion Cleveland Browns.

> Walsh being Walsh,
> he was determined to
> name his successor.

But internal and external pressures made it impossible for
Walsh to make those decisions. Privately, he was saying that Rice
and Young had to go, but in a postseason press conference he said
the two could stay if their salaries were reduced. Why the waf-
fling? He was being lobbied intensely by Mariucci to keep the
two—and other veterans as well—because Mariucci understood
that he would be blamed if the 49ers had another bad year. His
contract extension meant only that the 49ers would have to pay
him if he were fired; it didn't guarantee job security. Meanwhile,
Walsh was agonizing because he was so close to Young and Rice.
He had not allowed himself to get close to players when he was a
coach, but in the interim between his coaching retirement and
return as general manager, he had been a friend and advisor, especially to Young.

Walsh's postseason press conference was a disaster. He was
sick with the flu, which made him seem feeble. His voice broke

often as he talked. The tone of the press conference made it seem as if he were leading up to an announcement that he would retire, but he insisted he was staying on.

I learned the reason a couple of weeks later, when Walsh and I sat down for a long talk: He didn't think Donahue was ready to take over, mostly because he didn't understand the ramifications of the salary cap. Walsh being Walsh, he was determined to name his successor, just as he had done when he retired from coaching.

When I talked with Donahue later, he said he thought he was ready to take over, but he wasn't going to push for the general manager's job until Walsh said he was ready to leave. Donahue also said he was committed to the 49ers, though he had kept his home in Newport Beach. "We built that as our dream home, one we hope will be our family home, to pass on to our kids," he said. "We had been in the house just six months when Bill called me and said he wanted me to come up here. So, we've kept that house and rented an apartment near the 49er facility.

There were other problems. The 49ers badly needed a new stadium, but nothing could go forward on the original plan until the ownership settlement was final and Denise DeBartolo York had the authority to proceed. Because the animosity between brother and sister had continued to escalate, there was squabbling every time they got together to discuss the settlement. San Francisco mayor Willie Brown was miffed because John York wouldn't return his phone calls—and because York had told him earlier the city would have to kick in more money on the project, which Brown knew was impossible. A final settlement between the DeBartolos was reached in March 2000.

The 49ers' scouting department had been depleted by cuts in the mid-1990s—another unfortunate legacy of Vinny Cerrato's—which meant that the scouting evaluations weren't the best.

Though both men continued to deny it, the infighting between Walsh and York in the front office was intense. York was feeling ever more confident, telling me that he felt qualified to judge the coaches in the next season, even suggesting that Mariucci needed to back down from his hands-on approach and let his assistants do more direct coaching.

In the meantime, Walsh made the decisions to get the team under the salary cap by the February 10 deadline, though Mariucci's influence was clear in the way Walsh hung on to as many veterans as possible.

Young's contract was restructured, reducing his salary to $2.25 million for the 2000 season but giving him a signing bonus. Rice was offered a new contract with a substantial cut but did not accept, so Walsh tabled that discussion until later.

The contracts of guard Ray Brown, center Chris Dalman, and linebacker Ken Norton were restructured. A bitter Tim McDonald was released after he refused a contract that would have given him just $500,000, though incentives made it possible for him to earn $2.6 million. Linebacker Lee Woodall was another casualty.

The maneuvering pleased nobody. Walsh had just postponed the tough decisions, and the team would still be fighting salary-cap problems for the next two seasons at least. But the team that was left still had so many holes that even a .500 record in the 2000 season seemed an unreasonable goal.

In early June, Jerry Rice signed a restructured, five-year contract at a much reduced figure, but the one veteran player who could have made the 49ers significantly better, Steve Young, decided to retire instead of playing and risking another concussion. In a move that relieved the sports world more than it shocked it, Young announced his retirement, despite speculation that he might continue with the 49ers or move to Denver to captain the Broncos. The 49ers gave Young a $1 million retirement gift for his years of dedication and leadership on the field.

The 49ers had had a glorious run but the party was over.

CHAPTER TWENTY-FIVE

A Team for the New Millennium

THE WAY for the 49ers to get back to the championship level is simple but drastic: They must cut their ties to the past, making changes from top to bottom.

The first change should be in ownership. There is simply no reason for Denise DeBartolo York to own the 49ers. She has never been interested in football, nor in running a football team. At the time she took over for her brother, the 49ers were among the league's premier teams, and she had little to do beyond signing the checks. That is no longer true. The 49ers need a massive overhaul, and they need local ownership.

Denise's husband, John York, thought he could run the club, but he lacks specific football knowledge and judgment. He told me once that a horse racing operation was more difficult to run than a football team, which only underscored his lack of knowledge. He doesn't know what he doesn't know. Even if he did, he couldn't be in the area full-time, and nobody can run an operation well from 2,500 miles away.

The settlement worked out between Denise and Eddie provides that the Yorks will suffer serious tax consequences if they sell the club any sooner than two years from the time of the settlement, but if they hang on to the team for that period, they'll also lose money, with revenues reduced because of a drop in attendance. If they sell to local buyers, the Yorks can make enough money to compensate for the increased taxes.

There has never been a better time to sell. Though the team's performance has dropped sharply from the championship years, the price of NFL teams has escalated dramatically in that time, so the 49ers' value is higher than ever. With the explosion of Silicon Valley, the Bay Area probably has more wealthy people than does any comparable area in the country, so there should be no shortage of potential buyers.

The new owners should immediately make changes in the front office. Bill Walsh did an incredible job in building up both the team and the organization in the 1980s, but he was clearly not the man to take the 49ers into the twenty-first century. Walsh tried to relive the past, relying on men like John McVay, Bill McPherson, and Bobb McKittrick for advice; they had been very important to him in the 1980s but, like Walsh himself, had neither the vision nor the time and energy to deal with the greatly changed circumstances.

> There has never been a better time to sell.

Today the 49ers need a younger man for the daunting task that lies ahead, one with the energy to work the 16-hour days that will be necessary, one with thick skin to withstand the inevitable criticism. They need a man who can make the complete and ruthless changes the younger Walsh made when he first came to the 49ers and who can bring a fresh approach to the team. It is past time for trying to reward players for past service. For two years, the 49ers have postponed the tough decisions, restructuring contracts of veteran players so they could get under the salary cap, but also extending the period during which the team will be suffering from a salary-cap burden. Now, finally, they must move on.

There are two distinct methods for structuring an NFL team. One is the system Walsh used when he was both the coach and general manager, when he made all the important decisions on players. That system eliminates the problem the 49ers often had in 1999, when coach and general manager had very different ideas about what needed to be done, but it is also more difficult to find a man who can do both.

Two men with 49er ties, Mike Shanahan at Denver and Mike Holmgren at Seattle, act as their own general managers; and either one would be perfect for the 49ers, but it's unlikely that either one would leave his current job to take on a team with more problems. The 49ers' current coach, Steve Mariucci, has not sought that kind of dual responsibility, and he has yet to demonstrate the ability to make personnel decisions.

If the 49ers do try to find somebody who can do both jobs, they'll probably have to find a relatively young college coach who is eager to move up to meet this kind of challenge. Walsh, remember, came from college (though he had had extensive NFL experience) and had the resiliency that was necessary in his first two years with the 49ers.

The second way to build, and the path the 49ers will probably have to take, is to have a general manager to make the personnel decisions and a coach to prepare the team on the field. To make that process work, the general manager must work closely with Mariucci. Terry Donahue can do the job; the question is whether he'll leave before Walsh decides he's ready to retire. If Donahue isn't there, Matt Millen would be a good choice.

The new general manager should make it clear to the 49er fans that it will be a rocky couple of years while the team rebuilds, and the coach will not be responsible. But he must also make it clear to Mariucci that the team has to rebuild by developing its youth, not by hanging on to veterans past their prime.

The 49ers must take as many salary-cap hits as they can in 2001, to reduce the burden in future years. They must identify their key young players and keep them around, players like Bryant Young, Lance Schulters, Terrell Owens, Greg Clark, Jeremy Newberry. They must find a way to get rid of the overpaid underproducers, with J. J. Stokes leading that list. The litmus test is simple: They should be ridding themselves of all the players who don't project as key players two to three years down the road, which is the earliest the 49ers could expect to rebuild to a championship level.

Then the 49ers should go back to the formula for success they found in the '80s, building through the draft, always bringing in younger players for both starting roles and depth. Before they can do that, they have to bring in more and better scouts, so they have the evaluations to make the correct decisions on draft day. As any 49er fan knows, that hasn't been true very often in recent years.

The 49ers made a start in the right direction with their April 15–16, 2000 draft. After trading down to get two first-round and two second-round picks, they selected three potential starters—outside linebacker Julian Peterson, cornerback Ahmad Plummer, and defensive end John Engelberger—with their first three picks. But much more needs to be done.

> Most 49er [decisions] made in the last two off-seasons have been based on the salary cap, not the playing field, and that is no way to build a football team.

Bringing in younger players has another important benefit: They have lower salaries, making it easier to manage the salary cap.

In common with many other teams, the 49ers in the '90s became captives of the quick-fix solution, bringing in free agents to plug holes. And in common with many other teams, they discovered that such an approach can backfire. At times, as in the '94 season, the strategy worked perfectly, and the 49ers put together a team that won the Super Bowl. At other times, they've wound up paying good money—and being stuck with heavy salary-cap obligations—for players who have been of little help.

As they climb back into championship contention, the 49ers must be certain to make judicious decisions on free agents, because bad decisions paralyze a team. Most of the decisions the 49ers have made in the last two off-seasons have been based on the salary cap, not the playing field, and that is no way to build a football team.

Finally, the 49ers must address the stadium issue; and if they get new owners from the Silicon Valley, they might finally be able to drop the pretense that this is really a San Francisco team.

Though the 49ers carry a San Francisco tag, the majority of their ticket buyers live south of Candlestick, down the Peninsula. The team already has its practice facility in Santa Clara, and a stadium near there would be closer than one at Candlestick. It would be farther away for their fans in San Francisco and north of the city, but the extra distance is minimized because most games are played on Sunday, when fans don't have to buck the heavy weekday business traffic. For fans coming from Sacramento, which has always had a sizeable pocket of 49er fans, the extra mileage would be a trade-off for not having to cross the Bay Bridge, a terrible bottleneck on game days.

> Building a new stadium and bringing in new ownership and management is the only way the 49ers can regain their place at the top of the NFL.

The proposed new stadium on Candlestick Point has been stymied for a number of reasons, and one of the main problems has been the cost of building in that area. Most stadiums are sunk halfway into the ground, with fans entering at mid-level, so the ground acts as a support for half the seating area. Because the water table at Candlestick is barely below field level, the stadium has to be built entirely above ground, which means more support has to be built into the stadium itself. It also means that pilings have to be sunk. Building anywhere in the San Francisco Bay Area is more expensive than in other areas around the country, but a stadium on Candlestick Point is probably half-again as expensive as a comparable stadium would be in Santa Clara.

Building a new stadium and bringing in new ownership and management is the only way the 49ers can regain their place at the top of the NFL. Hanging on to the past, glorious though it was, has kept the 49ers from addressing their problems. It's time to cut the ties.

INDEX